J. MERRICK 1996.

C000109444

QUESTIONING
FOUNDATIONS

Editor
Hugh J. Silverman

Associate Editors
Stephen H. Watson
Forrest Williams
David Wood
Wilhelm S. Wurzer

Assistant Editors
Gary E. Aylesworth
James Barry, Jr.
James Clarke
James Hatley
Lajla C. Lund
Norah Martin
Brian Seitz

Bibliographer
Hélène Volat

Advisory Board
Hazel Barnes
Robert Bernasconi
Edward S. Casey
Jacques Derrida
M. C. Dillon
Thomas R. Flynn
Michel Haar
Irene E. Harvey
Patrick A. Heelan
Dominique Janicaud
Dalia Judovitz
John Llewelyn
J. N. Mohanty
Graeme Nicholson
Tony O'Connor
Adriaan Peperzak
William J. Richardson
John Sallis
Charles E. Scott
Jacques Taminiaux
Gianni Vattimo
Bernhard Waldenfels

CONTINENTAL PHILOSOPHY V

QUESTIONING FOUNDATIONS

Truth/Subjectivity/Culture

Edited by Hugh J. Silverman

ROUTLEDGE
New York • London

Published in 1993 by

Routledge
29 West 35th Street
New York, NY 10001

Published in Great Britain by

Routledge
11 New Fetter Lane
London EC4P 4EE

Copyright © 1993 by Routledge

Printed in the United States of America on acid free paper.

All rights reserved. No part of this book may be reprinted or reproduced or utilized in any form or by any electronic, mechanical or other means, now known or hereafter invented, including photocopying and recording, or in any information storage or retrieval system, without permission in writing from the publishers.

Library of Congress Cataloging-in-Publication Data

Questioning foundations : truth, subjectivity, and culture / edited by
    Hugh J. Silverman.
        p.   cm.—(Continental philosophy ; 5)
    Includes bibliographical references and index.
    ISBN 0-415-90623-7 (CL).—ISBN 0-415-90624-5 (PB)
    1. Philosophy. 2. Truth. 3. Subjectivity. 4. Culture—
Philosophy.   I. Silverman, Hugh J.   II. Series.
B29.Q475   1993
190′.9′04—dc20   92-39449
                                                                              CIP

British Library Cataloguing-in-Publication Data

Questioning Foundations : Truth,
Subjectivity and Culture. — (Continental
Philosophy Series;Vol. 5)
    I. Silverman, Hugh J.   II. Series
    121

    ISBN 0-415-90623-7 (HB)
    ISBN 0-415-90624-5 (PB)

CONTENTS

CONTENTS

Notes

Bibliography

Notes on Contributors

INTRODUCTION

Hugh J. Silverman

"The center cannot hold"
—William Butler Yeats

As a dominant moment of modernism, William Butler Yeats announced the crisis of the center, the threat that the long-admired focus of experience, of thought, of society was rattling in the wind. After so many centuries—following upon Descartes's reiteration of the Augustinian *cogito*—it could be expected that the concept of a unitary and central foundation would come under critical scrutiny. The early modern empiricist tradition (marked by Locke and Hume) could not believe in a center of experience. By contrast, Kant sought to find an alternative by linking his *Ich Denke* to the manifold of experience. What Foucault called the "empirico-transcendental doublet" prevailed for almost two centuries. Yeats's confrontation with the abyss (the *Ab-Grund*) foretells the concept of center shaking at its very foundations. The centered self—still dominant as a pure or transcendental ego in the philosophies of Edmund Husserl, William James, and Henri Bergson and in the ego-oriented psychoanalysis of Sigmund Freud—was matched by a centered body, a centered social grounding, and a centered historical epoch. These notions pertinent to a metaphysics, a philosophical psychology, and a civilizational context were themselves foundational for concepts of truth, subjectivity, and culture. Many figures of the postmodern age—the age of multiplicity, of juxtaposition, and of fragmentation—have questioned this persistent desire for a centered grounding. They have noted the self-circumscription that Yeats

1

and other dominant proponents of modernism had announced and feared but were unable to realize as critical delimitations.

The concept of foundations is at the base of all Western thought. This fifth volume of *Continental Philosophy* delves into the grounds of the Western tradition only to find that foundations themselves are open to question—even to the extent that there is nothing peculiarly "Western" about such a conception. Furthermore, the very idea of "Western thought" itself is an artificial construction of a set of foundations that themselves require further investigation.

Much of the project of continental philosophy as it has come to be understood has articulated deep concern about the viability of "foundations" and "foundational thinking." The contributors to this volume have addressed particular areas of thought: truth, science, ontology, the subject, signs, gender, civilizations, and cultural representations, all to discover that the notion of "foundations" hangs seriously in the balance.

I. Truth

Djuna Barnes has written that "truth is the last lie." Truth has been the centerpiece of Western thinking. For Plato, truth was that to which all philosophizing would aspire. Truth, associated with the good and the beautiful, was the end of knowing, the orientation of thought. To know was to know *the* truth. Once achieved, knowledge of the truth could improve society, eliminate evil, achieve ideality. Truth is the identity of the forms, the ultimate perfection of things replicated in the actual world. With Aristotle, rendering proofs for what is true through the observation of natural processes or through fallacies and validities in argumentation resituated the concept of truth from its central place to wherever truths can be found. When Christian truth was divinely revealed, its source came unquestioningly from the divine. Translated into clear and distinct ideas or a diversity of impressions, truth was again multiple. To reunite the manifold of experience into a transcendental unity of apperception would combine both the rationalist and empiricist conceptions at once. The options were then for truth to be either an ideality—the Hegelian *Absolute Geist*—or for it to be a Nietzschean extramoral sense that was more likely to be abused than used.

So when Heidegger attempted to understand truth as *a-letheia*, as disclosure, as the coming out of concealment, he was both de-centering truth and offering an Open, a place in which truth could happen without at the same time being a center. Truth as disclosure means understanding truth as at once focal and marginal. The discourse of truth that Heideggerian *Unverborgenheit* has occasioned reiterates the notion of truth as Ground, as principle of reason, as the *sine qua non* of thinking. Reading Nietzsche through Heidegger, Derrida remarks that "Truth is a woman." Truth is female unveiling (*Unverborgenheit*) accomplished in writing with a male style (stylus, stiletto, spur, phallus). Derrida's interest is in the traces (*Spuren*) of truth as they permeate discourses in which truth is hardly at issue. The Foucauldian *paresia*—the will to say the truth—is an unfulfilled desire inscribed in a discursive practice that is always available for reformulation. It results at best in what Derrida would call: truth in writing, truth in disclosure, truth in thinking, and even truth in painting. In this case, truth as foundation has meaning only as a will to speak the truth, or as a discourse of truth in which the inscription of knowledge is the writing of truth (and correspondingly, the truth of writing is difference as inscribed). What this all comes to is that truth, understood traditionally as center, as foundation, is now displaced into spaces of disclosure, into moments of appearance—as the *aletheia* of modernity (Vattimo), as truth-logos (O'Neill), as a hermeneutic of empirical science (Crease), as the language of semiotic sign-systems (Hrachovec). The origin of truth—as Merleau-Ponty would have called it—is the repetition of truth in the places of difference: where truth itself is interrogated, questioned, placed in parentheses.

II. Subjectivity

With modern philosophy, the subject becomes a center. The Renaissance subject was a link in the great chain of being—lodged somewhere between beast and angel, a free-willed being capable of choosing between the actual and the ideal. The Cartesian subject distinguished itself from bodily extension—the thinking thing was an "I" that thinks, dreams, and hopes. As a foundation, the Cartesian subject—seeking to distinguish itself from its own body because of an ideal of certainty, reason, and the innateness of ideas—anointed itself indubitably and uncontrovertibly. The early modern subject was the basis of all knowledge—whether reliable or not. By contrast, the empiricist subject depended upon experience—knowledge drawn from the outside world for its evidence. Hume could not even affirm the semblance of a unitary self as ground of all knowledge and experience. For the empiricist, sense impressions were far more reliable than the rational subject.

Kant resolved the conflict by bringing together a rational subject as a transcendental unity of apperception with the manifold of experience. The metaphysical foundations of all experience would rest in the transcendental domain of pure reason, but the necessities of moral action and judgment would also have to take account of conditions for universalizability through the categorical imperative and the pleasures of the sublime. Unbeknownst to Kant, the value of his schematism was to offer a space of difference *between* the transcendental and the empirical. But it left the subject in crisis—a crisis that it would not realize for almost two centuries.

The Hegelian subject was the universalization of the Kantian subject rendered Absolute. From sense-certainty to self-consciousness to Absolute Mind, the Hegelian subject suffered from a case of engulfment. By devouring all that is, the Hegelian subject would be the ultimate unification of all difference into identity. Totality would be its foundation. To the extent that the Hegelian subject was also a Romantic (pantheistic) subject, the ideal of being at one with nature was to be fulfilled by establishing a ground, a foundation, a unity in Nature.

The Husserlian subject returned to the Cartesian idea of a pure ego but now imbued with a concept of the self as standpoint, a transcendental ego from which all acts of knowing are derived, a source of intentionality for a pure phenomenology. At the same time, the Freudian psychical realm with its ego-centered id-ego-superego structure and the Jamesian pure ego with its stream of consciousness correspond with the Husserlian conception of the transcendental ego. The concept of the centered self, the self as ground, as foundation of all conscious experience had reached its highest point. It remained now for such a centered self to be open to the kind of ontological critique that Kierkegaard and

Nietzsche had already raised but which found its realization in Heidegger's hermeneutics and Merleau-Ponty's notion of embodiment. In Kant's schematism, difference became critical, but in Heidegger it was thematized as the ontico-ontological difference. The self, formulated as difference, could no longer be understood as ground without difference.

The postmodern re-inscription of subjectivity re-formulates the self as difference or abyss (*Ab-Grund/mise en abîme*), as placing the grounding concept of the self radically in question (Hatley). The self as difference is read as fragmented and de-centered, affirming multiple values rather than a single set of unitary self determinations (Bordo-Moussa). The subject is embodied ontologically (O'Connor), gendered (Butler), and culturally charged (Spivak).

III. Culture

Culture is a curious thing. To speak of "culture" is to suggest that there is a unity to it. And indeed, Western culture has a kind of unity—a tradition built upon tradition. As with other traditions, Western culture is identifiable, traceable, and narratable. There is a story to be told: from the Ancient Greeks, through the Roman Empires to the Renaissance, Modern, and on to Contemporary Worlds. But what of those multiplicities that continue to inscribe themselves on the surface of Eurocentric culture? Even Bacchus was a stranger to the Athenian Olympic culture that westerners call their own. And what of the barbarians or even Christians for the Romans? American culture is built on multiplicity and yet there is a myth of an American heritage. And the European is constantly confronted with alterity—otherness for a national pride, otherness because of its own colonial aspirations, otherness because to be European means to have neighbors who are either friends or foes. And what of the ideal of a European community? If realizable (and despite its aspirations), it cannot be other than a multiplicity.

Culture as a foundation shakes even at its roots. Hence the third section includes essays on European culture—the world of Picasso (Johnson) and Heidegger/Celan (Hatley)—and from several alternative cultures: India (Spivak), Mexico (Lingis), and America (Watson). The task here is to show that while economic foundations are built in the financial centers of the world: London, Paris, Milan, New York, Tokyo . . . , these foundations need to be questioned in their histories and in their cultural representations as well as in their social-political-economic bases—not in terms of third-world culture, but as postcolonial cultures, cultures after the breakup of European dominance, cultures seeking to redefine themselves without reaffirming their arborescent roots.

With the return of Europe as a concept—the return comes as multiplicity. Even nations incorporated into a multiple unity—the Soviet Union, Yugoslavia, Czechoslovakia, Canada, etc.—seek national identity (as, for instance, Lithuania, Latvia, Slovenia, Croatia, Slovakia, Südtirol, Québec, etc.), but their need for purity and an identity of their own serves only to give force to the minoritarian concept that minorities can become majorities. No one culture is or can be foundational—any nation will of necessity be divided into multiple components and constituencies, with multiple cultures and multiple cultural representations. Indeed, cultures found themselves in order to avoid foundering, and yet only by having formed themselves can they ultimately founder. Founding or forming a culture means establishing an identity. An identity requires a history (or various histories), an aesthetics (or competing art concepts), a set of politics (or alternative governments). But it is precisely the concept of a cultural identity that calls for reexamination. The fragmentation of identity is the breakup of culture as a center of knowledge, tradition, security, and self-certainty. By moving to the edge of these foundations, there can be a place for a critical examination of the values and virtues of a particular culture, of what is to be reaffirmed, and what needs to be reformulated.

This fifth volume in the *Continental Philosophy* series comes at a time when many foundations are in question, including the very ground of universities—what makes them function, the support that provides a basis for their survival, and the values that underlie their commitments. Among these is the necessary encouragement for projects such as this series. For this volume, I am especially grateful to Patrick A. Heelan, continental philosopher and Dean of Humanities and Fine Arts for 1990–92, whose interest and support of this and related work has been a godsend at a time when budgetary cutbacks threaten the basic research obligations of a major state university such as SUNY at Stony Brook. As of the summer of 1992, he became Executive Vice President for Academic Affairs at Georgetown University. While we did not always agree, his philosophical vision and his administrative energy in rethinking the very structures of the Humanities in the university has animated serious reconsideration of long-standing and outmoded habits of interaction and disciplinary practices. His important contribution is greatly appreciated.

Only a year after initial work on this series began, James Clarke joined the group of Assistant Editors who have devoted endless hours to the functioning and communications that a project of this nature requires. I am particularly cognizant of his tireless commitment—even at a time when he has been diligently completing his doctoral thesis. This volume has also benefitted from the continuing efforts of James Hatley, who has contributed an essay on Heideggerian grounds, Brian Seitz, and the newer members of the editorial staff: Lajla Lund and Norah Martin at Stony Brook, and Gary Aylesworth, whose active interest in the series antedates his actually joining the group in the past two years. Each essay in this volume has been read by at least one outside referee as well as by our editorial group. In many instances, contributions have been revised and improved. The help of the outside referees is extremely valuable in maintaining the high quality of these volumes; I am pleased once again to thank these specialist readers for their time and anonymous labors. More than anyone, Maureen MacGrogan my editor at Routledge will, I hope, be rewarded for her patience and continuing interest in the *Continental Philosophy* series by the publication of this volume.

Finally, the wide range of provenance of our contributors is especially noteworthy: Basil O'Neill (Scotland), Tony O'Connor (Ireland), Gianni Vattimo (Italy), Herbert Hrachovec (Austria), Richard White (England/USA), Gayatri Spivak (India/UK/USA), and the North Americans: Judith Butler, Alphonso Lingis, Galen Johnson, James Watson, Susan Bordo, Robert Crease, Mario

7

Moussa, and James Hatley. Their diversity of background and interests is testimony to the multiplicity and difference that animates this volume. If its readership is of even greater dispersal and dissemination, this particular task of thinking will have accomplished its ends.

PART I
TRUTH

PART I

TRUTH

Chapter 1

THE TRUTH OF HERMENEUTICS[*]

Gianni Vattimo

How does hermeneutic ontology speak about truth? This question must take into account the widely held suspicion that the philosophical position of hermeneutics is relativist, anti-intellectualist and irrationalist (or, at best, traditionalist). For it lacks that instance of truth which the metaphysical tradition has always thought in terms of patency (the incontrovertible givenness of the thing) and the correspondence of the proposition to the evidence of the thing. The Heideggerian critique of the notion of truth as correspondence seems to deprive hermeneutics of this instance, and even to make it impossible for hermeneutics to "save the phenomena," to acknowledge the experience of truth common to us all. This experience occurs when we openly espouse the validity of an affirmation, put forward a rational critique of the existing order (a mythical tradition, an *idolum fori*, an unjust social structure), or correct a false opinion by passing from appearance to truth. Without these usages of truth, thought seems to abdicate its vocation. Yet can they still be guaranteed without some idea of patency, and thus of correspondence?

One can reply to such a question only by trying to reconstruct, or perhaps construct, the positive terms of a hermeneutic conception of truth. This must be done on the basis of, and beyond, the "destruction" of correspondence-truth as carried out by Heidegger. At the beginning, however, let us recall the essential motives for Heidegger's rejection of the notion of truth as correspondence.

We are concerned to put to rest the misapprehension that in

---

*Translated by David Webb.

11

Being and Time Heidegger looks for a more adequate description of the meaning of Being and the idea of truth, as if the notions of Being handed down to us by the metaphysical tradition were partial, incomplete, inadequate, and therefore false descriptions of Being as it is *really* given, and truth as it *really* occurs. That this might not be Heidegger's intention is, from the very beginning, less than clear. However, it may be appreciated well enough if one reflects that such an intention would inevitably be contradictory, even in light of the features at play within truth as correspondence itself. With the evolution of Heidegger's work after *Being and Time* it becomes clear that his ontology cannot in any way be taken for a kind of existentially phrased neo-Kantianism (the structure of reason and its a priori having fallen into the thrownness and finitude of Dasein's project).

At the same time, it is clear that the objection to the conception of truth as correspondence is not made solely on the basis of its being inadequate to describe the experience of truth faithfully. For with the acknowledgment of inadequacy, one sees that one cannot retain a conception of truth as correspondence, since this implies a conception of Being as *Grund,* as the insuperable first principle which reduces all questioning to silence. Moreover, precisely the meditation on the insufficiency of the idea of truth as the correspondence of judgment to thing has put us on the track of Being as event. Admittedly, to say that "Being is event" (as Heidegger, quite rightly, never actually said)[1] is apparently *also* to give a descriptive proposition that claims to be "adequate." But to remark upon this superficially, as occurs repeatedly in all the "winning" arguments of metaphysics (the argument against skepticism is a typical example), is to placate and satisfy only those who bow before the ontological implications of the principle of noncontradiction. It does not persuade anyone to change their view, however. And above all, it does not allow thought to take a further step. In general, Heidegger has taught us to reject the untroubled identification of the structures of Being with the structures of our historical grammar and language. Thus, he has also taught us to reject the immediate identification of Being with what is sayable without performative contradictions in the context of the language we speak.

To say that Being "is" event means to pronounce in some way, still in the language of metaphysics, consciously accepted and *verwunden*, the ultimate proposition of metaphysics. The logic of foundation is being carried to extremes. It is the same process of unfounding [*sfondamento*], albeit experienced differently, that Nietzsche "described" with the proposition "God is dead."

It would not be rash to reconstruct the middle Heidegger's thought as an elaboration of this contradiction. This would resolve (dissolve) the *Kehre* entirely in *Verwindung*, in the resigned resumption-distortion-acceptance of metaphysics and nihilism. We recall this ensemble of problems only to remind ourselves that, in attempting to construct a hermeneutic conception of the experience of truth in positive terms, beyond the destruction of correspondence-truth, we must let ourselves be guided by the same motives that led Heidegger to that destruction in the first place. Such motives are not reducible to the search for a description that is truer because it is more adequate. They have, instead, to do with the impossibility of still thinking Being as *Grund*, as first principle, given only to the exact contemplation, panoramic but soundless, of *nous*. Recalling the motives for Heidegger's criticism of correspondence-truth is crucial if we are to overcome the aporias that seem to threaten the hermeneutic conception of truth, and not only in the view of its critics. Such a conception must be constructed on the basis of what Heidegger calls "opening." It will avoid the risks to which the critics of hermeneutics have drawn our attention (irrationalism, relativism, and traditionalism), only to the extent that we remain faithful to the motives of the Heideggerian destruction. This destruction did not set out to propose a more adequate conception of truth, but aimed to "respond" to the meaning of Being as event.

Referring to this guiding thread, we can resolve, or at least articulate in a more positive manner, a problem that post-Heideggerian hermeneutics does not seem to have posed in the right terms: the question of the relation between truth as opening and truth as correspondence (or, what is in many ways the same thing, between truth in philosophy and the human sciences and truth in the positive sciences). Every reader of *Truth and Method* will appreciate that it is not clear whether Gadamer intends to suggest that the human sciences have a truth of their own, founded upon interpretation, or whether he wishes to affirm this "model" of truth as valid for every experience of truth in general (and thus for the experimental sciences too). Either way, this "obscurity" in Gadamer may be easily explained by noting that in *Truth and Method* the Heidegger to which he makes most constant and wide-ranging reference is the Heidegger of *Being and Time*.[2]

Now, on the basis of *Being and Time*, we can say that the simple presence to which both banal everydayness and scientific objectivism are reduced arises from a partial attitude that cannot serve as the only model for thinking Being. Inauthentic thought, which is the ontology that needs to be destroyed, and will later become the metaphysics that forgets Being in favor of beings, takes simple presence and the objectivity of objects as models for thinking not only entities within the world, but also Being itself. To escape inauthenticity or the "lethean" distortions of metaphysics, we must avoid this undue extension of the simple presence of entity-objects to Being.

Gadamer does not seem to venture further than this in his criticism of modern scientism in *Truth and Method*. For him, such scientism is not the fatal outcome of metaphysics. Still less is it a fact bound up with the destiny and history of metaphysics, as it clearly is for Heidegger after *Being and Time*. Even Rorty's thesis in *Philosophy and the Mirror of Nature*, in which he distinguishes between "epistemology" and "hermeneutics" in terms that may well be drawn back to correspondence and opening, seems to be a reformulation ("urbanized" like Gadamer's) of a position whose basis may be found in *Being and Time*.[3] Epistemology is the construction of a body of rigorous knowledge and the solution of problems in light of paradigms that lay down rules for the verification of propositions. To be sure, these rules do not necessarily imply that whoever follows them gives a truthful account of the state of things, but at least they do not exclude it. Moreover, they allow a conception of science and scientific practice to survive which are for the most part in harmony with the traditional metaphysical vision of the proposition-thing correspondence.

Hermeneutics, by contrast, unfolds in the encounter with different paradigmatic horizons. Resisting evaluation on the basis of any correspondence (to rules or to the thing), such horizons manifest themselves as "poetic" proposals of other worlds, of the institution of different rules (within which a different "epistemology" is in force).

We will not pursue the suggestions or problems that arise

from Rorty's hypothesis, which seems common to a Gadamerian perspective, although Gadamer has always been very reticent on the subject of the relation between knowledge in the interpretive sciences and knowledge in the strict, or natural sciences. One relevant difference between his position and Rorty's consists in the fact that, on the moral plane at least, Gadamer grants a kind of supremacy to knowledge in the human sciences (especially in *Reason in the Age of Science*). The natural sciences, inevitably linked to technology and with a tendency toward specialization (not only in knowledge, but also in pursuing ever more specific ends, possibly in conflict with the general interests of society), must be "legitimized" by a thought which relates them back to the *logos*, to the common consciousness expressed in the natural-historical language of a society and its shared culture. The continuity of this consciousness, even in the sense of a *critical* reconstruction, is assured precisely by the human sciences, and by philosophy above all. In the terminology of *Being and Time* (and later, *Vom Wesen der Wahrheit*), the opening, which occurs in language and its founding events (like the work of art), is truth in its most original sense. It serves, too, as a point of reference for the legitimation of correspondence-truth in the sciences.

The sciences, however, insofar as they specialize via the construction of artificial languages, "do not think," as Heidegger and Gadamer have said. As for Rorty, his position seems to be more radical than Gadamer's. There is no residue of the distinction between the natural sciences and the human sciences. Each form of knowledge may be in either a hermeneutic "phase" or in an epistemological one, according to whether it is living through a "normal" or "revolutionary" period. However, this excludes any possible hierarchy between types of knowledge. It also excludes any privileged place for human rationality in general, such as Gadamer's logos-language (and common sense, dense with history).

Yet just how radical is this difference between Gadamer and Rorty? Both relate truth as correspondence back to truth as opening. This is understood either (in Gadamer) as an historico-cultural horizon shared by a community that speaks the same language, or (in Rorty) as a paradigm that, without necessarily being identified with a linguistic community or cultural universe, nonetheless contains the rules for the solutions of its own problems and shows itself to be a foundation that is not founded, not even by that historical continuity still active in Gadamer. However, the problem ultimately remains the same for both thinkers. For Gadamer too the historical continuity which legitimizes the opening, and prevents its reduction to an arbitrary and casual paradigm, is nonetheless a limited community. It cannot be extended to a limit such as would link it with humanity in general, at least not explicitly. There holds for Rorty, but probably for Gadamer as well, a certain "Weberian" relativism. One can speak of truth in the sense of conformity with rules, given with the opening itself, only within an historical-cultural opening or paradigm. At the same time, the opening as such cannot be said to be "true" on the basis of criteria of conformity, but is (at least for Gadamer) original truth. For it institutes the horizons within which all verification and falsification are possible. The "hermeneutic" experience of the opening is more or less explicitly "aesthetic." This is clear in Rorty, who thinks the encounter with other paradigms as an encounter with a new system of metaphors.[4] Not by chance does Gadamer himself begin *Truth and Method* by affirming the significance of truth in art. But in Gadamer the encounter with other openings of the world, which is interpretation, is an aesthetic experience only to the extent that the latter is thought in historical terms, as an integration, or better, as a present "application" of a call whose origin lies in the past.

In effect, we should turn more to Gadamer than to Rorty for an articulation of the hermeneutic doctrine of truth as opening. This is so even if in Gadamer the problems entailed by this conception are brought into relief, forcing us to return to Heidegger, to his thought after *Being and Time,* and to what have seemed to be the fundamental demands motivating the critique of correspondence-truth found in that work.

If truth as opening is not thought as the incontrovertible givenness of an object possessed by a clear and distinct idea and adequately described in a proposition that faithfully reflects the idea, then the truth of the opening can, it seems, only be thought on the basis of the metaphor of dwelling. At bottom, this holds not only for Gadamer, but for Rorty as well. I can do epistemology, I can formulate propositions that are valid according to certain rules, only on the condition that I dwell in a determinate linguistic universe or paradigm. Dwelling is the first condition of my saying the truth. But I cannot describe it as a universal, structural, and stable condition. There are two reasons for this: because historical experience (and that of the history of science as well) displays the irreducibility of heterogenous paradigms and cultural universes, and because in order to describe the opening as a stable structure, I would need a criterion of conformity which would then be the more original opening.

I shall speak, then, of truth as opening in terms of dwelling. I call it truth because, like rules with respect to individual propositions, it is the first condition of every single truth.

Dwelling in the truth is, to be sure, very different from showing and rendering explicit what already is. In this respect Gadamer is right when he observes that belonging to a tradition, or even in Wittgensteinian terms, to a form of life, does not mean passively undergoing the imposition of a system of prejudices. In certain contemporary readings of Nietzsche, this would be equivalent to the total reduction of truth to a play of forces.[5] Dwelling implies, rather, an interpretive belonging that involves both consensus and the possibility of critical activity. Not for nothing, one could add, do modern dictatorships give an ever greater place to the techniques of organizing consensus. Dominion through consensus is more secure and more stable. There is a certain difference from pure constriction established here, which perhaps humanizes the exercise of even the most despotic power. It certainly recognizes, albeit paradoxically, the decisive significance of a conscious adhesion to a tradition, and the always active interpretive character of staying in a tradition. As a metaphor for speaking of hermeneutic truth, dwelling would need to be understood as though one were dwelling in a library. Whereas the idea of truth as correspondence represents knowledge as the possession of an "object" by way of an adequate representation, the truth of dwelling is, by contrast, the competence of the librarian who does not possess entirely, in a point-like act of transparent comprehension, all of the contents of all the books among which he lives, nor even the first principles upon which the contents depend. One cannot compare knowledge as possession by command of first principles to the competence of the librarian. The librarian knows where to look because he knows how the volumes are classified and has a certain idea of the "subject catalogue."

It is therefore senseless and misleading to accuse hermeneutics of being reduced to relativism or irrationalism, whereby each articulation within the opening, each epistemology, would be merely the revelation of what always already is. The conflict of interpretations would then be nothing but a conflict of forces that have no "argument" whatsoever to offer, other than the violence by which their predomination is secured. But thrownness into a historical opening is always inseparable from an active participation in its constitution, its creative interpretation and transformation.

However, these suspicions about hermeneutics are always renewed by the fact that it seems incapable of describing "original" truth as dwelling without recourse to a metaphor rooted deeply in the metaphysical tradition: that of "community," or in Hegelian terms, of "beautiful, ethical life." The persistent force of this reference may be seen, most recently, in Habermas's *Theory of Communicative Action* where the *Lebenswelt* is thought in reference to the ideal of an organic community characterized in terms of ethical life, and has both a normative and a foundational role. If there is to be a moment of "patency" included in hermeneutic dwelling without recourse to the model of correspondence, then "ethical life" seems to be indispensable. In other words, truth as opening also seems to involve a moment of "recognition," a "sensation" of incontrovertibility, of full patency. In accordance with the characteristic aesthetic quality of the hermeneutic experience of truth, but also with its links to pragmatism (those promoted by Rorty are legitimized by the pragmatist approach of the existential analytic of *Being and Time*), this comes to be understood as the recognition of a harmonious integration rather than the appropriation of a content via an adequate representation. Classical doctrines of patency as characteristic not only of certainty but also of truth (until phenomenology) have always forced themselves to accept this sensation of integration and harmony as a sign and symptom to which the truth of the content of experience could not be reduced. Yet they have done so without ever producing convincing proof that this difference really existed.

Nietzsche acknowledges this, too, when he invites us to doubt precisely what appears to be most evident, certain, indisputable. In the hermeneutic conception of truth as opening, this transition is comprehensively eliminated. The truth of opening is not an object whose cognitive possession may be attested to by the sensation of patency, completeness, and integration that we may feel in any given moment. This integration is the original truth itself, the condition of our Being in the true, upon which depends the possibility of making true judgments, verified in the light of rules of correspondence.

Can these complications and problems connected with them be avoided by reducing truth to merely "secondary" truth, to correspondence-truth, as metaphysics has always done (with the exception of Kant)? Yes, but only by "reducing Being to beings," or at the price of remaining prisoners of ideology by identifying the paradigm or cultural universe into which we are thrown with the real world *tout court*. This, it is understood, *we cannot do*. We cannot knowingly reconstruct myth, we cannot artificially assume a natural attitude—so the problem of truth as opening poses itself in such a way that it cannot be ignored. And it does so in the form of the problem of opening as truth. Not to consider the historical-cultural condition into which we are thrown to be a problem of truth means to take it, more or less consciously, as a brute fact, whose fatal reduction to an effect of force is only a sign of its remaining within the sphere of a metaphysics of foundations—a prisoner once more of *Grund* as the ultimate point of reference beyond which we do not pass and which silences all questioning. Thus we cannot help but pose the problem of opening. Why should we consider the world to be identical to our historical description of it, which in the meantime, as a result of the revolution of metaphysics into nihilism, has appeared to us *as such*? We cannot help but pose the problem of opening in terms of truth, for otherwise we shall end up by taking it to be a brute fact, a *Grund*.

Yet this seems to be "prohibited" for two reasons: first, by the need to distinguish the opening from its articulation (the hermeneutical from the epistemological), which can no longer be ignored after Marx, Nietzsche, and Heidegger; second, because what becomes unthinkable with the experience of the distinction between the opening and single truths (with the ontological difference), is precisely something like *Grund*. The impossibility of continuing to think Being in terms of *Grund* inspired Heidegger to his critique of correspondence, which simply could not have been motivated by the desire to find a more adequate description than that founded upon adequation.

Yet, does the difficulty posed by this impossibility find a repose in the reduction of the givenness of an object to an aesthetic experience of *fulfilment*, of the harmonious integration into a community, of the with-itself of Hegelian spirit? It is not simply a matter of regarding with suspicion the aestheticism which this hermeneutic conception of truth seems necessarily to involve. For in the end, such is the referal of the sensation of objective patency back to a recognition of integration within the world in which one "dwells" and in which one feels at home, as though in beautiful ethical life. This aestheticism is suspect only insofar as it does not take its leave of the true as the *Grund*, but seems instead to be a still more monumental and preemptory version of it.

The solution of the problems and discomforts created by life in a "society" held together only by contractual, mechanical, and conventional links is not the reconstruction of an organic community. Just as the recovery of a notion of virtue within a concrete historical horizon of shared values (through belonging to a common tradition) is not the solution to the subjectivist aporias in which modern rationalist ethics has issued. As in MacIntyre, the criticisms of modern ethical rationalism conclude—perhaps not by chance—with the proposal of a return to a premodern morality. This outcome illustrates a risk run to an equal degree by the hermeneutic conception of truth.

On certain pages of Gadamer, it seems to be something more than a risk. Yet, in Gadamer, as in Rorty, there are the instruments needed to prevent the "aesthetic" model from leading to "aesthetical" results. Recognizing these elements maintains the proposal that guided the Heideggerian critique of truth as correspondence. In this way, one would also be more faithful to an "aesthetic" model no longer thought in anachronistic classical terms.

Hermeneutics replaces truth, as the appropriation of a thing via its adequate representation, with thought as dwelling and as aesthetic experience. But this aesthetic experience is in its turn thought on the basis of its actual configuration in the epoch of the end of metaphysics, to which hermeneutic ontology also belongs. For this experience, the false work of art, *kitsch*, is presented today with the characteristics of completeness, roundness, and the harmonious reconciliation and perfect compenetration of content and form that were thought to be characteristics of art in the classical sense. The connection between hermeneutics and aesthetics in the epoch of the end of metaphysics could also be formulated in this way: to assert the importance of aesthetic experience with respect to truth, and to propose it as a "model" for a conception of truth free from scientism (from the idea of truth as correspondence and the patency of the object) only becomes possible when aesthetic experience is modified to such a degree that it loses its "classical" characteristics. Corresponding to this transformation of the aesthetic, which, with Heidegger, must be considered as a feature of the destiny of Being, there is also a radical transformation of cognitive experience in the sciences. Indeed, this occurs to such an extent that the function of a "model of truth" put forward for aesthetic experience might no longer appear foreign or opposed to the very self-knowledge concurrently matured in the sciences.

The critique of the idea of truth as correspondence leads hermeneutics to conceive of truth on the model of dwelling and aesthetic experience. But this experience still tends to be presented according to classicist images of integration, harmony, and roundness which correspond to art in the epoch of metaphysics. If hermeneutics gives in to this tendency, it will end up opposing correspondence-truth with nothing more than an idealization of the beautiful ethical life. Instead of escaping the peremptoriness of *Grund* (and its forgetful identification of Being and beings), it would merely reassert an even more monumental foundationalism, expressing itself in the pure and simple identification of the opening with the brute factuality of a certain form of life not open to discussion.

A more accurate recognition of the aesthetic experience serving as a model here leads instead to a different outcome.[6] It leads away from the emphasis that metaphysical thought has always placed upon the subjective sensation of certainty as a sign of truth. Regardless of every effort to the contrary, it seems impossible, after Nietzsche, to still think of clear and distinct ideas as the model for truth, or of the experience of the true as the incontrovertible certainty of consciousness before a given content. The Nietzschean "school of suspicion" cannot but lead to a demystification so radical as to demystify the suspicion itself. Such a result, however, is not equivalent to a recuperation, pure and simple, of the experience of patency. If it wishes to be faithful to the intentions (and the good reasons) that motivated the Heideggerian critique of truth as correspondence, hermeneutics cannot simply offer another explanation of the experience of patency, referring the sensation of fullness back to a cause distinct from the manifestation of the thing in its simple presence (for example, the sense of integration in a community thought as the Hegelian beautiful ethical life).

For hermeneutics it is a matter, rather, of recognizing completely the link between that very patency of consciousness and metaphysics. Indeed, the manner of truth's being given as a clear and distinct idea and as incontrovertible evidence belongs to the very history of metaphysics. Here too, as with all elements of the history of metaphysics, thought cannot remain under the illusion that it can perform a true and proper overcoming. Instead it must work at a *Verwindung*, a resumption and distortion, which will maintain the model of correspondence as a secondary moment of the experience of truth.[7]

After Nietzsche, but in the end simply after Kant (whose transcendental foundation already places single truths and corresponding propositions on a secondary level), we no longer think of truth as the correspondence of a proposition to the state of things. Truth as correspondence, even as incontrovertible patency experienced in the certainty of consciousness, is only a secondary moment within the experience of truth, and reveals itself as such when metaphysics matures toward its completion. This can be seen, for example, in the advent of modern experimental science. Its technological consequences and its transformation of the scientific undertaking into a social project of gigantic proportions have rendered irrelevant the mythical moment of discovery and certainty of consciousness, upon which metaphysics constructed its idea of truth. Just as conceiving the encounter with the work of art in classical terms is anachronistic, illusory, and decidedly *kitsch* (nowadays only merchandise promoted in advertising is presented in this way), so to conceiving the "eureka" of the scientist in his laboratory as the supreme moment, as the very model for the significance of the experience of truth, is ideological and mystifying. Perhaps the experience of truth *begins* from there, as one then sets out toward certainty on a voyage to discover the conditions which render it possible (or perhaps belie it), where these are never given once and for all in sheer patency.

In opposition to *Erklärung*, to positive-scientific "explanation" which subsumes a single case under a general law (which is itself given as evident), hermeneutics does not propose a *Verstehen* which, as a lived experience of sympathy and common belonging, reproduces the same "silencing" peremptoriness of objective evidence, only at the level of vitalistic immediacy. Instead, it sets in opposition what one might call, with Heidegger, an *Erörterung*. This is an unfounding [*sfondante*] "collocation" which indeed has many traits of aesthetic experience, but as it is given at the end of metaphysics (and as a moment of its "overcoming" in the form of a *Verwindung*). Perhaps the research opened up by Kant on the conditions of possibility for physics as a science reaches its culmination here. Physics as a science, or modern technical science as it is set out in the world of *Gestell*, is possible only on the condition of no longer thinking truth according to the model of patency given to consciousness. The modern scientific project itself heralds the consummation of that model and the relegation of correspondence-truth to a second level. Ultimately, this is the ever more accentuated divarication between the real, as that which is given in the immediacy of a cogent intuition, and the true, as that which is established only by virtue of its being situated within an unfounding horizon [*un orrizonte sfondante*].

All of which, naturally, one would have to argue in greater detail via reconstruction of the rise of self-consciousness in the sciences between the nineteenth and twentieth centuries. This would also have to include a consideration of the debates over realism and conventionalism, and a discussion of such examples as the methodological anarchism of Feyerabend, as well as the reproposal of "realism" and its various significations.

From the point of view of hermeneutics, the features of *Erörterung* as an alternative to the metaphysical "model of truth" (and to its variations in the sense of the organic community) are brought out more clearly if we reflect further upon the metaphor of dwelling. To offer a declension of this metaphor with the example of dwelling in a library merely serves to underline a feature which is, however, common to all dwelling: being introduced not into a "natural" space thought as an abstract, geometrical space, but into a landscape marked by a tradition. The library in which late-modern man lives, and in which his experience of truth is set, is a "library of Babel," to use Borges's expression. The elements for this specification of the concept of *Erörterung* can already be traced in the distinction marked out in *Being and Time* between tradition as *Tradition* and tradition as *Überlieferung* (the latter understood as the active inheritance of the past as an open possibility, not as a rigidly determined and determining schema). What constitutes the truth of single truths given in propositions (that "correspond") is their referral back to conditions of possibility which cannot be articulated in propositions (which themselves correspond).

Such conditions are given as an unending network of references, a network constituted by the multiple voices of the *Überlieferung*, of the handing down (not necessarily from the past), which resound in the language in which those propositions are formulated. These voices speak as an irreducible multiplicity resisting every attempt to draw them back to a unity. This is an especially modern experience, making inevitable the link between the happening of truth as *Erörterung* and the ending of metaphysics.

Does the closed and definitive system of Kantian categories not also crumble because of the discovery of the multiplicity of cultural universes, and thus of the irreducible plurality of a priori conditions of knowledge? This multiplicity, however, would remain only a factual given, lacking any philosophical significance, if philosophy, for its part, did not link it to the discovery of temporality as constitutive of Being. The irreducible multiplicity of cultural universes becomes philosophically relevant only in light of the mortality constitutive of *Dasein*. This mortality does not confer upon the *Überlieferung* the character of a confused superposition of perspectives, but rather the dignity of the *Geschick*, the giving of Being as the sending of openings which vary from time to time, as do the generations of man. This must be kept in mind in order to understand how the tradition, within which propositions (that correspond) acquire their most authentic truth, is not only a Babel, but is also "impoverished." This marks it as an unfounding provenance compared to a giving of Being as simple presence.

This aspect of the *Überlieferung*, in which the sense of transmission and the more specific sense of sending and source are brought together, is recognized explicitly here in order to avoid yet another metaphysical equivocation. This equivocation can be seen in all versions of hermeneutics as a philosophy of the irreducible multiplicity of perspectives. In Heideggerian hermeneutics this multiplicity is opened by the mortality constitutive of *Dasein*, which finds itself always already thrown into a project, into a language, a culture, which it *inherits*. The awareness of the multiplicity of perspectives is *also inherited*. The conception of truth as dwelling in the library of Babel is not a true description of the experience of truth that would ultimately replace the false one given by metaphysics. It is, rather, the outcome of the articulation of metaphysics as the reduction of Being to presence. This includes its culmination in techno-science and the consequent dissolution of the very idea of reality in the multiplicity of interpretations. Situating truths, propositions that "correspond," within truth as opening does not mean suspending their ultimate cogency within a multiplicity of perspectives. (This might stand as a description of the deconstructionist version of hermeneutics proposed by Jacques Derrida). By contrast, the hermeneutic *Erörterung* places truths against the background [*sfondo*] of the irreducible multiplicity of voices which make them possible. It experiences this collocation as a response to a call that comes from the *Überlieferung*, and which keeps this groundlessness [*sfondamento*] from being mere confusion or arbitrariness.[8]

This seems to be the only way to pose not only the problem of truth as opening, but also the problem of opening as truth. The horizon cannot be reduced to a brute fact, insuperable and equipped with the same peremptory authority as a metaphysical *Grund*. The multiplicity of voices against which single truths acquire authenticity is not an ultimate structure given as true in place of Being as unity, *arche*, foundation. It is, rather, provenance. Being, given in metaphysics as simple presence, is itself always on the point of turning into an object (of measurement, of manipulation, etc.). It is given today as multiplicity, temporality, mortality. To recognize this giving as an event, not as an already-

given, peremptory structure, means to find in the multiplicity of voices not merely an anarchic confusion, but the call of a *Geschick*. This is a destiny that no longer has the characteristics of a metaphysical ground. The *Geschick* retains something of the metaphysical *Grund* and of its capacity for legitimation, but only in the paradoxical, nihilistic form of a propensity for dissipation that cannot present itself with a metaphysical cogency. It represents, nonetheless, a possible rationality for thought, a possible "truth of the opening." Thus, in the sphere of this dissolute destiny of Being, the succession of scientific paradigms and science's growing awareness of its own historically situated character are not to be resolved by substituting a relativistic metaphysics for the realist metaphysics of the tradition.

The divarication of the *true* and the *real*, one of the most striking implications of the development of modern science, would become an aspect of the completion and dissolution of metaphysics. In this history, Being is given, at the end, as that which *is not*, at least in the sense of an object. It occurs as the opening which, while making possible single truths as propositions corresponding to the given, withdraws itself explicitly from any kind of appropriative stating. The conquest of the true would thus follow a path leading away from the real as the immediate pressure of the given and the incontrovertible imposition of the *in itself*. To use an example from psychoanalysis, this is similar to the fascination of the imaginary and its games of identification, as in Lacan, from which we can only withdraw via a passage at the level of the symbolic.[9]

The unfounding [*sfondante*] horizon within which the single truths (even as "corresponding" statements of the sciences) acquire their authentic truth, i.e., come to be "founded" [*fondati*], would not be the historically determined paradigm containing the rules of their formulation, which cannot be interrogated further (like a form of life which legitimizes itself by the very fact of its existing). Nor would it be the disordered multiplicity of the paradigms that would effectively suspend any pretensions to the definitive status of single truths. To stand in the opening is not to achieve a harmonious (traditionalist, conservative) integration in a received canon shared by an organic community, but neither is it the pure relativist-historicist separation of the blasé. For the Mannheim of *Ideology and Utopia*, this constitutes the only possible point of view not limited by ideology, and which is taken up not by the Marxian proletariat, but by the European intellectual formed in and by the knowledge of many cultural universes.[10]

By contrast, we get back to truth as opening by taking the unfounding [*sfondamento*] as destiny. If the developments of science demonstrate a growing divarication of the true from the real, then this destiny means that the divarication attests not only to the insuperable historical relativity of the paradigms, with all the consequences this involves (first among which is the temptation to skepticism), but it also attests to Being's propensity for reduction, for the dissolution of strong characteristics. This presents itself as a possible guiding thread for interpretations, choices, and even moral options, well beyond the simple affirmation of a plurality of paradigms.[11]

What remains in this perspective of the "traditional" notion of truth as correspondence and the patency of the object? Paradoxically, the *critical* function of truth is enhanced here, in the form of a leap into the *logoi*, an ever renewed passage "from here to there," to use the Platonic expression. This is so inasmuch as even the consciousness of patency is forever reinterrogated regarding its conditions, forever drawn back into the horizon of the opening that constitutes its permanent unfounding [*sfondamento*]. In scientific research today the "discovery" itself is increasingly entrusted to measurements, instrumental verifications, and the establishment of continuity and "tests" between objects. Consequently, the sensation of success and the feeling of fullness that accompany "discovery" are relegated to the range of secondary effects of truth. Or they serve as points of departure too heavily compromised by the pressure of the "real," from which one must therefore separate oneself—a separation that began with the distinction between primary and secondary qualities, and in general with the ideal of disinterestedness and scientific objectivity.

The growing historical-political self-awareness of science can probably be counted as one of the aspects of this transformation of the notion of truth. The ideal of correspondence is not thereby explicitly denied, but situated on a second and lower level with respect to truth as opening.

Despite appearances, this does not amount to a reaffirmation of the supremacy of philosophy and the human sciences over the physical sciences. Even Rorty's distinction between "epistemology" and "hermeneutics" is probably too schematic: it draws too rigid a distinction between a work of articulation within a paradigm, i.e., the solution of puzzles, and the revolutionary transformation of the paradigm itself. But scientific work, from the viewpoint of Popperian falsificationism, is not readily described as a simple articulation of rules given when checking the correspondence between propositions and states of things. On the other hand, the institution of historical openings, of new horizons of truth, is perhaps a less aesthetically emphatic event than Rorty seems to think.

Nor is the other metaphysical usage of truth (guaranteeing the universal validity of true statements on the basis of the thing being given "in person") entirely lost in the hermeneutic reformulation of truth as opening. Here, the merely postulated universality of true propositions—always linked to the surreptitious identification of the "we" of a determinate scientific community or specific cultural universe with humanity in general—is replaced by an assemblage of single truths with the multiplicity of perspectives constituting the network that supports them and makes them possible. Once again, the hermeneutic conception of truth is not an affirmation of the "local" over the "global," or any other "parochial" reduction of the true. To articulate the connections and the stratifications that echo in every true statement means to activate the memory of an indefinite network of relations. (I am thinking of Wittgenstein's family resemblances). This network constitutes the very basis of a possible universality, namely, the persuasiveness of that statement, ideally, for everyone.

It is a case of universality and criticality *verwunden*. They are taken up again in their earlier metaphysical determinations, pursued and distorted accordingly, that is, in hearing a call of Being which resounds in the epoch of the completion of metaphysics. These, too, are the transformations on account of which Heidegger believed it necessary to refer the more original essence of truth to "freedom."[12] Hermeneutics must always reflect upon this turn.

Chapter 2

TRUTH AS FUNDAMENTAL AND TRUTH AS FOUNDATIONAL

Basil O'Neill

The concept of truth is implicitly transcendental. What I think, what you think, what anybody thinks may not be true; what is true transcends our best endeavors to think what is true, transcends also any ideal limit of logical systematization of our thinking. Philosophy seeks to think and to understand truth; it does so either by thinking it as something which is not transcendent, or by constructing an understanding of a transcendent mode of being to be the bearer of truth, thereby losing the world and man unless these also are transposed in a wholly unbelievable or unbearably alienating way. These are the aporias of philosophy, from which the thinking of our own time, "thinking at the end of philosophy,"[1] seeks to free itself. A strange freedom it has to be, achieved through and within the thinking of that very history of philosophy which follows the twists of the aporias, but a kind of freedom nevertheless, and one which will carry with it a reorientation in many other ways than in respect to the problem of truth. But how can the concept of truth be rethought without adding another chapter to the history of truth which, as Derrida tells us, is an illusion, and one which cannot quickly be dissipated?[2] Truth is unavoidably fundamental for philosophy; the problem is how to avoid thinking of it as foundational. But for that task it is essential to understand more closely what it is to think truth as foundational.

Within analytic philosophy of our time it is usually agreed that *epistemology* must do without foundations—i.e., without a set of data given as true in virtue of their status within human experience. Indeed, it is the clear realization of this rejection of foundationalism and its consequences which is claimed to lead to "post-analytic philosophy."[3] Certainly, the rejection of foundations in epistemology does have far-reaching consequences; it leads, one might say, to the triumph of hermeneutics. For the absence of given certainties, of pretheoretical data, leads at once to the thought that interpretation is everywhere, that no judgment can avoid assessment and possible revision in the light of other judgments. Rorty saw that this placed him closer to Heidegger, that for both of them philosophy operates within a hermeneutic circle (or rather within many such circles).[4] Rorty's own description of the outcome, however, is that "nothing will explicate 'theory-independent truth'," so philosophers should drop truth in this sense from their vocabulary as a useless concept, and confine discussion of truth to what can be established about the semantics of whatever language and theory we actually find it useful to employ. Transcendent truth with all its problems is in this way removed from philosophy by the simple tactic of refusing to discuss what we can't explicate, even though Rorty admits that "that we have such notions of truth and goodness—notions which float free of all questions of justification—is unquestionable." It seems rather a short way to dispose of philosophical problems which must recall those to which Kant devoted the Transcendental Dialectic and which motivated much of the architectonic of his thought. In its conclusions, however, this position may seem to be close to Heidegger's rejection of eternal truths as a corollary of his locating truth always with a previously established horizon of interpretation.[5] Actually Heidegger's view is quite remote from Rorty's, and transcendence plays a central role in his thinking about truth, as I shall try to show.

Rorty's position is motivated by engagement with the problems of epistemology, whereas for Heidegger epistemological problems and their possible solutions are secondary; the question of Being must be pursued at a more fundamental ontological level. An epistemological problem is one which requires that for some propositions or sets of propositions there is a question about whether they are known to be true or not, and if they are known what kind of grounds justify or ground this knowledge.[6] The propositions themselves must be assumed to be available to us for us to make their epistemic status a problem. What must be available is not just uninterpreted sentences but propositions (involving meanings, determinate enough that it is clear what it is for them to be true, and so what it is for them to be known to be true). For epistemological foundationalism, this requirement is no problem—it is secured for the foundational propositions by the immediate givenness of their meanings with their truth (e.g., the innate truths of reason relating logically simple ideas to each other in Descartes, or the immediate awareness of one's own ideas in Locke), and for other propositions by a semantic derivation parallel to the epistemic derivation in which more complex ideas are derived from the given foundational ones. For modern antifoundationalists like Rorty, on the other hand, propositions are not *given* in that way—we *make* them by our linguistic and associated nonlinguistic practices, thereby determining their truth-conditions which remain logically tied to the practices. Such propositions are not isolated, because practices are complex and interrelate their elements in structurally specific ways so that a group of propositions will form part of at least one "theory." Theories are judged successful or not by whether their truth-conditions usually turn out to be determinable and to be satisfied, especially in cases we regard as "important."

So truth is the satisfaction of the truth-conditions of a proposition within a theory, according to that understanding of what it is for a proposition of this kind to be true which that very theory determines. A proposition may not yet have been formulated or thought of, but "it" (i.e., the abstract and timeless entity we envisage) may still be true provided that the language of a theory which we already possess makes that proposition available to us "in principle." In the view of these antifoundationalists, only in this limited and theory-bound way can truth transcend what we now believe to be true. Thus in 1492 the proposition "Across the Western Ocean there lies a large continent separated from the Indies by another wide ocean" might have been formulated and considered by nobody, but the theories held by Columbus, Diaz, and others at the time about land-masses and oceans made that proposition available to them in principle. But the proposition "The nucleus of an atom can be split" was not available before 1897 even in principle, because the theory within which it can be understood and some conception of its truth-conditions grasped was not available before at least 1897, and the proposition can only be said to have been "true" before then from within the

31

assumed framework of the relevant twentieth-century theory as a narrative frame.

This conception of truth, then, can only be understood as part of a binary conception of truth-related-to-language-of-theory. Truth is explicated in terms of available propositions, which in turn are explicated in terms of theories within whose language they can be formulated and understood. The meaningfulness of theories is explicated in terms of the determinacy and accessibility of the truth-conditions which they assign to their propositions. The relation of truth to a proposition is that the proposition can only be grasped as what it is (as meaning what it does mean) by grasping how it would be valued as true or not true. Truth may itself be explicated as a relation of a proposition to a fact. More formally, the truth-predicate may be defined in Tarskian fashion—provided that we have available a metalanguage in which to specify its truth-conditions. In the "practice" of philosophers, the metalanguage is usually just a trivial extension of the object language whose truth we are seeking to elucidate. But this is not a definition which could eliminate the term "true" and replace it with another term.[7] Thus this philosophical doctrine can properly be said to make truth foundational, along with the notion of a language and the basic syntactic terms required for specifying the structure of sentences. "Foundational" here is not meant in the sense that the content of derived knowledge is developed from the basic terms or justified by reference to them, but in the sense that philosophical understanding is based on them, is formulated and discussed and problematized always by relation to these fundamental concepts and the way they can be applied to the issue in question.

This is true even for philosophical theories elucidating something as *not* involving assignment of truth-values, like noncognitivism in ethics. For there the fundamental character of ethics is determined by the (alleged) impossibility of assigning determinate truth-conditions to moral judgments. The status of moral judgments *must* (it is argued) be based on some kind of convention or social norm or attitude of the speaker, just *because* of the failure of moral judgments to fit into the truth-value assigning model of a fact-stating language. Such a view naturally engenders (within the same philosophical viewpoint of truth as foundational) its opposite, the view that truth can after all be assigned to moral judgments, in which the motor of the philosophy is the working out of how the truth-value assigning model could be applied to moral judgments and of what implications this would have for the status of ethics.[8] Again, even in speech act theory, part of whose purpose was precisely to bring into clearer focus for philosophy the role of nonconstative language, the idealizing character of the analyses as they are systematized in Searle's account is surely generated by the idealizing character of the analyses of constative language already so familiar within analytic philosophy, idealizing constatives precisely in order to make each proposition be defined by determinate truth-conditions.[9] Thus the sense in which truth is foundational for a great part (not all) of analytic philosophy is that it is pivotal in determining the kind of being anything has, and in the sense that all philosophical discussions presuppose the fundamental binary relation of truth and the languages of our theories: truth and logos.

The phrase "truth and logos" sets us into a very different framework of philosophical discussion, that of Heidegger, Derrida, and Levinas. All of them reject the foundational truth-and-logos pair, seeking rather to uncover what lies behind the idea of truth and the possibility of ideally determinate logos. They do so, however, in different ways. Heidegger's thinking of truth and logos as nonfoundational (with some reference also to Derrida) raises the following question: If a "foundational" concept means that its application is fundamental and criterial, can one pursue philosophy without making some concepts foundational? Or are critiques of foundationalism anything more than relocations of the status of foundation from one concept to another; or do they entail the complete disintegration of philosophical inquiry?

Derrida's critique of the truth-logos pair is directed primarily to the ideality of *logos* in the pairing from which "metaphysical truth" is derived. "All the metaphysical determinations of truth . . . are more or less immediately inseparable from the instance of the *logos*" (*OG*, 10), declares Derrida, and the metaphysical illusion diagnosed in this way is called not "veritacentrism" but "logocentrism." Similarly, when Derrida approaches metaphysics by stressing the overemphasis of the voice, which "effaces the signifier" by encouraging us to think in terms of a supposed self-heard immediacy of meaning, he remarks that the "experience of this effacement of the signifier" is "the condition of the very idea of truth" (*OG*, 20). Derrida sees logos as primary, while truth is derivative from a metaphysical concept of meaning "in the element of ideality or universality."

In the light of the close interlocking of truth with logos discussed above, this order of explanation looks like a mistake. Metaphysical truth is not just *derivative* from idealized meaning; its telos generates and defines idealized meaning. This is true for Frege (for whom reference is defined by what determines truth-value in a proposition), for Russell, and for the doctrines and traditions of (mostly) extensional logic which derive from their work. I think this telos also orders the thinking of Descartes, while the empiricist tradition essentially consists in reinterpreting the meaning of what is claimed to be known as true, so as to make it coincide with the meaning of the mental states (or the sentences expressing them) which are our awareness of them. Metaphysics does indeed presuppose idealized and abstractly determinate meanings lying in the words which express them. But it does so in order to see language as expressing truth. For a meaning to be determinate, according to this metaphysical philosophy, it must fix a determinate set of truth-conditions for propositions, thus enabling reality to be articulated and expressed "as it is" (which includes the possible sense "as our best current theories make it out to be"). As Heidegger says, "The Being-question unfolds into the question about the correlation [*Zusammengehören*] between unconcealment and presence ('truth' and 'Being')."[10] The metaphysical understanding of this correlation supposes an articulation of truth and being within an idealized logos which fixes the articulation as eternally valid. (For Rorty what is eternally valid is the truth of a given proposition within the context of theories and practices in which its truth was originally established). Heidegger's understanding of it rather seeks "what determines the correlation as such" (*HQT*). Heidegger's interpretation of the essence of metaphysics as a pairing, a correlation, of truth and idealized logos better captures the roots of metaphysics than does Derrida's interpretation of it as an idealized understanding of meaning (logos) deriving from mistaken assumptions about the primacy of the voice, the dominance of the phallus, etc., *from* which a metaphysical concept of truth is in turn derived.

It might seem that not much hangs on this issue, that what

matters is not which features of metaphysics we regard as its essence, but in what direction a freeing movement out of meta- physics is indicated by its diagnosis. And here it may seem that Derrida's diagnosis has an advantage over Heidegger's. Language in general has many modes other than truth-asserting, and an adequate grasp of the many ways in which writing and talking are possible may be better promoted if we de-emphasize the truth-stating mode by displacing truth from the central role it has enjoyed too long in philosophy. Indeed, even where truth- stating *is* the ostensible purpose of a text, we may fail to under- stand it unless we see the truth-stating as embedded in a rhetori- cal context, which is the really essential aspect of the text.[11] In light of these considerations, it may seem that Heidegger's thought preserves too much of the ghost of metaphysics (as Derrida in fact alleges in *De l'esprit*). Yet when Derrida, speaking of the double guard of memory and chance, says that it "will be assigned, as its responsibility, to the strange destiny of the university. To its law, to its reason for being, and to its truth," he invokes a conception of truth which makes it central the way Heidegger does: "Let us risk one more etymological wink: truth is what keeps, that is, both preserves and is preserved. I am thinking here of *Wahrheit*, of the *Wahren* of *Wahrheit* and of *veri- tas*—whose name figures on the coat of arms of so many Ameri- can universities. It institutes guardians and calls upon them to watch faithfully—truthfully—over itself."[12] No doubt the irrup- tion of Heideggerian etymologising into a Derridean text has an ironic smile behind it, but it is a gesture Derrida felt to be neces- sary at just the point where thought engages action. So perhaps we should see as already inscribed in Derrida's texts the Heideg- gerian thinking of the essence of truth, and of the way it can be guarded.

The concept of truth explained by Aristotle as the *homoiosis* (agreement) of the *logos* (i.e., the *logos apophantikos*—the declara- tive sentence) with a *pragma* (a thing or a state of affairs) is the origin of the common understanding of truth as correctness. In this sense, "the proposition is the seat and place of truth—but also of untruth, of falsehood and the lie."[13] Heidegger starts his inquiry from this everyday concept which is the kernel of the metaphysical and representational thinking from which he seeks to free us. The Tarskian formula does no more than express this concept of truth in a finitely axiomatized theory for an arbitrary language. Heidegger leads his inquiry *from* this everyday concept *to* a deeper concept of truth. In 1925, in the Marburg lectures, he distinguishes the two concepts of truth in a radical way, as a binary opposition: "Truth on the one hand, and being-true or being-false on the other, are completely different phenomena."[14] But in later lectures and writings on truth he is careful to relate them closely together—to show that reflection on the representational character of truth *leads us to* the deeper concept of truth, as from phenomenon to essence. It does so in this way: a sentence is the specification of a thought—a state or event or process in the understanding (the *dianoia*). Aristotle says that truth is in *dianoia*, not in things (*ouk en pragmasin*); but this view cannot be right if we understand it "in a purely external manner" (*BPP*, 214). For a true proposition is true in virtue of the way things are, i.e. the way the things referred to in the proposition are, and this cannot be sufficiently secured by the intrinsic character of the proposition itself or of the thinking articulated by it. So a proposition must be taken as reaching right out to the things in the world (cf. Wittgenstein); directing (*richten*) out toward them so that the things meant in the proposition are part of it as it is meant in the understanding. Only in this phenomenological sense of what a thought in the understanding is can Aristotle's dictum be defended. But in that case truth as correctness (*Richtigkeit*) presupposes and requires the prior establishment of this directedness (*Gerichtet sein*) to things. "Representation [*Vor-stellen*, placing before] must give itself a relation of equivalence [*sich angleichen*] to the being in each case; that is, as re-presentation [*Vor-stellen*] it must bring forward the encountered thing before us and hold it brought forward [*hingestellt*]" (*GP*, 15).

We might say Heidegger is stressing that the establishment of the meaning and reference of a declarative sentence must be established and operative before any question of its representational truth can arise. That would be a correct but superficial way of seeing what Heidegger is doing. The inner connectedness of a proposition with things in the world is for him not a relation of a sentence, an abstract linguistic entity, to things, as abstractly "referred to" (*bedeutet*) by expressions in the sentence (as it is for Frege), but a characterization of thinking as a human activity or process which is (he will argue) made possible by the form of human involvement in the world, the In-the-World-Being of *Dasein*. For he goes on to characterize what makes this direct-edness of the proposition to beings possible in this way:

> If our representing and asserting—for example in the sentence "The stone is hard"—is to be directed to the object, then this being—the stone itself—must previously be accessible, so that it can offer itself as criterially open for this directing to itself. In short the being—in this case the thing—must lie open. More than this: not only the stone itself, but also the range of beings which the directing to the thing must assess all through, must lie open; for the directing to the thing must read off it re-presentingly what characterizes the being in its thus-being. Moreover the man—who represents and directs himself representingly toward the thing—must also be open *for* what meets him, so that it can meet *him*. Finally, the man must also be open for men, so that he can direct himself *with* other men, and out of Being-with with them, toward the same thing, co-representing what is communicated to him in the proposition, so that he can be agreed and united with them about the correctness of the representing." (*GP*, 19)

Openness, in four different dimensions, thus governs the cor-rectness (or, indeed, the incorrectness) of propositional repre-senting. This openness is "the ground and basis and operative space for all correctness" (*GP*, 20). Correctness is only inadequate because everyday thinking neglects its ground and takes it to be self-sufficient, and is thereby led into metaphysical thinking. Heidegger's phenomenological questioning about the essence of truth leads from this everyday notion of correctness to its ground and essence—in the first instance, to this fourfold openness. Thence, in the attempt to think the unity of this openness and to follow the dynamic of the questioning, we are led via a medita-tion on the texts of Aristotle, Plato, and Heraclitus toward seeing the essence of truth as *aletheia*, unhiddenness. We can then see that "the ground of correctness (*homoiosis*) is *aletheia*, the unhid-denness of beings" (*GP*, 98). This is what "gives its ground to the true, so far as the latter is understood as correctness." *Aletheia* also means the fourfold yet unitary openness which Heidegger has already shown to be presupposed by correctness. So, for the mature Heidegger, correctness and truth are not at all "quite different phenomena"—one is grounded by the other and is its essence.

Heidegger is thus not leading us *away* from concern with truth in the sense of representational truth. He is revealing what lies hidden in it, what governs it. Truth shows itself to have a deeper or more authentic layer or stratum, to which we men of the technical age must redirect our thinking and our questioning. Thus Heidegger could not write, as did Derrida, that a metaphysical illusion (phonocentrism) is "the condition of the very idea of truth" (*OG*, 20). Rather, he would say that the metaphysical idea of truth fails to reveal its true essence, what truth really is, and that it is thereby led into a series of illusions in philosophy; whereas questioning along the way of phenomenology, authentic questioning concerned to find what truth is, *can* reveal correctness as derivative from the kind of truth which is fundamental.

But why, one may ask, should the ground of correctness be called *truth*? Why shouldn't correctness have its ground in something other than truth, so that we could continue to attach the label "truth" in the familiar way to correctness? Its ground could be called "the open," or "the horizon of discourse," perhaps. After all, what's in a label? Then a large issue on the nature of truth could die away, and we could all agree.

Again, this suggestion would wholly fail to grasp the depth of Heidegger's thought. His inquiry is fundamentally concerned with the way *Dasein*, thinking being, is in the world in a sense-disclosing way; it is therefore concerned with the self-revealing character of Being. To seek the essence of truth is to seek what is most worthy of being questioned, and what most needs to be questioned. Far from being discarded, the concept of representational truth will acquire a new dignity and a new weight for us in a time when the wasteland grows, when it can be seen as deriving its role and decisiveness from its prior essence, *aletheia*. Heidegger sees the essence of truth as a way to open Being, to make it accessible in such a way as to escape the illusions which representational thinking involves if conceived as independent. But the opening of Being is not an invented concept Heidegger has tried to foist on us in place of truth. Rather, it is what men already sought without knowing it; indeed, what they sought was barred from them by the structure of the sending of Being in the modern age.[15]

Location of truth in a movement of Being rather than in the proposition (or in the understanding while it thinks the proposition) makes possible the resolution of many philosophical knots. In 1937 Heidegger was preoccupied with the way it might make possible a response to Nietzsche's skepticism about truth as arising from the nihilism of the will to will. But I should like to focus on the issue with which I began this paper—the problem of transcendence. Like Rorty, Heidegger rejects the idea of eternal truths as ideal propositions eternally holding the truth-value "true." But he is not thereby led to fix truth in what our current theories make accessible. He can avoid this because for him truth is not tied to propositions representing what is true in an ideal (or historically located) logos. Truth precedes such representations; the presencing of Being makes such representations possible. This presencing happens in the event of appropriation, the *Ereignis*. To this extent Heidegger ties truth to historical uncovering. The event of appropriation is not eternal (the very idea of eternity is for Heidegger a misunderstanding of the nature of time and of Being), but the transcendence which was the main provocation of the idea of eternity is captured in Heidegger's thinking of the essence of truth. In the Fourfold (*Das Geviert*) which is the space of *aletheia*, the Earth, the veiled source, the inexhaustible origin, is beyond any particular state of theory, any particular giving of Being.

Furthermore, Heidegger's critique of the metaphysical distinctions (form and matter, essence and existence, subject and its attributes, etc.) by which representational thinking structures the thing is essentially a critique of finite and fixed specifications of a being.[16] Representations must indeed start with an identification of the thing designated, under some sortal description or other. But if we understand the Being of the thing as no longer exhausted by the designation, though understood through it, we are no longer fixed into the metaphysical subject-and-attribute mode of thought. The designation employed in the proposition arises from a prior understanding of the sense within which we understand it, a prior opening of truth, in which this apophantic structure is shown to rest on a more primordial disclosing of the

being. This more primordial disclosing is not structured proposi-
tionally, even though fragments of it can be expressed in propositions. In this way the grip of the subject-predicate structure
on our understanding of Being is loosened. Indeed, the same
loosening would happen for any other structure identified as
syntactically central, in any language form.

Alert readers will no doubt have remarked that this theory of
truth is archaeological; it valorizes by reference back to an origin.
They may also have noticed that I called *aletheia* "fundamental."
Apart from the shift from the word "foundational" to the word
"fundamental" (which still awaits explanation in this paper), it
may seem that Heidegger's thinking is still caught in the basic
metaphysical pattern. Does not Derrida's objection to Searle also
apply to Heidegger: "The enterprise of returning 'strategically,'
ideally, to an origin or to a 'priority' held to be simple, intact,
normal, pure, standard, self-identical in order then to think in
terms of derivation, complication, deterioration, accident, etc.
. . . is not just *one* metaphysical gesture among others, it is *the*
metaphysical exigency" (*LI*, 93). So is this theory of truth merely
the last of the great metaphysical systems? Does it solve the
problems of one foundationalism only by retreating to another,
one in which the *arche* of truth in presencing is privileged as the
determinant of value and the lever for shifting the aporias of
transcendence, but whose own aporias will eventually make
their appearance?

Derrida's remark, quoted above, specifies the metaphysical
move as a return to an origin which is held to be "simple, intact,
normal, pure, standard, self-identical." All these terms require
further elucidation, but perhaps we can best elucidate them, in
this context, by showing how they do *not* apply to Heidegger's
understanding of the origin and essence of representational truth
in the unconcealing of Being. An origin does not need to be
metaphysical; it may be an *arche*-trace whose character is precisely to resist self-identity, simplicity, normality. What is certainly true is that any such *arche*-trace must suffer from a vulnerability to misunderstanding which is built into any route by which
we might understand or specify it. Janicaud correctly remarks:
"The interpreter of Heidegger encounters the same type of difficulty as the interpreter of Wittgenstein: 'He must, so to speak,
throw away the ladder after he has climbed up it.' Impossibility

40

of gathering together definitively and synoptically the discourse and the trajectory: the latter must always drive further and more deeply than the former." The misunderstanding of Heidegger is basically this: "that a thinking of the unthought and the presupposed could play the role of a fixed referential centre, organizing and sovereign" (*ML*, secs. 7, 9). But is not the idea of the unconcealed that of something brought into the light and so no longer concealed? Answer: that is precisely the thinking of the discourse of truth and not its trajectory, against which Janicaud warns us. Heidegger's thinking does indeed lead us by this route, and it has to do so; but the trajectory of his thinking continues by understanding the no-longer-concealed not as result only, but as process. To the understanding of unconcealment the process of unconcealing is essential. "For the unhidden not only is it still essential that it makes the seeming accessible in some way and holds it open in its appearing, but also that the unhidden constantly overcomes a hiddenness of the hidden. The unhidden must be torn out of a hiddenness, in a certain sense plundered from it. . . . For the Greeks originally hiddenness as a self-hiding governs the essence of Being."[17] Thus the negative, the not-yet-revealed, indeed that which resists being revealed, is as essential to truth as coming into the light.

But how can this be right? Presupposed and preestablished before the correctness of "The stone is hard" is precisely the *openness* (in four dimensions) of the stone and of man, within which "The stone is hard" is accessible. Nothing was said at the time to show that the *hidden* was also presupposed or that the process of unconcealment rather than its result must be presupposed. No—but the inquiry was into the essence of truth, in pursuit of the questioning toward truth on which Heidegger and his hearers had already embarked, seekers of what was needed by a culture in a wasteland. The logic of presupposition takes us some way along this route but not to the essence. Questioning to the essence takes us into the situation of human being-in-the-world taken as a whole; what is presupposed not by the specification of the sense of the proposition, but by the giving of sense to it within a context of understanding.

Heidegger fully recognized the special character of the questioning which follows what Janicaud calls the trajectory; at least he made it increasingly clear and gave it increasing emphasis as he got older. By 1937 he characterized what draws our questioning toward the essence as a "need" which is "the not-out-of-knowing and the not-into-knowing [*Nicht-aus-wissen und Nicht-ein-Wissen*]; out of and into what is opened up as this untrodden and ungrounded 'space' through this kind of knowing. This 'space' . . . is that Between in which it is not yet determined what is being and what is unbeing" (*GP*, 152). This need is "not a lack or a deprivation, but the excess of a bestowing"; "man himself first arises from this need, which is more essential than he is"; "it belongs to the truth of Being itself," (*GP*, 153). The awkwardness of the phrase which Heidegger latches onto at the beginning—"Not-out-of-knowing and Not-into-knowing"— contains already the refusal of normality and simplicity needed to avoid metaphysics, according to Derrida; this is a knowing which is not a knowing, which is not out of a space and not into it but which opens it up through this kind of knowing. Such a space is a Between, not a result. In Heidegger's thought, the fundamental *arche* of truth is not a being, so not a foundation; it is a Between. Truth is not the unhidden only. Nor is it the hidden only. Nor again is it a kind of package-deal in which both the hidden and the unhidden are bundled up together. It is the ontological difference *as* difference. Truth is unconcealment as a movement, an event-of-appropriation. Heidegger thinks it in a way that would be contradictory if we were to understand it as being fully one thing or the other. As Zarader has emphasized, it is "the play of veiling and of unveiling, and thereby the mysterious unity and movement of both these";[18] in this it repeats the double determination of *phusis* as presencing and as withdrawal. Zarader notes that lighting as the essence of *aletheia* "not only makes a sign towards what is hidden beyond what unveils itself, towards presence beyond what is present, towards Being beyond beings, but also towards the self-hiding constituting the essence of Being" (*HPO*, 69).

This difference-essence enables us to say that with Heidegger philosophy escapes from the trail of arguing toward establishing this or that thing as a foundation, and then getting entangled in the resulting aporias. Truth—the essence of truth—in the sense given it in Heidegger's texts, is fundamental but not a foundation. It is not a foundation in the sense in which Frege's "The True" is a foundation for him, and in the way the truth-value true is for the main part of the analytic tradition in philosophy (and even, as I have claimed, for the "post-analytic tradition"). Thinking, in Heidegger's sense, aims always to uncover the ground of phenomena (that is the dynamic which first leads us beyond representational truth in search of what *grounds* it), but it is ultimately led to what is groundless, an abyss (*Abgrund*)— and this abyssal character of the fundamental keeps it from being a foundation. The ungrounded ground then infuses back into every aspect and topic of our thinking at the end of philosophy a nonfoundational, differencing character (which is the aspect of Heidegger's thought that best chimes in with Derrida's).

This paper has not to any serious extent sought to argue for nonfoundational thinking, only to make clearer what it is, as it works in Heidegger's thought. The issue between a foundational thinking (metaphysical, in the sense I have been discussing) and a nonfoundational thinking is not a shallow one. According to Heidegger, no argument as such could resolve it, for we are led on the path of this questioning by a need, a mood, an attitude which looks to the future as much as it interprets the past. At least, no argument in the sense of an abstract movement of logic could resolve it. But what an argument properly is, is just one of the issues at stake here. Can an argument, a philosophically cogent movement of thought, itself be the expression and the trajectory of a thinking need?

Chapter 3

SCIENCE AS FOUNDATIONAL?

Robert P. Crease

The philosophy of science has been one of the last bastions of foundationalism. Different versions of foundationalism have been found in each of the two major philosophical perspectives on science, one stressing its factual, observational side, the other its theoretical side. In general, foundationalist programs in the philosophy of science have been maintained by overlooking the significance of experimentation—or the planning, executing, and interpreting of actions—the implications of which are profoundly antifoundational. The first-mentioned, empiricist perspective, conceived of facts or observations as ready-made building blocks of science, and theories as ways of organizing these blocks, arrived at by some process of generalization or induction. Certain "new empiricists" deny the possibility of an observation language, but still hold that science is principally structured over a growing empirical base—without, however, seriously examining the character of the experimental acts which produce that base.[1] The other, anti-empiricist perspective recognized the role of theory in data statements, and therefore that experimentation alone does not and cannot decide between competing hypotheses or theories. Carnap, for instance, ultimately adopted a variant of this view, rejecting belief in foundational statements in science and insisting that the adoption of a theoretical framework was required before observation sentences could be formulated. Nevertheless, along with many contemporary partisans of such a position, he maintains a version of foundationalism in his assumption of a stable level of some sort in science, and in his belief that instability enters only through the different conceptual frameworks with which that level is apprehended. For Karl Popper, "the empirical basis of objective science has thus nothing 'absolute' about it. Science does not rest upon rock-bottom. The bold structure of its theories rises, as it were, above a swamp."[2] But the swampiness Popper saw was not due to the recognition of ambiguities in experimentation, only to the fact that observation statements depend on the frameworks in which they are made. As he wrote, "observations, and even more so observation statements and statements of experimental results, are always *interpretations* of the facts observed . . . *interpretations in the light of theories*" (*LSD*, 107, fn. 3). Experimental data constitute a swamp not due to factors that arise in the performing and interpreting of actions, but because of the various conceptual frameworks with which data can be constituted. Choose a single framework, and the swamp turns into bedrock.[3]

One reason philosophers have avoided raising the problem of experimentation is a certain understanding of the nature and goals of philosophical activity that encourages a preoccupation with theory and a neglect of action as a philosophical theme, which has left them without adequate tools to handle experimentation in a philosophically appropriate manner. The move away from action as a philosophical theme was practically contemporaneous with Western philosophy itself, and was at work when Plato began using *episteme*, which for Homer and others could mean practical skill and ability, with an emphasis on its ideational content. The notion that genuine knowledge is cognition, and cognition the mind's beholding of fixed and immutable forms, became a recurring theme within Western philosophy. The neglect of experiment is but another manifestation of a more general neglect of action within traditional philosophy.

In the past few years, however, a few philosophers, sociologists, and historians have begun to focus on science as an activity rather than as a body of statements, and in the process begun to view experimentation more attentively.[4] That examination could be expected to encompass, in principle, the full range of issues involved in planning, executing, and witnessing experiments, and to disclose how these issues are similar and different from those involved in planning, executing, and witnessing other kinds of actions. Such an approach to the philosophy of science, however, must be qualified in two respects. Since the same phenomenon can show up in utterly different guises or contexts, the inquiry must be phenomenological, for it must address the constitution of scientific entities: how they can appear as "the same" throughout radically changing contexts. And since history and culture are ineluctably present at the heart of any human action not only in execution but also in meaning, such an inquiry must also be hermeneutical, for it must recognize that meaning arises through actions of communities of historically and culturally bound individuals. A phenomenological and hermeneutical philosophy of science might not only solve many traditional problems, but also answer the challenge posed by certain historians to broaden the language of the philosophy of science.[5] And insofar as such an approach restores the importance of experimentation, and thus recognizes the role of craft and the holistic relation between a particular and the system within which it appears, it might also begin to answer the challenge posed by certain philosophers for a holistic or "feminist" approach to science.[6]

Science as Praxis

Foundationalist programs in the philosophy of science have been beset by numerous recurring difficulties, both scientific and philosophical. Empiricist programs must at some point confront the fact that the "given" is a "myth"; observations are perceptual, and the meanings of perceptions are never given once and for all but are always susceptible to reconstitution and reinterpretation. The same holds for the products of experimental actions. A line on a cloud chamber may be interpreted at one time as an electron, and at subsequent times as positrons, muons, or other particles. Shall we say that the "datum" consists of a simple line, which acquires meaning only when the scientific community interprets it correctly or incorrectly? But that line, like data of every experiment, no more arrives on the scientific scene "naked," with a meaning to be supplied by scientific investigators, than a color arrives in my head as a mere "patch," to be subsequently interpreted as, say, the red of an apple or strawberry. A scientist's understanding of that line is contextual, grounded in the web of background assumptions that went into producing it, and this web of background assumptions opens up certain possibilities and forbids others. Continual changes in these background assumptions alter the meaning of past observations as well as expectations for the future, and cut the ground out from under any attempt to understand the dynamics of science in terms of observation alone. If the history of science embarrasses empiricist programs, it embarrasses rationalist programs as well. Scientists are constantly advancing new theories and new concepts to replace existing ones, changing the alleged referent of theoretical terms. The theories of Stoney, Thomson, and Dirac each involved different conceptions of the electron, as do electroweak and string theories, and do not involve progressively less ambiguous descriptions of the same thing.

Data and theory, in short, are both *fragile*. They can be adjusted and reworked depending on how the phenomenon shows itself; they are *relative to* the phenomenon. A set of data, for instance, means nothing in itself. It is like having just a side view, a single appearance, of a cup. It only comes to mean something—and to legitimate itself as a set of data—when it is incorporated with other sets of data that present other appearances into one picture of a phenomenon as appearing through different profiles. One set of data is in the same situation as that figure, used as an optical illusion, that can be seen either as a duck or rabbit profile, depending on the rest of the context; the figure only emerges as a picture *of* something, and hence as a picture at all, in the presence of that context. In the actual practice of science, "data" constantly have had to be recalculated, reworked, or adjusted because the appearance of the phenomenon has shown additional factors in play; "data" even have had to be thrown out because they are discovered not to have had anything to do with the appearance of the phenomenon in question. Thus, the empiricist insistence on the priority of observations or data is misplaced, as is the rationalist assumption of the priority of theory. One must distinguish between the *phenomena* that are disclosed in the praxis of experimentation and the *data* by which they are presented in specific experimental contexts, on the one hand, and the *theories* by which they are represented, on the other. To do so, however, a philosophy of science must possess an adequate notion of disclosure.

The work of Martin Heidegger, the philosopher of disclosure par excellence, would seem to be a natural place to turn at this point. According to Heidegger, human beings are not thinkers but doers first and foremost. We relate to other human beings and to nature primarily through our practices, which range from the ability to move about to the use of tools and language. The total network of these practices is not a thing itself but a background or "world" against which things appear and have meaning. This network of practices discloses the world to us; only because of such disclosure is anything like "discovering" possible. As our practices change, so does this network or world and the meaning of things in it. Activities, rather than beliefs or propositional sentences, form our most intimate alliance with the world.

The difference is crucial.[7] If our fundamental relation to the world is through beliefs, then we can accept or reject this relation through acts of will; we become, in effect, lords of the world. If, on the other hand, we are engaged with the world—and it with us—through practices, then we lack that independence. We are stuck to the world, adapting ourselves to it even as we cause it to adapt to us. We may choose to explore particular possibilities opened up by the world, and through this exploration bring about changes that ultimately affect the world and us along with it, but we are not free to choose that field of possibilities itself.

Heidegger's "existential conception of science" is nonfoundational, for it envisages scientific entities and observations as products of a prior engagement of *Dasein* with the world; a scientist never confronts an entity or makes an observation purely and simply, but through a process of making-present. However, it also envisages science as a derivative activity with respect to other activities of the lifeworld; the making-present involves the transformation or "change-over" of something ready-to-hand to something present-at-hand, and thereby the removal of scientific entities and observations from the lifeworld—from human culture and history. For Heidegger, science, in short, is *not* disclosive. These views remain largely intact in his later writings, with the difference that the change-over is now for the sake, not of the theoretical attitude, but of turning objects into resources for exploitation. "Nature," Heidegger says, "becomes a gigantic gasoline station, an energy source for modern technology and industry."[8] Through science we come to look upon nature, others, and even ourselves as calculable, manipulable resources.

Beings become means to ends, and subordinating means to ends becomes the end itself.

Many other phenomenologists who were either contemporaries of Heidegger or inspired by him held similar views. "To return to things themselves," writes Merleau-Ponty, "is to return to that world which precedes knowledge, of which knowledge always *speaks*, and in relation to which every scientific schematization is an abstract and derivative sign-language, as is geography in relation to the countryside in which we have learnt beforehand what a forest, a prairie or a river is."[9] The danger that such phenomenologists saw was that this abstraction would be substituted for the lifeworld and mistaken for it. H.-G. Gadamer, for instance, says that "modern physics has departed radically from the postulate of perceptibility that comes from our human forms of perception. . . . the impression is created that the 'world of physics' is the true world that exists in itself, the absolute object, as it were, to which all living things relate themselves, each in its own way."[10] Opposing modern *theoria* to the ancient notion of participation at a religious event, Gadamer concludes that "the modern theory is a tool of construction, by means of which we gather experiences together in a unified way and make it possible to dominate them" (*TM*, 412). Strangely, we find the phenomenological tradition to have rejected the traditional foundational approach to science while nevertheless to a large degree adopting without question certain of its views, including the priority of theory, the detachment of scientific objects from human culture and history, and the derivative status of science with respect to the lifeworld and to the essential task of philosophy itself.

That the continental tradition possesses the resources for an antifoundationalist, nonderivative philosophy of science is argued by Joseph Rouse in his *Knowledge and Power: Toward a Political Philosophy of Science*. Rouse's book has two principal theses. The first is that the sciences need to be regarded, not as networks of theories or beliefs or propositions, but as fields of practices. When the sciences are so regarded, so runs the second thesis, it becomes evident that science is a profoundly political activity, where "political" means constitutive of human self-understanding and of the field of human possible actions. "[T]he very practices that account for the growth of scientific knowledge," Rouse writes, "must also be understood in political terms as power relations that traverse the sciences themselves and that have a powerful impact on our other practices and institutions and ultimately upon our understanding of ourselves" (*KP*, xi).

Drawing upon Foucault, Rouse attacks the traditional notion that power and knowledge are extrinsic to each other—that, for instance, knowledge can be applied to obtain power, and power to suppress knowledge, but that power cannot *create* knowledge, a view Rouse summarizes as follows: "The way the world is, is not produced or changed by the exercise of power; only our beliefs about it may be changed" (*KP*, 15). To the contrary, Rouse argues, power is productive as well as repressive:

> The power relations that open up a field of scientific practice are also relations of disclosure, of truth. In working on the world, we find out what it is like. The world is not something inaccessible on the far side of our theories and observations. It is what shows up in our practices, what resists or accommodates us as we try to act upon it. Scientific research, along with the other things we do, transforms the world and the ways it can make itself known. We know it not as subjects representing to ourselves the objects before us, but as agents grasping and seizing upon the possibilities among which we find ourselves. The turn from representation to manipulation, from knowing that to knowing how, does not reject the common-sense view that science helps disclose the world around us. (*KP*, 24–25)

Drawing upon Heidegger, Rouse argues that the meaning and development of scientific activities, like all others, must be understood against an ever-changing background context. Thanks to this context, the scientific world comes preinterpreted, and no "objective" way of assessing, for instance, a good research opportunity is possible. "[T]he reasons for such assessments cannot be usefully disentangled from one's involved, skillful 'craft knowledge' of a field of objects and practices or from one's practical needs—what one aims to do and hopes to achieve"— (*KP*, 92). Nor are there objective criteria for "rational acceptability." "There are no generally applicable standards of rational acceptability in science. There is only a roughly shared understanding of what can be assumed, what can (or must) be argued for, and what is unacceptable for any given purpose and context" (*KP*, 124).

When scientists advance claims, what is involved in their evaluation is not an objective standard but the very specific intentions and method of a very specific group. "Scientific claims are thus established within a rhetorical space rather than a logical space; scientific arguments settle for rational persuasion of peers instead of context-independent truth" (*KP*, 120). If there are standards, they state "what one does" in that field; to be taken seriously, a scientist must address "what one does," and those who do not are not taken seriously. Rouse accurately points to the large role that ad hominem arguments play in the evaluation of a new discovery—how reliable this or that investigator has been in the past—an insight that could be supported by numerous examples in the history of science. The other side of the coin, of course, is that scientists go out of their way to maintain their respectability. "The standards scientists employ, then," Rouse says, "are what they take to be the practical standards of their fellow participants. Note that this understanding involves two distinct claims: the standards are *practical*, based upon the perceived needs of ongoing research activities, and they are *situated*, within localized social networks" (*KP*, 122).

For Rouse, therefore, scientific practices are disclosive. Missing from Rouse's account, however, is an account of *how* scientific entities are disclosed, of what plays the analogous role to what Heidegger called thematization. Again and again, Rouse uses hermeneutical tools to show that practices interpret the world in science as everywhere else, and that an uninterpreted world would be unintelligible. And he also denies that this makes the world our creation: "the interpretation does not make the world the way it is; it allows it to show itself the way it is. . . . Our practices at most determine the possibilities for what there can be, not what there is" (*KP*, 159). But having come to this important threshold, Rouse refrains from taking the next step, and asking how the things of science show themselves—how scientists recognize "what there is." Rouse is content to leave it that the question of what there is is "an entirely objective matter" (*KP*, 159).

But it is critical to discover the nature of that objectivity. Astrol-

51

ogy and witchcraft each had their own practices, their own interpretations, their own power relations, their own standardizations. What makes them pseudosciences? Numerous pseudodiscoveries were made thanks to certain practices and power relations. We need to ask, therefore, how X rays showed themselves as scientific entities in a way that N rays did not.

Traditionally, this question is handled by the role of theory. Realists, for instance, may take a representationalist tack by asserting that the real presence of theoretical entities such as X rays makes theories about them true. Rouse rejects this kind of approach, but offers nothing in its stead. While rightly insisting that science is an activity that discloses entities in the world, he wrongly neglects the question of the being of the entities that are so disclosed. The small role that theory plays in his account is symptomatic of this neglect; theories are best viewed, he says, as "strategies for dealing with various phenomena" (*KP*, 116). Rouse is evidently afraid that granting a large role to theory would force him to surrender the insights of hermeneutics and the disclosive effects of power relations. In effect, Rouse has taken the traditional priority of theory over praxis and stood it on its head, when what is needed is perhaps to recast that relation.

Scientific Praxis as Performance

Such a rethinking has been carried out in the work of Patrick A. Heelan.[11] Heelan views science as a disclosive activity, employing tools provided by Heidegger's existential phenomenology. But he also addresses the question of the being of scientific entities by insisting on the perceptual character of scientific phenomena. While some phenomena are *natural*, that is, ordinary parts of the lifeworld directly accessible to the senses, Heelan argues that scientific phenomena are *naturalized*, or brought into the lifeworld by the mediation of specialized instruments, technologies, and practices. Heelan is then able to bring into play concepts of Husserl's constitutive phenomenology.

Following Husserl, Heelan argues that in science as elsewhere phenomena reveal themselves not all of a piece but only through profiles. Just as I never experience all there is to see about a chair in any individual encounter with it but only a single profile, so I never experience all there is about electrons in a laboratory encounter with them. In the case of the chair, the specific profile I see depends on the relative position of me and the chair. In the case of the electrons, however, the "positioning" is not just spatial, but depends on the particular selection of experimental equipment and techniques I have chosen.

Profiles of phenomena can be transformed among themselves in two ways: the chair can reveal different profiles either when it itself turns (an active transformation, in scientific terminology), or when I walk around it (a passive transformation). Similarly, different electron behaviors produce different active transformations of the profiles, while different methods of sampling electron profiles will result in different passive transformations. In Husserlian language the active transformation group is the noema and the passive transformation group the noesis; the point is that the two transformation groups are the same. The horizon of profiles that can be generated through transforming the respective "positionings" of observer and observed is called the inner horizon, and the law of invariance (or transformation group) governing the profiles is called the eidos.

Following Heidegger, however, Heelan argues that phenomena do not reveal themselves apart from specific human worlds, meaning that their profiles bear the irreducible stamp of human culture and history; a phenomenon, Heelan says, is "fleshed out" or wears a particular "dress" depending upon the particular context in which it appears. The latter metaphor, of course, is imperfect in that there is no such thing as a "naked" phenomenon; there are no "nonsocial occasions." The metaphor is useful, however, in its implication that it is through the dress that a phenomenon belongs to the world in which it appears; the "dress" is provided by the particular instruments, technologies, and practices employed by the scientist. Electrons as they appeared to J. J. Thomson in 1896, for instance, were dressed differently from those that appear to experimenters utilizing a modern particle accelerator. In Husserlian terms, the horizon of profiles that can be generated by phenomena appearing in different historical and cultural circumstances—the "wardrobe" of possible dresses—is called the outer horizon.

The result is a rethinking of the role of theory and experiment in science. A scientific theory, for Heelan, attempts to describe through mathematical models the law of invariance of the profiles of a phenomenon—its inner horizon. However, insofar as those profiles never appear except in particular human cultural and historical contexts—they never appear except "dressed"— a scientific theory is incomplete apart from a concrete social-historical-technological context and a standardized set of experimental praxes. Heelan refers to the theorist as S_t and the experimenter as S_x, using Dirac state vector notation, Heelan refers to the abstract theoretical model, which describes the law of invariance of the profiles generated by the inner horizon, as $|X>_t$ (the model state vector), and the set of empirical profiles of a phenomenon (the phenomenological state vector) as $|X>_x$. He writes:

> The theoretical model $|X>_t$ now appears from the standpoint of S_t to be a kind of language under which the reference phenomenon with its empirical profiles $|X>_x$ is described. . . . The syntax of that "language" is mathematical; of itself it provides no more than what Husserl would have called a *formal ontology* or a *possible* formal ontology, that is, empty schemata of categories of things. Its semantics, however, is tied up with the standardized experimental praxis within which it is used. (*ETCR*, 521)

Theory, therefore, cannot be viewed as picturing entities that exist apart from the lifeworld. The meanings of theories are intrinsically tied up with particular standardized means of producing the phenomena they address in the lifeworld; the vocabulary of theory is thus "praxis-laden." A theory has the abstraction, Heelan says, of a script or score in relation to possible musical or dramatic performances. "Theory alone can no more witness to the authentic presence of a phenomenon than can the same score alone of a piece of music witness to the authentic presence of a musical performance: there are hosts of other relevant factors in each case" (*ETCR*, 516).

Experiments, therefore, do much more than confirm or disconfirm theories; they are performances constitutive of the content of theories. The phenomenon itself, like the play or piece of music, is not a material object in space and time. It only appears "in performance," and the way it appears depends on its "staging." Experimentation therefore acquires a kind of priority over theory: "The last word in scientific research is then with S_x" (*ETCR*, 522). But this corresponds to no more than the priority phenomenology, and science itself, has traditionally placed on seeing things first-hand—which is, after all, the ancient meaning of *theorein*. And what else can "the scientific method" mean if not the skillful performance of acts programmed by theory and witnessed by a suitably prepared audience?

The two scientific roles—S_t and S_x—are thus quite different. The experimenter, S_x, prepares and examines phenomena with the aid of instruments. In science, as in dramatic art, such a production is not automatic; experimentation is not a matter of switching on a device and checking the dials if we are speaking of real science as opposed to demonstrations or lab exercises. Nor is it a matter of Ryle's "knowing how" in the simple sense of knowing how to operate a single piece of machinery. Instead, the production of a scientific phenomenon is a *performance,* one requiring the integration of a battery of different kinds of skills and judgments. There is even a sense in which one might speak of a scientific performance as being so virtuosic as to be unrepeatable, as the masterful and extremely difficult experiment in 1911 by Rutherford and crew demonstrating the existence of the atomic nucleus.

The theorist, S_t, analyzes a performance or set of performances carried out on an instrumental set-up and compares them with others. But while the experimenter "reads through" an instrumental set-up to encounter a phenomenon, the theorist analyzes the instrumental setup itself as a possible representation within a field of possible representations—the way a musicologist, for example, might analyze a score with an eye to seeing whether and how it exemplifies sonata form, or the field of possible sonatas. A scientific example might be the way C. N. Yang and T. D. Lee analyzed a series of experiments producing tau and theta particles in such a way that they were able to treat the experiments as possible representations of the same field, that is, as revealing profiles of the same phenomenon, namely, parity violation in the weak force.

Though S_x and S_t may be executed by the same person in practice, it is crucial not to confuse them, as commonly happens.

The word "electron," for instance, differs when used by the experimenter and theorist. For the experimenter, "electron" is a real phenomenon, a piece of *material ontology*, which is involved in causal explanations; the real presence of electrons in the instrumental set-up is causally involved in the events that take place there. For the theorist, "electron" is an abstract term, part of a *formal ontology*, which is involved in nomological explanations; the theorist delivers an abstract model for the phenomenon consisting of a set of equations.

Performance and Production

Just as the score does not manifest the authentic presence of a piece of music, Heelan observes, theory does not manifest the authentic presence of a scientific phenomenon; many other factors pertaining to the concrete cultural and historical context must come into play. What is now needed is a way of specifying the different hermeneutical dimensions at work in the appearance of scientific phenomena in the laboratory. This might happen if the process by which experimental performances are executed were to be examined more closely.

A way to do so, for instance, would be to examine the process by which phenomena are prepared in an experiment. The *preparation* of phenomena might be viewed as a necessary intermediary stage between theory and experimental performance. Indeed, it might be compared to a "production" in dramatic art, which is a necessary intermediary stage between a script and its dramatic performance.[12] The need for a preparation arises as follows: Theories are abstract testimonials to the presence of phenomena in several respects. They do not specify, for instance, when or where the phenomenon is to take place, or many of its perceptual features—its "dress," to use Heelan's term. Before the phenomenon puts in an appearance it must first be dressed or prepared, a process requiring the experimenter to make a set of decisions in advance of the actual experimental performance. The preparation, in short, specifies that particular environment or special context within which the phenomenon is to be concretely realized in the experimental run or performance. This

56

special context then provides a stable content to the runs or performances of that experiment, making it possible to speak of repeating runs and even of repeating experiments; the latter would occur if, elsewhere, the same set of decisions regarding the phenomenon were to be made and the same environment recreated. And just as there may be different "runs" of one preparation, there may be different ways of preparing the same phenomenon. The Glashow-Weinberg-Salam electroweak theory, for instance, lent itself to several different kinds of preparations—in measurements of neutral currents, in measurements of the scattering of polarized electrons, and in measurements of atomic parity violation effects among others. These all amounted to different ways of preparing the same phenomenon, the electroweak force, on the basis of one theory.

Preparation, in short, "dresses" the phenomenon through the choice of one particular costume from among a wide variety that a phenomenon can have and creating the condition for it to be worn. A further elaboration of this will allow us to pick out several different hermeneutical dimensions involved in experimental preparations—several different ways in which the presence of human culture and history enter into the being of a scientific phenomenon.

First, an experimental preparation embodies a decision about *when* the theory or "experimental script" is to be given a performance. At any given time, thousands of experiments might be performed; indeed, national laboratories and observatories can accommodate only a fraction of the requests for lab time put to them. The choice is dictated by a variety of motives, including the reputations of the scientists who make the proposals, the facilities of the laboratories, and political and economic considerations. One crucial factor, however, is a judgment about the pressing scientific questions of the day and which of the proposed experiments best addresses them. The Glashow-Weinberg-Salam electroweak theory and Grand Unified theories, for instance, were judged to be important theories in the 1970s and 1980s, respectively, and proposals to prepare phenomena on the basis of them received priority over other proposals in the hands of laboratories and funding agencies. The decision to prepare a scientific phenomenon, in short, embodies a judgment about the state of the scientific "world"—just as a decision to produce a dramatic work involves a decision about the state of the theatrical world.

Second, an experimental preparation embodies an entire set of judgments about how that phenomenon is to appear in experimental performances. If the above-mentioned hermeneutical dimension concerned the fact *that* a particular experiment addresses the pressing scientific questions of the day, this one concerns *how* that phenomenon is to be realized in performance. The Glashow-Weinberg-Salam electroweak theory was a "script" with a variety of possible performances; experimental preparations could involve vastly different contexts in which these performances might take place, contexts calling for vastly different instrumentation, power sources, computers, monitors, and the like. The Grand Unified theory in its simplest form, on the other hand, was a "script" with few possible performances with contemporary instrumentation—one, however, being proton decay. Setting up the conditions for this performance, however, required environments unlike any hitherto created. (Several groups of scientists with different preparations proved unable to execute performances in these environments, suggesting that the script had to be revised.) An experimental preparation must also include selection of individuals whose specific skills will shape the experimental performances; poor execution of an experiment is likely to prevent scientists from correctly judging a performance.

While the above two hermeneutical dimensions of experimental preparation refer to decisions made in advance of the performances in order to realize them, a third has to do with the way the performances are studied by scientists. Here we must invoke the distinction between the experimental and the theoretical role. In the experimental role, scientists prepare phenomena and conduct performances, while in the theoretical role they work on the theoretical models by which performances are "scored." This may involve attending only to the internal logic of these models, or it may involve attempting to pick out the essential features of experimental performances and comparing them to those of similar performances. Stretching Heelan's analogy, we might compare experimenters to directors, and theorists to dramaturges. The theoretical role, however, involves its own kind of judgment, and thus its own kind of hermeneutical dimension. Data, for instance, can come to be "seen as" denominating profiles of a new phenomenon rather than as just machine-generated numbers. This seeing-as results in a new perception, a perception which supplies its own standard for correctness inasmuch as seeing something as an object implies an infinite number of further profiles belonging to this object, which may themselves be sampled. Sometimes theorists may pick out what subsequently turn out to be irrelevant features of experimental performances, such as the early classification of particles by mass; though initially illuminating, mass ultimately had nothing to do with what is now thought to be scientifically relevant. Murray Gell-Mann's judgment that the techniques of group theory could be used to classify the particles on the basis of strangeness and isotopic spin, on the other hand, turned out to be inspired, and subsequent experimental performances disclosed other profiles implied by the theory he had described. His judgment, running against the conventional wisdom about the nature of particles, made it easy to find other new particles—just as Becquerel's discovery of radioactivity in uranium, for instance, subsequently made it easier for the Curies to spot radioactivity in other elements. No "standard of rationality" could possibly make interpretive judgments of such novelty for us; we could no more write a program to pick out the scientifically relevant properties of an experiment than one to write drama criticism.

But scientific research may be conducted in several different ways. First of all, it may be directed to looking for the theory behind a series of repeatable performances—performances that experimenters know how to prepare with stability and consistency. Examples of this include Roentgen's efforts to understand what was making his scintillation screen glow and the search of present-day scientists for the theory behind high-temperature superconductors. In this kind of research, theorists are looking to write the script, as it were, for a series of performances that have been consistently executed.

Second, scientific research may be directed to preparing a performance for the first time—in more traditional language, discovering a phenomenon predicted by a theory. Examples of this include the first creation of a superconducting material and the discovery of certain types of subatomic particles. In this kind of research, experimenters look to prepare and perform, so to speak, a new phenomenon on the basis of an existing script.

Third, scientific research may be directed to seeking out deviations between experimental performances and theoretical scripts. Experimenters or theorists alike may engage in this kind of research program. Experimenters may try to prepare performances in novel conditions to see whether such performances still "fit the script." Instances of this include measurements of phenomena, such as the position of hydrogen spectral lines, to an unprecedented degree of accuracy. Theorists may try to see in already executed experimental performances indications of another script and attempt to write it; Gell-Mann's classification scheme for elementary particles was an example. It is as if, in a theatrical performance, directors continually tested the limits of how a play can be performed while critics sought to pick out novel features of the performance not codified in the script— and as if, furthermore, this information required scripts to be reworked. The closest theatrical analogue here might be certain forms of experimental theater.

The analogy between science and dramatic arts, therefore, opens the possibility for liberating the philosophy of science from foundationalism without incurring a slide into relativism, on the one hand, or making science a derivative activity with respect to the lifeworld, on the other.[13] It is useful not simply for its descriptive value, but for its ability to bring a certain philosophical canon—that of hermeneutical phenomenology—to bear upon the activity of science.[14] The point of the analogy is that both theatrical and scientific productions involve an interaction between world, performance, and audience. Just as the dramatic world changes by the critical evaluation of performances, calling for new scripts and new performances, so the scientific world changes by the evaluation of experimental performance, which calls in turn for new theories and new performances. Analyzing this interaction in greater depth will require tools of both hermeneutics and phenomenology while keeping an eye on the practice of science. Such a study is likely to shed light not only on the philosophy of science, but also respond to demands on the part of historians and even on the part of certain scientists for a more meaningful language with which to speak about science.

Chapter 4

DELETION OR DEPLOYMENT: IS THAT ANY WAY TO TREAT A SIGN?

Herbert Hrachovec

Edmund Husserl's treatment of signs as derivative from the lived presence of human consciousness[1] has evoked quite divergent critical comments. Two can paradigmatically be singled out. Whereas Jacques Derrida, in a Heideggerian move, shows the metaphysical assumptions hidden in unmediated presence,[2] Ernst Tugendhat exchanges Husserl's emphasis on phenomenological explorations of the human mind for the tools of analytical philosophy of language.[3] Although Derrida and Tugendhat eventually move in very different directions, their objections start from similar concerns. Talk about signs is almost incomprehensible unless a certain dualism between something that is employed to indicate, refer to, mean . . . something else is assumed. It can be argued that, consequently, Husserl's attempt to tie such a dichotomy back to the presumably unshrouded clarity of Cartesian consciousness threatens the very idea of signification. According to this consideration semantics cannot be grounded in the noetic realm. "Signs are foreign to this self-presence of consciousness" (*SP*, 58), since their possibility rests on some systematically antecedent set of differences governing the relations between what is present (the signifier) and what is indicated or expressed by it (the signified). This idea can be expressed not only in the Saussurian terms the early Derrida draws upon, but also by using the distinction between syntax and semantics familiar in analytical philosophy.

The consequent complexity of a sign calls for a careful description of its constitutive elements as well as of the overarching structure that keeps those elements from disintegrating into mere givens, lacking significative value. In outlining these relationships I shall link the terminology of formal semantics to considerations that are closer to the European tradition. The outcome will justify Derrida's observation about "the sign [being] from its origin . . . marked by this will to derivation or effacement" (*SP*, 51). Derrida's insight (which coincides with analytic philosophy's insistence on mediation by language) raises the question of how to deal with the permanent unfulfillment such a status inflicts upon a sign. Husserl's concern with the fulfillment of intentional (semantical) phenomena, however, also deserves to be taken seriously. I will, therefore, develop an account of "the sign" that retains its metaphysical nonprimordiality, while accommodating the fact that in describing its successful employment we constantly find ourselves referred back to just the language of originary insight attacked by Derrida. Introducing an illustrative simile and relating its discussion to the traditional distinction between first and second nature, I hope to show how the autonomy of intentional and semantical notions can be upheld even as attempts to ground them in some basic intuition or successful employment are conceived as perfectly legitimate. It will become clear in the course of the argument that only by abandoning the rhetoric of exclusiveness can a satisfactory account of the sign be given. In general terms: signs are characteristic examples of transient satisfaction. The fundamental constituents of any semantic theory have to be able to fit smoothly into a pattern of originary relations while preserving the susceptibility to disruption that marks their nonprimordiality.

Formal Semantics

It can be doubted whether the idea of formal semantics arising from Gottlob Frege's work makes any sense at all. Meaning, as it is ordinarily understood, is clearly distinct from abstract representations of meaningful utterances. To clarify some basic points these constructions may, however, serve as a useful starting point. What is a sign? We already characterized it as something pointing to, or standing for, or representing something else in an orderly fashion. It seems natural to assume that such relations can be described systematically. "Model theory" is a completely abstract way of doing this, building up an increasingly complex structure starting with interpretations of signs that are not considered to be complex (elementary things) and moving on to configurations of signs, presenting configurations of things in a formally suitable way.[4] It is not necessary to go into the details of this approach in order to discuss several presuppositions exhibited by this approach. Let me explain some implications of the underlying picture.

Perhaps the most fundamental assumption is this: something serving as a sign is not regarded simply by itself, as an element of syntax. It is incorporated into a semantical relation that can be understood as directing attention away from the given inscription, drawing it to something else, its semantical value. Such values (entities, relations, truth) are readily defined in formal semantics, and as a consequence little emphasis is normally put on the fact that they are constructs of a special kind, not on the same level with syntactic marks. Nevertheless, it is commonly conceded that a qualitative jump separates concatenations of inscriptions from the "meanings" they represent "under an interpretation." Theoretical ideality marks the realm of the signified in any semantical theory worth its name.

Now, if we follow our intuition that words have meaning we seem committed to an explanation of where they get it from. There is considerable theoretical disagreement about how to proceed at this point, but one fundamental move cannot be in dispute, since it establishes the semantical enterprise itself, namely starting from a split, introducing two different kinds of entities before proceeding to interrelate them systematically. Formally speaking, variables, constants, and terms refer to something; well-formed formulas are satisfied by sets, and sentences characterize models. This structural pattern should not distract attention away from the fact that a certain tension between presence (of the signifier) and absence (of the signified) lies at the heart of this analytical account. Can such a gap be allowed to stand at the beginning of a discipline? Mustn't it be retracted immediately because it would be impossible to explain the interrelation of the components of the scheme? Consider formal languages designed to refer to mathematical structures that are supposed to have a certain existence of their own. On the one hand, they are conceptually separated from their reference; on the other hand, exactly the same language of set theory is used to introduce the elements of both the system of signification and of the signified. It is in fact by assuming a common logical structure that the split is made to work as an inducement to bridging the gap. This can be generalized.

A sign enacts an essential distinction of realms, but it cannot function without the possibility of their fusion either. If semantics does not simply occupy itself with empirical investigations, it has to reflect on this apparent contradiction. The essentials of this situation are a double perspective and a unifying overview, the *relata* of the procedure of interpretation, on the one hand, and its underlying logic, on the other. In model theory the interchange between presence and absence that constitutes a signifying unit is couched in prescriptive mathematical metalanguage. Thus, the difficulty of having to explain how two domains, by definition separate, can function as a whole is avoided. From this perspective they are not at all unrelated to each other, since they form part of a more inclusive pattern, held together by the rigor of a formal discipline. But this explanation obviously fails when metaphysical, epistemological, and deconstructionist questions are raised.

The Use of Signs

The most prominent objection against formal semantics is that it rests on an uncritical reification of meaning. As long as a distinction between making noise and making sense is upheld, however, some account of the gap opened up by the deferment accomplished by signs has to be given.

A great variety of theories, reaching from cognitive science to hermeneutics, is currently offered to deal with the division and fusion of syntactic and semantic modes of analysis. From information-processing to (post)metaphysical thinking, the characteristics of signs have received wide attention. But there has also been a countercurrent, which, starting with Husserl's attempts to ground signification in some prominent features of human consciousness, tries to set aside such an uncomfortable dualism.

Ordinary reconstructions of our intuitions about meaning seem to produce a very peculiar relation, bridging two incommensurable realms. In Wittgenstein's words: "Naming appears as a *strange* connection between a word and an object."[5] Whatever the results of an empirical investigation into our cognitive capacities might be, and however impressive a case could be made for (or against) our civilization's tendency to reify meanings, according to Wittgenstein such a strategy does not address itself to the most elementary question that can be asked concerning a sign, namely why it needs some explanation at all. Why should there be such a puzzling dichotomy calling for mysterious integrative elements in the first place? To quote him again: " 'The sentence, a peculiar thing!': the sublimation of the whole presentation resides in this. The tendency to assume a pure intermediate being between the *sentence-sign* and the facts" (*PI*, Sec. 94).

According to the picture of linguistic elements that depicts them as linked up to corresponding elements of the world by a special, epistemologically relevant relation, signs appear as extraordinary constituents of the universe. But once one starts to wonder about signifying entities, there will be constant puzzlement about the unity of the world and man's position within and/or outside the course it takes. This reconstruction of our use of language establishes a fundamental ontological priority of speakers, i.e., beings that are somehow able to create the world of which they are part. This is the predicament nonsemantical theories of understanding try to escape from. Wittgenstein, for example, in his later work worries about the legitimacy of the initial astonishment and considers substantialized meanings as consequences of a misguided picture of language. There are no signs to start with, rather contexts of use that serve as complex, multilayered units of communication. Furthermore, a basis of unquestioned agreement in behavior has to be assumed before bits of language relating to pieces of the world can even be considered.

Jacques Derrida, as I have indicated, arrives at similar conclusions starting from a critique of Husserl's phenomenology.[6] But his line of argument is completely different. Realizing that the phenomenological concept of a sign is firmly linked to traditional metaphysical assumptions, he tries to find a way out of the dilemma of this foundationalism. In Derrida's view signs cannot but disturb metaphysical securities by their nonprimordiality. His philosophical strategy of thinking at the edge of metaphysics, consequently, unlike Wittgenstein's antimetaphysical thinking, demands a more complicated procedure. His efforts divide into establishing a protoprimordial grounding of signification *and* an overcoming of the established concept of a sign. The claim is that "to restore the original and nonderivative character of signs, in opposition to classical metaphysics, is, by an apparent paradox, at the same time to eliminate a concept of signs whose whole history and meaning belong to the adventure of the metaphysics of presence" (*SP*, 51).

Where does that leave us regarding the initial astonishment indicated by Wittgenstein? Derrida occupies a peculiar position between semantic dualism and its systematic opposite, the dissolution of ordinary signification within the context of the living presence of consciousness or actual use of language. He hints at an ultrafoundational attitude toward the sign, although he recognizes that we would lose our current concept of a sign if we were successful in establishing its proper nature. Something like a primordial *"différance"* is supposed to ground signs and cannot be understood in established semantical terms. As it unfolds it cancels the "metaphysics of the presence" on which, according to Derrida, the common notion of signification rests. At this systematic juncture, analytic philosophy and deconstruction obviously part company in their attempts to clarify the structure of semantics. So where does that leave my argument?

Schematically speaking, the preceding considerations have been drawn in two different directions. On the one hand, there is the discovery of a constitutive dualism inherent in every attempt to conceptualize signification; on the other hand there is insistence on a fundamental simplicity of human communication. Very different schools, ranging from transcendental phenomenology to ordinary language analysis, regard this unity as anterior to a subsequent split. In taking up the discussion at this point the next section will deal with a traditional concept that receives scant treatment in Derrida's critique of Husserlian self-givenness of consciousness, namely intentionality. This concept will eventually supply us with a pattern underlying the strangeness of the semantic relation and the intuitive ease of signifying behavior.

How Can Signs Fulfill Their Functions?

Intentionality can be established as a fundamental semantical relation or regarded with suspicion as resulting from an inherently dualistic worldview. The activities of reference, belief, desire, and the like are characteristically described as of another kind as what is referred to, believed, or desired. This difference poses a constant challenge to philosophical attempts to eliminate the classical epistemological dichotomy. Taking a closer look at so-called intentional phenomena, however, reveals that neither undisturbed belief in their existence, nor unrelenting attempts to remove them from the picture altogether are satisfactory. Common-sense examples of fulfillment, such as discovering a solution to a problem or keeping a promise give a good starting point for showing this.

Two types of situations are relevant in such cases, one marked by an uncertainty, a question, generally speaking by an unresolved tension between constituents of a certain state, the other one suggested by an overcoming of uncertainty, e.g., the determination of an answer or the achievement of satisfaction when a promise is kept. What one finds is a dichotomy that calls for resolution into a state of satisfaction. But how can the question (the expectation, the promise) be present in its fulfillment? These conditions of fit by definition exclude just the unfulfilled features. An answer, once articulated, does not exhibit the question to which it answers. To solve this problem it is important to realize, by looking at examples like the ones given, how artificially both our previous positions have been opposed. Utterances are *neither* simply isolated (and in need of interpretation), *nor* simply functioning in a satisfying way. We use them in particular circumstances in order to fulfill certain needs. It is loosely said that something answers a question. A more precise way of putting this would be to say that within a certain context something is accepted by someone as an answer. There is a peculiar logic at work here. By relating an unresolved situation to a state of comparative closure an extremely useful move of mastering the world is described. This bears on the process of signification and its fulfillment in unproblematic use.

Achieving satisfaction is not adequately described as making one final move toward an aim. It involves a qualitative change in the description of the whole enterprise. Here we can begin to see why fulfillment of intentional attitudes might (precariously) hold semantics together. In some sense, ordinary meaningful behavior must be described by excluding reference to possible disturbances. Nevertheless, the complexity of the overall situation can only be captured if the second descriptive approach, pointing at the lack of fit, is included. Fulfillment cannot be conceptualized as a result only, it has to be seen as fulfillment *of* something which by this very feature relates back to the state of unfulfillment. In proceeding from an explicitly objectified semantical situation toward its resolution, the problematic dichotomy can be eliminated, but the resulting one-dimensional account of successful communication loses its punch if it is divorced from this genesis. Pure satisfaction is a phantom.

Fulfillment of intentional structures, seen in this way, is a concept referring to both a process of satisfaction and its result, weaving together situations characterized by a lack of fulfillment and by the lack of this lack. It is crucial that when some want changes into accomplishment the whole apparatus employed to describe the respective situations is completely reshuffled, provoking claims of radical incommensurability. As long as signifiers can be viewed in isolation their correlates in the realm of sense are also bound to appear as single entities, causing the problem of commerce between signifier and signified. Lack of satisfaction produces the construct of something capable of satisfying this state. But it is exactly because of this that the constructed entity cannot fulfill its task of satisfaction as if it were a missing piece of equipment fitting into a predesigned slot. Its raison d'etre is to indicate the incompleteness of the situation by its absence, it cannot simply be added to it like another of its elements.

Thus fulfillment, seen as a process, relates two qualitatively different types of situations. Obviously, introducing a one-to-one correlation between its respective constituents will not work here. This is why the apparatus of formal semantics is of no use in clarifying the situation. Establishing a metaphysical link between the signified and the signifier likewise is a misguided way of grasping what happens when the patterns of description switch. Thus, Derrida is right against Husserl insofar as he stresses the uneliminable strangeness within this relation. But he misses Husserl's legitimate concern with intuitive closure. Talk about satisfaction amounts to a decision to see those patterns in the light of each other, and more precisely to regard a lack of disruption as a state internally connected with a particular disruption and its removal. Only by resorting to the analysis of a preceding problem and the logical space it opens up can some features of a state of the world be recognized as solutions. Taken by themselves they remain mute, just as a question without the prospect of an answer is mere rhetoric. Various philosophers have attacked the inclination to be inside and outside of a particular language-game at the same time. Such tendencies can certainly be a source of confusion, but, if my remarks on fulfillment are correct, we cannot dismiss them out of hand. The course of investigation suggesting itself here, rather, is to find out more about this simultaneity.

First Nature, Second Nature

Let me explore the tension between abstraction and involvement, starting with an example of harmless dualism. Someone owns a very old record player and has never heard of anything more refined than mono recordings, even though half his records are produced for stereo listening. He has to be taught the difference between mono and stereo, and only by being shown how a stereo system works will he be able to discover that his own collection consists of two significantly different types of records. In other words, only the proper use of a particular apparatus can bring out experiential distinctions. It is virtually meaningless to claim that they are present per se, without the availability of a certain corpus of knowledge and techniques. We can construct certain machines that enable us to subdivide one type of sound-event into two subtypes, depending on the information upon which the record player operates. The content of such an acoustical event, consequently, is relative to the interests and devices of those trying to extract the information from a given source. Everyday life characteristically consists in such multilayered situations. A wealth of data is ordinarily invested into the constitution of objects of our acquaintance, but there is no ultimate test that could ascertain how many levels of analysis there are and no guarantees that newly found features will fit together nicely with the ones already known. Signs figure within this same experience. They cannot simply be picked out as self-sufficient elements of the world (if there are any), just like stereo records are not recognizable without a special differentiating device. Earlier on I described the semantical stance as imposition of a duality of views on given data. This is nicely mirrored in my propaedeutic simile, stereo sound splitting the flow of impulses from the original source and processing it through a second channel.

The lesson suggested by this example is as follows. A sign is something that can be seen as just another piece of nature and, with the help of certain conceptual devices, as embodiment of some particular transcendence of supposedly "natural" interactions—namely lawlike causal processes or pragmatic communicative discourse. To see this more clearly, let us look again at the case of the record player. A crucial distinction has to be observed here. Stereo can be opposed to mono, but both stereo and mono are modes of reproduction of some previously given acoustical signal. The original sound underlying the record obviously is neither mono nor stereo. In reproducing it we use a given set of possibilities that implies and/or excludes others, all of them, however, remaining on this side of the representational divide. Stereo might invariably sound "better" to the well-informed listener, but this does not affect the point that there are distinct uses for either of both reproductive modes. (This is why more sophisticated audio equipment usually includes a mono-button.) Both recording techniques are, in a systematic sense, equidistant from the original source. This does not entail, however, that their difference in reproductive quality cannot be put to use according to changing requirements. Now it seems to me that naturalistic and semantical descriptions of human behavior can also be regarded along those lines. Taken *as* descriptions both share the same methodological status, neither being an a priori more accurate rendering of a certain phenomenon than the other. Only by specifying the circumstances do we set up a situation in which either mode of description is superior. Sound events are neither inherently mono nor stereo, but there can be an overwhelming case for preferring stereo reproduction against mono. Employment of the dualism inherent in intentional ascription can likewise be the best strategy available to make sense of the data. Claiming that semantical features of the world must be derivable from causal or pragmatic ones can then be compared to saying that stereo sound derives from basically mono acoustical sources.

Let us discuss this less picturesquely in the setting of our considerations about fulfillment as resolution of the semantical dichotomy. The general point is that there is no single exclusive way to describe how signs actually function. Whether simply substituting the semantical scheme in favor of a nondualistic one or remaining within the dichotomy, both offer an easy way out. This leaves the task of specifying the particular way in which fulfillment as nondichotomic state of affairs is affected by intentionality. As it turns out, it can be posited on either side of the semantic tension. An unmediated fit between significatory elements can be taken either as naturalistic or as a very special semantical description. One pertinent way of expressing the distinction is to say that operational signs are often regarded as "first" nature, whereas their particularity only shows under the light of what has traditionally been called "second nature," a combination of features of naturalistic interaction and fulfillment of meaning. Second nature is the quasicausal set of historically acquired dispositions posited, among other reasons, to capture the law-like quality of sign-governed behavior. Social compliance with signs is not present in conceptualizations of nature pure and simple. Second nature seems supervenient on nature in the literal sense and thus is open to well-known reductionist complaints. Is it just an invention useful to lay claim to a specially invented, dubious territory of humanistic fancy?

Why should we employ representational categories when meaningful behavior seems to lack explicit intentional features most of the time? Its characteristics can, on the contrary, often be convincingly described within the mechanical paradigm. Why take the trouble of introducing second nature? The answer turns on the degree of complexity and interference of simultaneous, mutually exclusive, perspectives one is prepared to countenance. The concept serves to introduce an additional coherence into the constitution of hermeneutical phenomena, namely, the historical dimension of communicating, failing to communicate, and re-opening communication by means of signs. To explain how something disclosed to us in an intentional mode and seen as fulfillment (hence elimination) of this very mode can be the same thing, we must be able to produce a story connecting sentences in the intentional idiom with standard assertions without reference to intentional states. It calls for an elucidation with different approaches that are much more flexible than their contraposition suggests. Assimilating second to first nature, on the other hand, amounts to opting against the delicate conceptual balance that allows us to treat fulfillment of the semantical quest as something distinct from a presemantical "fullness" of interactions. The question comes to whether semantics has its own distinctive foundation or whether it is forced to search for it within the confines of another paradigm. It follows that, if the former is conceded, the relation of first to second nature has to remain an open question. Attempts to address it have to include provisions not only for the stability but also for the possible disruption of the signifying process. Lack of the first requirement disqualifies something as adequate description, lack of the second falls short of characterizing signs, at least if they are understood as figuring in two distinct sets of circumstances capable of being integrated into unproblematic procedures, and yet readable as contingent resolutions of previously open configurations.

Multiple Simultaneous Descriptions

Starting from the controversy about Husserl's anchoring signs in the primordial realm of Cartesian consciousness, the preceding discussion has advanced to show how intuitions concerning their ultimate derivability and ultimate underivability may be reconciled. In its course we have touched upon three possible foundational accounts: naturalism, autonomy of dualism, and a kind of naturalism on the second level, embedded in use. Those alternatives are commonly regarded as mutually exclusive, competing approaches. But adherence to just one of those frames misses the essential complexity of the phenomenon we have been investigating. Such a story has to be built on the interplay between the various modes of reference. It would lose its point if only one would be allowed.

As a typical example, consider the attempt to reduce the intrinsic dualism of representation to some unmediated connective state of the world. There are, as I have pointed out, in principle two ways to go: first and second nature, both removing the challenge of dualism, though by very different means. The choice is between abolishing the category of intentionality or tracing its fulfillment. But why should one suppose that the same choice is adequate on all occasions? Cries of pain and utterances communicating intellectual achievements require different treatment. There are situations calling for the abandonment of dualistic complications, and others that need to be considered in the light of the difficulties they induce. Wittgenstein's puzzlement about the "strangeness" of the naming relation is probably best assuaged by recognizing that attempts at referring are ordinarily successful. But this does not exclude the possibility that, whenever a well-established praxis of relating to some segment of our world breaks down, the problem of reference remains.

Because of the linear order in which the three possible positions have been presented, one might be tempted to conclude that a hidden dialectic is at work here. But, taking contextuality seriously, it is impossible to produce general rules that could determine such a process. It is often difficult to decide whether the successful use of a sign should be seen as a matter of instinct or training. Naturalistic reduction of semantics and its assimilation to pragmatics are difficult to distinguish once the representational point of view is bracketed. First nature fuses with second nature as signs turn into one feature of a universal, vaguely causal framework. I do not possess an a priori program telling me in advance which option has to be taken. At this point the metatheoretical problem looms large. Which picture should help us to decide about the basic shape of investigations about meaning? Or can we opt for a variety of pictures? Would this simply amount to giving in to relativism?

Obviously, one cannot start a promising research project on the metalevel. But occasionally it is helpful to take a step back and review the overall situation. My proposal is to treat the semantical stance as an irreducible stage in the process I have been indicating. The existence of such processes cannot be demonstrated to a hypothetical outsider without getting him or her to agree upon some suitable ontological frame, but this dilemma is common to all the approaches mentioned. How, then, can the various stages be combined into one picture, keeping in mind that they follow entirely different descriptive patterns? Basically, I think, by granting that developments of any kind (think of the arrival of high fidelity) involve internally coordinated switches of perspective. There is no Hegelian Logic of History, but there are all kinds of expectations disappointed and fulfilled. Only by keeping the descriptive apparatus flexible can justice be done to them. It is neither entirely by chance nor by systematic a priori correlation within a singular pattern that a gestalt-switch can take place. On such occasions two patterns can profitably be employed simultaneously in an ad hoc fashion that is nevertheless born out by some set of data. (An underlying sensory stimulation has for example been arranged to give rise to entirely different interpretations.) Multiple readings of such information are not arbitrary even though they contain an amount of conventionalized subjective experience. In fact we are perfectly accustomed to live with simultaneous, mutually exclusive meanings; architects using elevators as decorative elements and children regarding toys as friends are just two examples. Considering a sign as causal factor, bearer of meaning, and as a social construct is no more mysterious than regarding a sweater as protection against cold weather, as a gift, and as a symbol of a certain lifestyle.

A signpost, as Wittgenstein describes it, sometimes leaves doubts regarding the direction in which it points, but sometimes it does not (*PI*, sec. 85). This remark does not sound very profound, yet in an inauspicious way it contains all the problems about fulfillment I have been discussing. There is no guarantee that doubts will not turn the seemingly automatic process of following a direction into an open question. Conversely, in terms of the resulting question, there is no explanation of how it is eventually settled. Instinctively, we want a theory covering both the reliability of well-established procedures and their potential to go awry. One way to respond to this challenge is to take signs as causal instruments and explain their failing statistically, introducing additional parameters wherever needed to assimilate them to more conventional scientific mechanisms. Another methodological option has been defended here: signs are regarded as something that *can* mislead in the sense of incorporating possible doubt about their particular function into their definition. The plasticity of signs emphasized by semantic theory derives from disentangling second from first nature, setting up and bridging the gap between them. Signs carry expectations, expectations risk disappointment, possible disappointment can be built into understanding. Nature will never again be what it seemed before it was recognized as partly man-made. Discussions surrounding semantical concepts are determined by this hidden fact. Bringing it into the open turns this lack of reliability into an asset of language-using animals.

PART II
SUBJECTIVITY

Chapter 5

AUTONOMY AS FOUNDATIONAL

Richard White

In the final pages of *The Order of Things,* Michel Foucault invokes Nietzsche's parable of the madman and the death of God as an expression of the last word on humanism and a prediction of the end of our anthropocentric age:

> In our day, and once again Nietzsche indicated the turning-point from a long way off, it is not so much the absence or the death of God that is affirmed as the end of man. . . . is it not the last man who announces that he has killed God, thus situating his language, his thought, his laughter in the space of that already dead God, yet positing himself also as he who has killed God and whose existence includes the freedom and decision of that murder? . . . Rather than the death of God—or rather, in the wake of that death and in a profound correlation with it—what Nietzsche's thought heralds is the end of his murderer; it is the explosion of man's face in laughter, and the return of masks; it is the scattering of the profound stream of time by which he felt himself carried along and whose pressure he suspected in the very being of things; it is the identity of the Return of the Same with the absolute dispersion of man.[1]

Foucault understood that Nietzsche was not just another nine-teenth-century thinker, in the tradition of Feuerbach, who celebrated the death of God in order to reaffirm the new divinity of man. Certainly, God *is* dead, but according to Foucault the real force of Nietzsche's parable does not lie in its atheism, since the ultimate issue is actually the death of "man" as the one who has defined and dignified himself *as* the murderer of God. We might remember, for example, that in Nietzsche's original passage those who are standing around regard the death of God as rather obvious and unremarkable. What they fail to recognize are the momentous consequences of this deed: " 'I come too early,' he said then; my time has not come yet . . . deeds require time even after they are done, before they can be seen and heard."[2] Thus, according to Foucault, the final meaning of the death of God is the death of "man," in the sense of the final passing of that *episteme* or order of things which has focused upon "man," human experience, and human history as the origin and locus of all meaning and truth.[3] In philosophy, the thought of Kant, Hegel, and Marx, phenomenology and existentialism may all be construed as representative versions of this modern anthropologism. And if it is allowed that such "humanism" has frequently defined itself in opposition to the religious hypothesis, then the surpassing of the latter must ultimately lead to its own demise: "To all those who still wish to talk about man," Foucault writes, "to all those who still ask themselves questions about what man is in his essence . . . who refer all knowledge back to the truths of man . . . [and] who refuse to mythologize without demystifying . . . we can answer only with a philosophical laugh—which means, to a certain extent, a silent one" (*OT*, 342–43).

Foucault's interpretation of Nietzsche is quite compelling. In his notebooks, Nietzsche explicitly condemned all the varieties of bourgeois humanism as so many forms of "incomplete" nihilism, which merely substitute "man" in place of God within the same Christian-nihilistic schema. And this is the point of the madman's apocalyptic warning: "What did we do when we unchained this earth from its sun? Whither is it moving now? Whither are we moving now? Away from all suns? Are we not plunging continually?" The death of God clearly implies the death of *all* fixed centers of meaning (all "suns," such as "man," "ego," "subject," "atom," etc.) which could provide a foundation from which we might derive a final account of the meaning of the world. Once God is removed, every other substantial unity must be challenged as a simple reflection of this central pole. So that, with the death of God, the self is effectively de-centered, and the traditional goal of self-possession becomes entirely problematic as we find ourselves straying through an infinite void.

In *The Order of Things*, Foucault follows the general program of structuralism, and its largely discredited attempt to reduce the variety of human existence to the static models or systems which are supposed to support it. In the final chapter, for example, Foucault expressly considers the need for short-circuiting the reliance upon conscious experience as the ultimate reference and truth. In order to study "man," he suggests a grid whose axes would be constituted by the sciences of ethnology and psycho-analysis. Such a framework would effectively dissolve "man" as a self-present subject totally in charge of himself; as Foucault suggests elsewhere, it would leave conscious experience as noth-ing more than a kind of "scum" or surface effect. Foucault's later work transcends this structuralist model, and in general the rational faith of structuralism has given way to the rigors of poststructuralist thought. Even so, Foucault's original rejection of humanism is still completely relevant and contemporary; for beginning with the Derridian critique of structuralism, in "Struc-ture, Sign and Play," poststructuralism has gone even further to unmask all of those principles—such as the subject, sign, and *structure,* which falsely represent themselves as the originary presence of truth.[4] Now, if Derrida is correct, there is only an endless play of *différance* which produces subjectivity as another "trace" of its overall effect; to follow Foucault's interpretation of Nietzsche, what we have to come to terms with is the "explosion of man's face in laughter" and "the absolute dispersion of man." Ever since Nietzsche, contemporary atheism has been unable to avoid such a crisis by appealing to a new transcendental ground.

Foucault's interpretation of the death of God may be read as a symbolic manifesto for much of recent continental philosophy, insofar as it encapsulates the attack on "man," humanism, and every ordinary notion of *self*-appropriation. By challenging the sovereignty of the enthroned subject of consciousness and pro-claiming the absolute dispersion of "man," recent continental thought has effectively cast suspicion on the received values of "reflection," "experience," and "history." More particularly, as we will see, it challenges a major current of modern philosophy which, from Kant to existentialism has focused upon the drama of the individual life, and grasped the autonomy of the individual as the foundation for every value and truth.

The debate between "humanism" and "antihumanism," or "modernism" versus "postmodernism," remains fraught with complexity and requires the distinguishing of several related positions.[5] Rather than attempting such a survey, in what follows I shall focus instead upon the single ideal of individual autonomy which appears to inspire all modern and humanist perspectives, while it is explicitly rejected by postmodernism and recent continental thought in general. First of all, I want to show what is at stake, by suggesting some ways in which the imperative of autonomy underlies the whole project of modern philosophy, so that it may become apparent that to call such an ideal into question is to effect the most decisive break with tradition. Here, I will offer a reading of Kant as the representative thinker of the modern age, since I think it can be shown that nineteenth- and early twentieth-century philosophy is largely bound by the Kantian "problematic" which gives priority to the project of autonomy. I will then consider three powerful critiques of autonomy that are embodied in the work of the later Heidegger, Derrida, and Foucault, respectively. In spite of their differences, these thinkers appear united in their insistence upon the perniciousness and redundancy of the category of sovereignty.[6] After evaluating their claims, I will conclude by returning to Nietzsche's timely example.

I

The imperative of autonomy summons each of us to the task of self-appropriation. It commands us to take command of ourselves and to make our existence our own. Thus it could be argued that were it not for this possibility of acting in one's own name, the individual could never emerge as a specific or singular individual in any significant sense. Following ordinary usage, we shall therefore say that autonomy describes the possibility of taking charge of oneself and living according to one's own law, whereas "heteronomy" describes the opposite possibility of self-abandonment. In this respect, autonomy has often been regarded as foundational for the establishment of any ethics or system of values which requires the accountability of the individual subject and the possibility of her own self-determination.

Perhaps a fully-blown ideal of autonomy first emerges with Christianity.[7] For here the task of individual salvation is viewed as the most urgent issue of all, as the individual is called to take charge of herself, not for convergence with a principle of Reason or Nature, but for her own sake and the final reward of eternity. Hannah Arendt has argued that the concept of the will is absolutely original to Christianity.[8] And if we now understand autonomy as the *will to will* oneself, then it follows that such a project requires something like the Christian schema in order to exist.

It may well be, then, that the imperative of autonomy is charged by a spiritual momentum that is originally Christian in character. What is indisputable is that such a concern with the individual has been a distinguishing feature of Western culture. And as we move forward to the "modern" age we are bound to acknowledge the growth of individualism and the insistent concern for the "value" of individuality as such. Of course, this development is not limited to philosophical texts, and we could follow its progress in more popular works—in the rise of autobiography, for example, or the perennial literature of "self-reliance."[9] But while it is generally accepted that Descartes inaugurates the turn to subjectivity in philosophy, it is Kant who offers a systematic justification of the priority of autonomy, and in this respect he lays the philosophical foundations of the age.

According to our received history of ideas, the distinctively "modern" period in the history of the west begins with the French revolution of 1789, when the revolutionaries sought to legislate the order of society rather than having it dictated to them by the force of custom and arbitrary decree.[10] Paralleling this, in Kant's work it is the subject who determines the limits of all possible experience. Indeed, Kant's "Copernican revolution" is an attempt to determine the ways in which objects must be given to the subject in order that they may be known. It is sometimes forgotten, though, that Kant also insisted upon the priority of the practical over the theoretical side of his philosophy. And while there is some dispute about the meaning of this priority, it can reasonably be argued that, for Kant, the constitutive activity of the theoretical subject depends upon the original constitution of the self as practical, which relies, in turn, upon the imperative of autonomy and the claim of our own higher self.

In the first section of the *Critique of Practical Reason*, Kant offers an extended argument to show that no heteronomous principle, such as the happiness of others or the will of God, can ever serve as a proper foundation for morality. Kant's claim is that moral principles as such have to be binding upon all of us; but since heteronomous principles exist outside of the will, their relation can only be contingent. If I don't care what God might do to me, or if the sufferings of others don't bother me, then these principles can reasonably be ignored. This leads to the following conclusion:

> The autonomy of the will is the sole principle of all moral laws and of the duties conforming to them; heteronomy of choice, on the other hand, not only does not establish any obligation but is opposed to the principle of duty and to the morality of the will.[11]

For Kant, we are simply not acting "morally" if we follow commands, or yield to our own finer *feelings.* A fully moral action depends upon the autonomy of the human subject, and this requires that she follow a particular principle not because it has been ordered, but because, in the final analysis she has chosen it as her own.

In various places, Kant claims that through the experience of obligation we are recalled to a "noumenal" or "intelligible" order, which we implicitly belong to because as well as being sensible creatures we also have a rational existence.[12] For Kant, the imperative to recover such a world, through moral activity, is necessarily inescapable, since it is at root the summons to a recollection of our own higher self. Rather than any alien or heteronomous principle, it is the intelligible or rational part of the self which seeks to subjugate its phenomenal counterpart to the principle of its own higher law. The radical implication of all of this is that morality is not primarily a debt that we owe to others, but a relation that we have to our own higher self. Through the intermediary of the Categorical Imperative, the self comes to realize which of its maxims are in accordance with its higher (rational) nature, and which of its maxims are not. Indeed, the very concepts of "good" and "evil" must be subsequent to these determinations, for "the moral law is that which first defines the concept of good . . . and makes it possible" (*CPR,* 66). I suggest that it is precisely this primordial and foundational sense of autonomy as the most urgent task which exists prior to (or beyond) any consideration of good and evil, that determines much of nine-teenth- and twentieth-century thought. And, in this respect, Kant's thinking is an exemplary manifestation of the modern age.

From a poststructuralist perspective, Kant's account of auton-omy might well be criticized as a conspicuous manifestation of the "philosophy of mastery" which should be overcome. For it seems to imply a godlike self-creation on the part of the individ-ual involved, and ignores the determinations of history, gender, class, and every other relevant factor. In fact, Kant argues explic-itly that in the freedom of autonomous activity we approximate to the ultimate self-mastery and self-sufficiency of God; he holds that in morality we can spontaneously create a realm of freedom (and reason) in exactly the same way that God himself created and sustains the world.[13]

Certainly, Kant may be charged along these lines. But even if his discussion embodies a "bad" form of individualism, it does not follow that every account of individual sovereignty is subject to the same problems, or that every model of autonomy presup-poses a self-constituting subject. Kierkegaard, for instance, re-jected Kant's account of autonomy as arrogant and self-serving.[14] And yet he consistently gives priority to the highest sphere of *individual* decision over the universal claims of moral law. Kierkegaard accepts the proper achievement of selfhood as the most important project, and throughout his writing he seeks to articulate its essential moments: the aesthetic, moral, and religious. Similarly, even though Nietzsche calls substantial ac-counts of the "self" and "ego" into question, the one issue which drives his work from *The Birth of Tragedy* to *Ecce Homo* is that of sovereignty, or "How one becomes what one is." In *Thus Spoke Zarathustra*, the discussion of the three metamorphoses (camel, lion and child) is an obvious attempt to delineate the necessary stages of self-appropriation, though in fact, *all* of the major themes in his work—the Eternal Recurrence, the Overman, Apollo and Dionysus, etc.—may be read as attempts to provoke the very sovereignty that he also seeks to describe.

Marx challenges the ideal of the self-constituting subject by uncovering the efficacy of economic determination. And yet—*pace* Althusser—he also accepts an implicit ideal of individuality, one which will finally emerge with true communism, when humanity reappropriates its productive powers and the individual regains control over the fundamental possibilities of her existence.[15] In Freud the subject is effectively displaced by the focus on *libidinal* determination; but once again, in a thought that is captured by the line, "where Id was, there Ego shall be," he suggests the ideal possibility of a reappropriation of sovereignty as the goal of every analysis.[16] Finally, while Heidegger's early theme of "authenticity" may seem to be another displacement of Kantian autonomy, it is clear that this ideal is not linked to the recovery of an original but alienated self. In *Being and Time*, Heidegger insists that all of *Dasein*'s possibilities are circumscribed by tradition and by the limiting conditions of our thrownness and being-in-the-world. This means that the individual's choice of authentic possibilities is strictly determined by the models which are available to her, and that resolution implies "choosing one's hero from out of the heritage of one's past."[17]

Further examples could be given, but I think it should now be clear that the attempt to think "sovereignty" and the truth of individuality is an overriding concern of modern thought. And while Kant may have been the first to formalize the issue, later thinkers have moved beyond him while still remaining within the same "problematic." Such considerations must force us to reject any blanket condemnation of autonomy as "self-presence," and oblige us to distinguish and evaluate specific models of sovereignty. In fact, I think it remains undeniable that every morality, as well as every account of human liberation and every discourse of "resistance," rests upon the possibility of human agency and hence the sovereignty of the individual subject, however this is to be construed. To give up on the *possibility* of autonomy is to reduce the individual to a cipher for whatever forces or systems have produced her. It is to deny "responsibility" (in any ordinary sense of the word) and to accept the basic inevitability of the historical process. On the other hand, if we do become nostalgic for such humanistic ideals, we have only to remind ourselves of the Christian origins of autonomy, to realize that the end of sovereignty may actually be unavoidable as a final consequence of the death of God. In celebrating the end of "man" or the radical de-centering of the self, recent continental philosophy has tended to abandon the autonomous ideal as a naive projection of illusory plenitude and mastery. Before deciding for ourselves, we should now consider some of its more specific claims against autonomy.

II

The later Heidegger, Foucault, and Derrida offer three complementary approaches to the problem of sovereignty. This is not to say that their work somehow circumscribes all of the available positions in continental thought. But with their explicit rejection of humanism and their deep suspicion of the traditional category of the subject, they are profoundly representative of the continental turn away from the possibility of autonomy. According to the later Heidegger, the individual project of self-mastery is inextricably bound up with the domination and violation of Being as a whole; for Derrida, the goal of autonomy can be viewed as an illusory attempt to achieve total "self-presence"; in Foucault, the very idea of autonomy is a self-serving myth that only justifies the creation and subject-ification of "responsible" citizens for the forces of oppression and control. Altogether, these are perhaps the three most important moments of recent antihumanism, and as such, I think we are obliged to consider their claims before we reach a provisional conclusion.

1. Heidegger's discussion of authenticity in *Being and Time* reflects his original emphasis on self-assertion and resolve as the only appropriate manner in which Being may be grasped in its truth. In his later writings, however, Heidegger is at pains to distance himself from such a "subjectivist" position. In the *Letter on Humanism,* for example, he opposes his own thinking to Sartre's existentialism by insisting that "humanism" of any kind has to be rejected, since it "does not set the humanitas of man high enough."[18] Heidegger claims that in the most original sense, before he is ever determined as a subject, "man" ek-sists in the openness of Being as neither subject nor object, but as *Da-sein,* or the one who is claimed by Being in order to speak its truth. This primordial imperative of attendance to Being undermines the subjective imperative of self-mastery: henceforth, the individual is to relinquish all willful and self-assertive attitudes, since the latter can only prevent her from attending to the original disclosure of Being.

In Heidegger's later writings, the attack on subjectivism directs his reading of the history of philosophy as the record of humanity's violent suppression of Being. This is held to culminate in the rise of technology, and Nietzsche's explicit avowal of the Will to Power (or the "Will to Will," as Heidegger often refers to it), as the basic character of everything that is. This "Will to Will," Heidegger comments, "forces the calculation and arrangement of everything for itself as the basic forms of appearance, only, however, for the unconditionally protractible guarantee of itself." And, he explains, "The basic form of appearance in which the Will to Will arranges and calculates itself in the unhistorical world of completed metaphysics can be stringently called 'technology.' "[19] For Heidegger, the Will to Will has triumphed insofar as technology now secures and arranges everything with a view to its own continuation and enhancement. Against the ravages of this objectification, he proposes the stance of *Gelassenheit* (or releasement) as the only appropriate remedy. *Gelassenheit* is a form of openness in which the individual resolves not to will any more. It is the resolve *not* to appropriate either oneself or the world, but to exist in a "patient noblemindedness [which] would be pure resting in itself of that willing which, renouncing willing, has released itself to what is not will."[20]

Thus, Heidegger uses the "Will to Will" to describe the epochal determination of Being. And yet, as I have already suggested, the "Will to Will" might also be construed as an excellent determination of the essential nature of autonomy itself. Heidegger would say that "man" is *willed* by the Will to Will. At the same time, however, I think it also follows that the project of individual autonomy represents the highest fulfillment of the Will to Will, since it achieves the most complete incorporation of this epochal determination at the level of the individual self. In an epoch of subjectivism, the project of autonomy may be regarded as an attempt to grasp the subjectivity of the subject, or the individuality of the individual, insofar as the latter can support and direct herself against everything that lies outside of herself. From Heidegger's perspective, the ideal of self-appropriation may therefore represent the final achievement of the Will to Power, and thus the final blasphemy against Being and the mark of its most complete oblivion.

Heidegger in no way regrets the loss of the "subject" or bemoans its subordination to the order of technology. In fact, the self-assertion of the subject is itself the corollary and accomplice of object-ification. So that if our task is, somehow, to think outside of the essence of technology, then the subjectivism or humanism which makes "man" the lord over beings must accordingly be abandoned. This means that Heidegger *must* view sovereignty as an entirely selfish project, in which the individual can only command herself as an individual by denying or dominating the world or the other—this is certainly the main thrust of his interpretation of the Will to Power in his writings on Nietzsche. What Heidegger does *not* recognize, however, is that in Nietzsche's work the Will to Power is simply not construed as a unitary principle. In *The Genealogy of Morals,* for example, Nietzsche makes a clear distinction between the Will to Power of the Master and the Will to Power of the Slave. Whereas the latter can only understand power as domination and control, the former experiences it as a joyful self-affirmation and celebration of strength which does not presuppose the subjection of the other. Heidegger interprets the Will to Power in purely slavish terms—as calculation, ordering, and control—and as a result, the only solution he can offer is one of quietism, where we must wait patiently for the "grace" of Appropriation (or *Das Ereignis*), the "event" of Being.[21] This suggests a monolithic critique which refuses even to recognize the possibility of an individual ideal that would not reduce to individualism. And in opposition to Heidegger, it may therefore be argued that the most important task today is to *rethink the nature of sovereignty.* For while Descartes or Kant may be criticized for their inherent subjectivism, this does not mean that *every* version of autonomy must be predicated upon a slavish self-assertion.

2. Perhaps a similar critique may also apply to Derrida, who has developed a more sustained argument which may be used to support Heidegger's proclamations. In *Speech and Phenomena,* Derrida rejects Husserl's account of the Transcendental Ego by demonstrating the incoherence of a pure consciousness which is supposed to grasp its own identity prior to language. For Derrida, there can be no such realm of "phenomenological silence" in which one could be directly related to oneself, since the determination of any object of knowledge, including one's own self, will always be mediated by the differential system of language.

Moving beyond this specific critique, Derrida has generalized his argument to show that any philosophy which seeks to comprehend the final nature of things is inevitably thwarted by its dependence on "writing," or the materiality of the signifier, which it is bound to suppress and deny. His deconstructive readings expose the logic of this suppression within particular texts, and, in general, they force us to reconsider language as the very fabric of meaning rather than its incidental cover. In this respect, the "subject" is not simply the one who *uses* language, since her very position is itself an effect of textual dispersion and difference.

In fact, Derrida seems to reject any substantive conception of the human "subject," since he holds that the latter must always rely upon the notion of self-presence which he has shown to be incoherent. In his essay on "Freud and the Scene of Writing," for example, he is quite unequivocal: "The last part of the lecture concerned . . . erasure of the present and thus of the subject, of that which is proper to the subject and of his proper name. The concept of a (conscious or unconscious) subject necessarily refers to the concept of substance—and thus of presence—out of which it is born" (*WD*, 229). In a text like "Limited Inc.," Derrida actively performs this erasure of the subject and his proper name, by showing how the author's claim to (legal or textual) mastery cannot be sustained. In this case, John Searle is singled out for signing and copyrighting his response to Derrida. Derrida shows that such ordinary claims of identity and propriety are deeply problematic. For given Searle's own admission of his indebtedness to others, as well as his final inability to fix and control the meaning of his own discourse, Derrida can argue that his proper respondent is not the singular Searle but "SARL," an abbreviation for the French "Societe á la Responsabilité Limitée," or Limited Inc.[22] In other texts, Derrida plays similar tricks with his own name, transforming the proper into the common, and thus generating an anonymous multiplicity of the self as an antidote to all dreams of self-appropriation and mastery.

Derrida's work effectively destroys the myth of the self-present subject who could create himself *ab nihilo* and thus mirror the activity of god. On the other hand, he seems to use this particular critique to dispense with *any* discussion of the subject or autonomy. And when he argues, as above, that every account of subjectivity relies upon an illicit notion of presence, this leads to some false alternatives, where we are obliged to accept *either* the self-legislating enthroned subject of consciousness *or* the disintegration of the self in infinite textuality. Like the later Heidegger, Derrida cannot countenance alternative models of autonomy which would recognize the thrown character of human existence and reject self-presence. The radical dispersion of the self leaves him no way to distinguish between the various levels and degrees of self-possession.

Perhaps in reply to this, it could be held that it is simply not Derrida's concern to give a full discussion of sovereignty, since his discourse operates at an "ultratranscendental" level, from which such considerations are really beside the point. In "Otobiographies" and "Interpreting Signatures," for example, Derrida meditates upon the singularity of the individual author, such as Nietzsche, which can neither be used to account for the text nor excluded as simply irrelevant.[23] "Otobiographies" begins with an account of the one page exergue from *Ecce Homo*, where Nietzsche announces his intentions for the text that follows. Properly speaking, the exergue exists at a point which is in-between the one corpus of Nietzsche's work and the other of Nietzsche's life. For Derrida, it thus represents an internal border, the place of a "programming machine," which engenders the text that is finally constituted by the one who reads it (or as Derrida would have it, the one who *hears* it—and hence the neologism, "otobiography"). As is to be expected, Derrida's essay forces us to challenge traditional ideas about the "autos" of autobiography, and the status of the proper name with Nietzsche's signature as "author." And insofar as autonomy is a matter of acting in one's *own* name, this discussion could be taken as a point of entry into Derrida's positive discourse on sovereignty. Once again, however, Derrida seems to use his own authorial position in order to forestall any more "concrete" appropriation of his work. In the roundtable discussion which follows "Otobiographies," he is asked how the auto-engendering of the text that he describes is related to the more traditional categories of autobiography. Derrida's response is that such questions are themselves deeply problematic given the reformulation that he has just effected. One suspects, though, that from Derrida's perspective *any* investigation into the forms of subjectivity is bound to use the outmoded categories of the "philosophy of presence." And hence, despite some later texts which seem to offer an evocation of singularity that *could* provide us with the space for sovereignty, Derrida's position obliges him to reject every articulate version of autonomy in advance.[24] It is another "monolithic" critique.

3. In a profound respect, Foucault's work represents a sustained illustration of Heidegger's claim that humanism must be rejected "since it does not value the humanitas of man high enough." In an early discussion with Foucault, for example, Noam Chomsky argues that a humanistic social theory would have to be based "on some firm and humane concept of the human nature or human essence."[25] Foucault responds that the concept of human nature is really dispensable, since all it describes are the products of various economic, technological, and political regularities—a position which he argues for most fully in *The Order of Things*. As well as questioning the theoretical status of "human nature," Foucault also insists that the very idea of some fixed human essence is inherently dangerous, since it can be used to dominate and control individual men and women, by foisting some ideal model upon them. And in a much later interview he repeats this claim: "What we call humanism has been used by Marxists, liberals, Nazis, Catholics. I think that there are more secrets, more possible freedoms, and more inventions in our future than we can imagine in humanism as it is dogmatically represented on every side of the political rainbow."[26]

In his writings on madness, sexuality, and the prison, Foucault describes various disciplines and technologies of power which control the individual and reproduce her as a docile utilizable "subject." In effect, Foucault shows how the concept of human nature—especially as it accompanies the growth of the human sciences in the nineteenth century—is fundamentally repressive; for it has always sanctioned a particular vision of "man" to serve as the norm, against which all deviations may be corrected and punished or reduced to silence. In the case of sexuality, for example, Foucault points out that the idea of perversion did not exist in the middle ages: intercourse during Lent, sodomy, and bestiality received equal condemnation as simple violations of canon law; the sexual life of children was not a matter of concern.

Yet in the nineteenth century, as a result of specifically bourgeois values becoming the focus of all humanism, the "perverted" homosexual "personality" was incarcerated and cured, while the campaign against child masturbation achieved an intensification of familial surveillance and control. All of this was justified and directed by a dominant version of "normal" or "natural" sexuality which could be supported, in turn, by the findings of "experts."

Now on the basis of this brief sketch, it might be supposed that Foucault's work is intended as a philosophy of liberation which seeks to uncover all of the ruses of power that have dominated and controlled us for so long. The problem with this, however, is that Foucault himself insists upon the complete and mutual implication of knowledge and power, and he is therefore bound to reject, as hopelessly naive, any argument which reduces to the simple assertion that "the truth will make you free." At the beginning of *Discipline and Punish,* for example, the horrendous account of Damien's execution in 1757 does not allow us to congratulate ourselves for our humanitarian "advances," since it is followed by the daily timetable of a nineteenth-century reformatory, which demonstrates that while power has changed its forms it is now perhaps even more efficient in controlling individuals and populations than it ever was before.[27] The very idea of a "liberation" from power remains deeply problematic. Foucault cannot assume any privileged position for his own work, and as a result he seems open to charges of fatalism and even nihilism.[28]

Marxist critics pointed out the existence of this theoretical impasse in *The Order of Things,* where the unequivocal emphasis on systems and regularities seems to deny the possibility of individual agency, and any suggestion that human beings might "make their own history."[29] Foucault's later work on the relations of power examines various practices of surveillance and control which developed in institutions like schools, factories, and prisons in the course of the nineteenth century. Once again, though, Foucault's claim is that these techniques of power do not so much capture as *constitute* human subjects, who therefore exist only within the relations of power by which they have been produced.[30] Such a view seems to make all "resistance" impossible. And indeed, Foucault is at pains to point out that at the very moment the subject rebels against the system she is always already constrained by the system in another respect. To return to our leading example, in the first volume of *The History of Sexuality*, Foucault argues that the whole discourse of sexual liberation is just as constrained by the "prison" of sex as prudish Victorian morality. For both pornography and prudery force us to think of ourselves as primarily sexual beings. This implies that power is the only subject, and that individual agency or autonomy is merely an illusory projection of power itself.

This brings us, then, to an apparent paradox in the tension between Foucault's theoretical position and the practical orientation of his work. On the one hand, Foucault, the antihumanist, seems to rule out any possibility of individual sovereignty. And yet, as a spokesman for the oppressed of history—the mad, the criminal, the deviant, etc.—Foucault's work is directed by an obvious revolutionary praxis. Such a discourse of liberation has inspired various dispossessed groups, including prisoners and women, and a thoroughly anti-authoritarian project that seeks to undermine the "givenness" of the present order by recollecting the forms of violence and oppression through which it has achieved its hegemony. Exactly as in the case of Heidegger, Foucault's attack on "man" and "humanism" is motivated by a profound humanistic impulse. And though he challenges theoretical constructions and models of subjectivity, it is only in order to liberate individual men and women from whatever represses and controls them. In that way, the real sovereignty of the individual—let us say, her "autonomy"—may be restored, at least as a possibility.

In the end, perhaps all of this comes down to a question of strategy: Given his rejection of "human nature" and his awareness that this has always functioned repressively, Foucault cannot really articulate an alternative version of sovereignty which would then prescribe how we *should* take charge of our lives. As we have already noted: "There are more secrets, more possible freedoms, and more inventions in our future than we can imagine," and this enjoins a very deep suspicion of any positive discourse of autonomy. Thus, while his work is clearly inspired by an implicit recollection of sovereignty—insofar as he values the "liberation" of human beings—Foucault is always bound to avoid the explicit thematization of sovereignty itself.

I conclude here with the observation that in Foucault's final writings, on the classical and early Christian problematic of sexuality, he opens up a theoretical space for the *possibility* of sovereignty by returning to the "subject" as a basic field of analysis. He argues that the *rapport à soi* which constitutes subjectivity is to be studied, along with "power" and "knowledge," as the basic object of a "historical ontology."[31] And while he continues to specify the workings of power upon the *rapport à soi*, his final account of subjectivity does not reduce it, as in earlier work, to the simple *effect* of power or discursive formations. Clearly, Foucault sought to understand the possibility of a genuine resistance and freedom within the economy of power itself: "I believe in the freedom of people," he insists in one of his later interviews, "To the same situation people react in very different ways." His renewed meditation upon the *rapport à soi* does not give us a theory of autonomy, but it does allow us to think the individual as a "fold" within the field of power which may cultivate itself so as to resist power's control.[32]

III

Recent continental philosophy has demonstrated the inadequacy of conceiving the subject as the center of all meaning, and has shown the absurdity of "autonomy" if this is construed as the complete and godlike self-presence of the subject. In this essay, however, we have seen that not all conceptions of autonomy are founded upon an absolute self-presence, and this conforms to our common-sense understanding that there are different degrees of sovereignty—something which would not be possible if the possession of sovereignty were an "all or nothing" affair. In this respect, we must also allow that autonomy remains foundational, not as an impossible goal, but as an empowering ideal that is implicitly presupposed by every movement of resistance and liberation.

Thus, rather than abandoning the goal of sovereignty, what is needed now is a renewed discussion of individuality which might allow us to articulate the nature of sovereignty in its nonabsolutist form. After proclaiming the death of man, recent continental philosophy has tended to avoid this issue as anathema. But elsewhere, in contemporary feminism, for example, the question of the subject and the need to rework traditional conceptions of selfhood have remained at the forefront—and I suspect that it is probably here that the elucidation of individual autonomy will be advanced.[33] In this regard, Nietzsche's call for new discussions of selfhood, for "new versions and representations of the soul hypothesis" remains profoundly relevant to the philosophical elaboration of sovereignty.[34]

This brings us to the problem of strategy. Foucault, at least, understood the dangers of prescribing any particular version of individual existence: for the sovereignty of the individual is effectively destroyed when it is made to conform to a prescription that is not of its own making. In Kantian language, to legislate the content of autonomy is to make it heteronomous. This may imply that, in the final analysis, a wholly "positive" discourse of autonomy is actually impossible. And our only recourse would then be to use an "oblique" strategy which evokes the possibility of autonomy without fixing it in any definite formulation.

One final example may illuminate this point. In *The Genealogy of Morals*, Nietzsche tells us a story of Masters and Slaves, in which the Slave, as one who is purely suffering and reactive, is the embodiment of heteronomy, while the Master, as the active one, is nothing but autonomy. Thus, Nietzsche's discussion of the Master raises the question of sovereignty, but at the same time, he stresses the murderous aspect of the Master as a bloodthirsty "beast of prey," so that it becomes very difficult to identify Nietzsche's exemplar of autonomy as a simple ideal which must be followed. Elsewhere in the same text, Nietzsche expresses a longing for the "return" of the Master (though now as one whose sovereignty is engendered *within* society), and he inspires us to try to grasp what the nature of such a sovereign will might be like:

> If we place ourselves at the end of this tremendous process, where the tree at last brings forth the fruit, where society and the morality of custom at last reveal what they have simply been the means to: then we discover that the ripest fruit is the *sovereign individual*, like only to himself, liberated again from the morality of custom, autonomous and supramoral (for "autonomous" and "moral" are mutually exclusive), in short, the man who has his own

independent, protracted will and the *right to make promises*—and in him a proud consciousness . . . of *what* has at length been achieved and become flesh in him . . . a sensation of mankind come to completion.[35]

In this way the question of autonomy is raised, and while a straightforward answer is not proposed, we are inspired to recollect, even if only for ourselves, this sovereign possibility which had almost been forgotten.

Nietzsche's example remains instructive, for it shows the possibility of an oblique strategy which could direct us toward sovereignty without circumscribing it in advance. Clearly, every version of sovereignty must accept the "risk" of articulation, but Nietzsche's discussion allows us to see how a particular account could still contain the possibility of its own critique as an immanent moment of itself. For we must now *rethink* the nature of sovereignty, even if we are obliged to avoid the ordinary forms of prescription.[36]

Chapter 6

INTENTIONALITY, ONTOLOGY, AND EMPIRICAL THOUGHT

Tony O'Connor

Merleau-Ponty, by returning transcendental subjectivity to the realm of lived or empirical experience, appears to be open to the objection that, ultimately, his philosophy offers merely a descriptive psychology of conscious processes. He would reject this objection, however, by arguing that his "existential transcendentalism" is grounded in an implicit ontology.

I argue that this ontology is explanatorily weak, or neutral, such that the objection stands unless it can be rejected on some other grounds. The underlying difficulty stems from his view that an adequate account of the ambiguities and complexity of meaning can be given in intentional-ontological terms. However, I will claim that this is a false, or, at best, only one way of approaching the issue. My position is that ambiguity and complexity can be acknowledged philosophically by allowing for a plurality of approaches to issues.

For Husserl the fundamental task of philosophy is to identify and describe the *a priori* that conditions and makes possible each and every experience. This *a priori* he names transcendental subjectivity. The essential forms of phenomena are to be identified in transcendental subjectivity, and the term also serves as the locus both for the identification and the description-cum-explanation of intentional experiences.

Identification of transcendental subjectivity involves a break with the natural attitude, or the realm of empirical, spontaneous, and naive beliefs about ourselves and the world in which we live. It gives knowledge a stable origin or foundation by allowing the investigator to be distanced from empirical beliefs and knowledge in order to view their *a priori* forms.

The core philosophical problem, then, becomes that of determining how objects take on meaning in terms of the essence of subjectivity. Insofar as what is revealed after the break with the natural attitude is the *a priori* form of subjectivity, it follows that both subjects and objects manifest themselves as part of the universe of the transcendental subject.

Merleau-Ponty reverses the Husserlian enterprise, however, and returns transcendental subjectivity to the realm of lived experience, not to reject the *a priori*, but to identify and expound it in a more fundamental and comprehensive way. This deeper intentionality he identifies as "operative intentionality," which, he maintains, is a "pure motor intentionality," and which underpins our reflective, deliberate, or fully conscious cognitive acts.[1]

Philosophical examination of this pure intention, Merleau-Ponty claims, can reveal the total intention operative in any specific situation, as well as the intending subject's unique modalities of consciousness—sight, motility, sexuality, etc.—plus the "intentional arc" that subtends and unites them. This he calls the "momentum of existence" that establishes the modalities of consciousness as part of a "phenomenal field" (*PP*, 136).

On this basis he describes consciousness as a projective function, or an "I can," a doer rather than primarily a reflective knower. He then proceeds to describe the various ways—visual, aural, tactile, motile, etc.—in which consciousness enters into relationships, both with itself and with things other than itself. But this appears to leave him open to the objection that what he has to offer is simply a descriptive psychology of human conscious process, insofar as he merely describes the various modalities of human behavior and how they interact. Ayer makes this criticism at various stages of his account of Merleau-Ponty's philosophy in *Philosophy in the Twentieth Century*. He claims that Merleau-Ponty distinguishes bodily space from external space on psychological grounds.[2] Likewise, Merleau-Ponty's account of shame and immodesty is described as "a good psychological description of a form of frustration that is sometimes experienced" (*PTC*, 223).

Merleau-Ponty would reject this objection on the basis of what can be called his "existential transcendentalism."[3] In other words, the problem is not simply one of psychology, or that of describing modalities of consciousness. Rather, these descriptions serve to identify the *a priori*, or fundamental grounding phenomenon, that links together all worldly phenomena. This *a priori* he believes is to be found not in the formal cognitive structures of consciousness where indubitable representations are obtained, as Husserl thought, but in the ontological structures through which the entities that we are, namely, consciousnesses, can be said to belong to being-as-such.

This is clear from his account of intentionality in the introduction to *Phenomenology of Perception*. He argues that the world is lived as ready-made, or already there, as prior to knowledge positing it in a specific act of identification. Here Merleau-Ponty takes his lead from Husserl's account of the teleology of consciousness, which deals with the problem of the world in terms of consciousness as perpetually directed toward a world, and the world as the preobjective unity which precedes knowledge. It involves two kinds of intentionality: (1) intentionality of act, including express judgments and decisive acts, and (2) operative intentionality, which is prepredicative, which is present in desire, and which furnishes the text that knowledge tries to translate into precise language. Operative intentionality leads the philosopher to be concerned precisely with the question of origins or foundations. Its task is to incorporate the total intention operative in any particular situation, as well as the unique modality of existing appropriate to the phenomenon under investigation (*PP*, xviii). Hence, the task of the philosopher is to clarify and define the proper meaning of our humanity, and to specify the conditions for the establishment of a common truth by means of a description of intentional history (*PP*, xviii).

What is specifically original in Merleau-Ponty's position, then, is this. Whereas Husserl's subjective transcendentalism moved from objects of experience to our *a priori* modes of knowing them, existential transcendentalism moves from the *a priori* modalities of consciousness—visual perception, motility, sexuality, etc.—to their rootedness in the entities that we are—our "being-as-consciousness." Merleau-Ponty's concrete descriptions of modalities of consciousness are accompanied by a variety of ontological expressions or statements, whose function is to ground or explain the concrete descriptions. Examples from his early work include: the linking of the diverse contents of consciousness by the "momentum of existence" (*PP*, 138); consciousness as "a being toward the thing through the intermediary of the body" (*PP*, 139); the claim that sexuality "follows the general flow of existence and yields to its movements" (*PP*, 157); and that the "I" is described as "a primordial field of presence" (*PP*, 92), as a "possibility of situations" (*PP*, 407), and as "a certain manner of Being."[4] In *The Visible and the Invisible* terms like "perceptual faith," "flesh of time," "brute or wild being," etc., take on the ontological function (*VI*, 115). Here the world is described as "a Being of which my vision is a part" (*VI*, 123). Language is "the most valuable witness to Being" (*VI*, 126).

Here the question arises as to whether, and in what specific sense, such expressions add explanatory weight to Merleau-Ponty's concrete descriptions of the modalities of consciousness. If explanatory weight is not added by such ontological expressions, then the earlier objection stands.

Consider the following statements:

1 That is a table.
2 The being of the table is revealed.

From Merleau-Ponty's perspective the first statement may be identified as a mundane, empirical statement of fact. The second statement, however, is an expressly ontological statement, and goes beyond the first one, because it indicates directly something that is given intuitively in every identification, namely, the "being" of the phenomenon in question. Being, the ultimate *a priori*, is given along with our perception or identification of objects as the particular things they are, i.e., in terms of their dimensions of size, shape, texture, etc.

However, no evidence is adduced by Merleau-Ponty in support of this claim, nor is any specific line of argument developed to justify it. Rather, it is a procedural feature of his enterprise. Against this, it could be argued that unless there is demonstrably a phenomenon called "being" given alongside, yet separate from, material objects, events, relationships, etc., it may be assumed that this is an error, or a misuse of language, or at best a weak grounding of empirical descriptions.

If this objection is correct, if there is not a phenomenon called "being" given alongside our identification of objects and events, then the second statement above says nothing that is not said in the first statement. In other words, the meaning of so-called ontological expressions such as "the being of the table," "momentum of existence," "flesh of time," etc., can be conveyed at least as well, if not better, by ordinary descriptive, or observation sentences, and/or by more technical or scientific statements. In other words, there are not special kinds of statements, namely, ontological ones given alongside ordinary, commonsensical, factual, or descriptive statements.

In fact, the statement "that is a table" is also an ontological statement. Ontological statements are simply ways of viewing and describing phenomena—events, activities, attitudes, ideas, etc.—as entities and substances. More specifically, they enable us to refer to phenomena, quantify them, identify aspects of them, identify causes, set goals, motivate actions etc.[5] Thus a series of supportive ontological statements around the original— "that is a table"—might be the following:

The table is one of a set of four.
The leg of the table is broken.
My sitting on the table caused it to break.
I use the example of identifying the table in my seminars to help students to think more critically.

Statements such as these fulfill the functions of referring, identifying, etc., which Merleau-Ponty explains in terms of "being." But from this viewpoint "being" has no explanatory function beyond its role in language as verbal noun, and as present participle of the verb "to be." Hence, Merleau-Ponty's *a priori*, "being-as-such," does not constitute a separate or deeper layer, but dissolves into a series of observation statements about behavior, sight, motility, sexuality, etc. The objection that he offers only a descriptive psychology has not been refuted, and the core issue then concerns the effectiveness of our philosophical statements.

The difference between the two approaches to ontology has its proximate root on the phenomenological side in Husserl, for whom being is not anything that can be perceived, but which, nonetheless is intuited in every perception. But the philosophy of transcendental subjectivity identifies being with consciousness. All that is, especially the object of intentionality, is in consciousness, present to consciousness. Hence, to be is to be represented, with the consequence that being cannot be grasped as objective presence (*HBA*, 67–69).[6]

This problem of the designation of being as objective presence is what gives rise to Heidegger's enterprise. In *Being and Time*, Heidegger identifies the conditions of the possibility of a philosophy of subjective consciousness. This leads to the existential analytic of *Dasein* which, by means of its ontological essence, is an origin more fundamental than consciousness. Heidegger hereby argues that the condition of the possibility of experiencing and knowing is to be discovered in terms of the relation of the human being to the Being of beings as a whole (*HBA*, 69). But a problem remains for Heidegger of distinguishing between the "beingness" (*Seiendheit*) of beings and Being that is independent of beings. Hence the stress in his later philosophy on the question of the Being of beings.

Although Merleau-Ponty appears to be Husserlian when he says that the central task of philosophy is to clarify and define both the proper meaning of our humanity and the conditions for the establishment of a common truth by means of a description of intentional history, nonetheless his philosophy is not intended to be a mere philosophy of subjective consciousness. Rather, a Heideggerian dimension is preserved in the attempt to articulate an origin deeper than consciousness, namely, the "beingness" of consciousness, world, other, etc. Hence, for example, his designation of the body as field of presence, which is the condition for the presence and absence of external objects (*PP*, 92).

Merleau-Ponty addresses this issue of the beingness of consciousness in his essay "The Metaphysical in Man."[7] Here he claims that metaphysics begins from the moment we apperceive the radical subjectivity of all our experience as inseparable from its truth-value, because knowledge communicates with a "way of being" (*SNS*, 93). To get over the Husserlian difficulty of reducing being to consciousness, he claims that the experience of consciousness, self-experience, is not the measure of all imaginable being in itself, but is coextensive with all being of which we can form a notion. This leads him to assert what he identifies as the twofold basic fact of metaphysics: certainty that there is being, but on condition that the only kind of being to be sought is "being for me" (*SNS*, 93). Thus, he concludes that a metaphysical view of the world cannot result in the establishment of a universal system. On the contrary, doing metaphysics is a matter of testing various paradoxes revealed by our inherence in a world (*SNS,* 94–97).

Viewed in Heideggerian terms, Merleau-Ponty's problematic can be seen as one of thinking being as a unity in diversity. Just as Heidegger identified the self-manifestation of being in terms of "lighting," "reaching," "giving," etc., so Merleau-Ponty appeals to "flesh," "perceptual faith," etc. The purpose of such terms is to justify his procedural assumption that being as such does not reduce to a manifold of appearances, but has a unity that can be ascribed in one specific sense.

This leads Merleau-Ponty to attempt to show the internal connection between Being itself and the form/content of worldly beings, because he assumes that priority must be given to Being in philosophical investigations. In other words, he assumes that access to the "true character of being" will involve the construal of the "principle of identity in itself" because, following Heidegger, he accepts that identity is a principle that is essential to the structure of Being in relation to beings. Identity must be expressed in the terminology of the ontological character of Being in relation to beings.

In his preface to *The Visible and the Invisible,* Lingis shows clearly how Husserlian and Heideggerian concerns with problems of being, identity, etc., come together in Merleau-Ponty's reflections. Phenomenology, as a philosophy of essences, takes as its task the intuition of the real as it interacts with the positive structure of the possible. The result of such an intuition is that the mind gains possession of the essence as the pure ideal possibility which the existing thing accomplishes, or specifies, in a moment of time and at a point in space. The phenomenological intuition of essences occurs by means of an imaginary variation carried out in relation to the primal topography of the visible. Being is available as a theme for variation because it announces and harbors, in the present, an immense latent content of past, future, and the elsewhere (*VI,* xlv–xlvii, 114).

The core of Merleau-Ponty's problematic then rests on three interacting factors: the role of the *a priori,* the status of intentionality analysis, and the character of psychology. These three factors come together initially in terms of his attempted reduction of empirical psychology to intentionality analysis, and their reduction to a kind of fundamental ontology in his later work, especially in *The Visible and the Invisible*.

Merleau-Ponty's intentional approach undoubtedly has the value of revealing certain limitations in the then extant empirical and intellectualist explanatory models of psychology, which viewed consciousness either as an amalgam of stimuli, or in terms of biochemical reactions related in automatic, causal circuits. Thus, he shows that psychology is not a matter of detached, unprejudiced listing of facts, but occurs as sets of procedures that presuppose certain operational norms and evaluative categories, which are merely used by the psychologist rather than explicitly justified. More positively, however, he shows the value of investigators in the human sciences incorporating self-awareness in their descriptions and explanations. Yet, by preserving being as the necessary and universal condition of spontaneous experience, and scientific and philosophical judgments, Merleau-Ponty gives undue weight to certain kinds of ontological statements, with the result that he fails to appreciate that explanations in terms of intentionality are but one type, namely, those that offer reason-explanations based on the desires, needs, motivations, expectations, etc., of the human agent.[8]

Despite such a serious flaw in his enterprise, however, there is a sense in which, from the very beginning, Merleau-Ponty allowed for alternative approaches to these issues. This is evident from his attempt to introduce into philosophical analysis a principle of discontinuity that recognizes that changes or developments in various fields of human endeavor occur not simply in a linear fashion, but by means of leaps and crises.[9]

To fully exploit this, Merleau-Ponty, having modified the transcendental assumptions of phenomenology, should have rejected its ontological presuppositions also. Despite his interest in art, politics, psychoanalysis, structuralism, etc., ultimately, his adherence to the explanatory ideology of phenomenology never wavered, insofar as his work consistently involved a mixture of empirical descriptions of events, and what Foucault calls "an ontology of the unthought."[10] Thus, as Foucault indicates, Merleau-Ponty shows that it is possible to break with "transcendental narcissism."[11] However, to be completely free from the "circle of lost origin" (*AK*, 203) Merleau-Ponty must break from what can be called his "ontological narcissism," or what he calls the "voices of silence," which for him are the "Being of every being" (*VI;,* 126–27).

Granted that notions such as the "voices of silence," "wild" or "brute" being, etc., help him to overcome problems of classical ontology, they do not, and cannot, give stability of meaning and homogeneity of experience "prior" to the representation of meaning in language. In other words, cultural variety cannot be controlled by a formal notion of being, even one as weak as wild or brute being, because the notion of being itself contains a variety of cultural items.

If this formal ontological structure were dropped from Merleau-Ponty's enterprise, he could then pursue his account of the wide variety of ways of viewing, interacting with, and interpreting the world, or better, worlds, in terms of events, actions, substances, etc. This would be a matter of giving free rein to the empirical and contextual side of phenomenological ontology, which can be appreciated then as its most valuable and long-term contribution to philosophy.

From a more empirical, or concrete, perspective, many of Merleau-Ponty's formal problems can be simply dissolved because insoluble, or because they offer only vague and unworkable solutions. For example, one can reject the implications of his claim in *The Visible and the Invisible* that it is necessary to bring the results of *Phenomenology of Perception* to ontological explication (*VI,* 183), suggesting that the findings of *Phenomenology of Perception* are merely preliminary and preontological and need to be more fully grounded in terms of a deeper and more fundamental study. If, however, as I have suggested, "ordinary language" is ontological through and through, then Merleau-Ponty's findings in *Phenomenology of Perception* are not preliminary, and in need of a more universal grounding, but perspectival, or contextual, contributions to a complex debate. In this respect, his notion of the "phenomenal field," for example, can be identified as an ontological metaphor whereby we identify our phenomenal environment as a container, and further, identify what we see, hear, taste, etc., as inside it (*ML,* 30–32).

Obviously, this is just one way of identifying and interpreting an aspect of the world, which must compete with alternative interpretations. The core point, however, is that just as phenomenology shows that the perceived thing is an identity open to a variety of perspectival views, so too are our descriptions-cum-explanations of things, events, situations, etc.

Two further consequences, among others, follow from this position. Firstly, it is necessary to deny Merleau-Ponty's claim that perception "teaches us, outside all dogmatism, the true conditions of objectivity itself."[12] For perception does not reveal in a neutral fashion "the primordial data of the problem" (*PrP*, 25). On the contrary, it is culturally influenced and shaped by the past experience, knowledge, and expectations of the observer. For example, Wittgenstein's duck-rabbit illustration shows that a single set of perceptual data can be interpreted differently depending on whether they are grouped under the guide-term "duck" or that of "rabbit." Likewise, Chalmers cites psychological experiments showing that members of certain African tribes whose culture does not include the custom of depicting three-dimensional objects by two-dimensional perspective drawings would not see the following figure as a staircase, as presumably most of us do, but as a two-dimensional array of lines.[13]

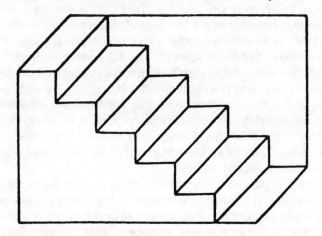

Secondly, the original objection in this paper that Merleau-Ponty offers merely a descriptive psychology of consciousness also disappears in that it is possible now to accept his rejection of the claims of the human sciences to offer purely objective truth. Rather, just as our "perceptual truths" are conditional on our linguistico-cultural inherence and are constantly tested by our personal and interpersonal experience, so the claims of the human sciences are not entirely independent of their professional presuppositions and expectations, i.e., of how practitioners understand and use their technical language, as well as their wider cultural presuppositions and expectations.

Thus, once the special explanatory status of ontological statements is removed from Merleau-Ponty's philosophy, the way is clear to break with universal generalizations, and with a view of philosophy as determining in a fixed way the sufficiency conditions that bind phenomena to a single grounding necessity.

More specifically, once it is recognized that observation statements are contextual, the central task becomes one of identifying their conditions of existence, their limits, their links with connecting statements, what they exclude, and the reasons for the exclusion. In other words, philosophy becomes a matter of strategic deployments, which is pluralist in the sense that it acknowledges the presence of various, and possibly competing, positions on particular issues.

In this regard Foucault points to an interesting way forward, insofar as he shows that our *a priori's* do not reveal pure, or constant grounds, but are ideological characteristics of the various kinds of reason explanations given in particular socio-temporal contexts. Although *a priori's* have a certain temporal constancy, there is nothing absolutely necessary about them. Hence, there are no pure phenomena—not being, not transcendental subjectivity, not consciousness, etc. Furthermore, *a priori's* are not simply relative to certain philosophical or scientific-type problems and solutions. Rather, they also involve various other sociocultural factors and techniques that are considered relevant within the particular context.

From this perspective it is not helpful to offer descriptions or explanations in terms of pure *a priori's*. For example, selfhood is not simply a matter of being conscious, or enjoying a certain kind of experience, namely, self-awareness, that, in turn, involves attending to one's activity, successes and failures, attitudes of joy and sorrow, etc. On the contrary, one must also take account of the various sociocultural techniques whereby human beings have learned to identify themselves as persons, or as subjects. What is at issue here can be clearly revealed in Merleau-Ponty's and Foucault's differing approaches to sexuality. Merleau-Ponty analyzes sexuality showing how reflex and representational models do not account for affectivity as a feature of sexual intention. (*PP*, 156). Foucault argues, however, that the analytical task is not simply to trace the features of desire, but to show how individuals are led to practice a "hermeneutics of desire."[14] This is not merely a matter of intentionality, but is expressly ideological in that it involves philosophical, religious, and other social factors.

The core task cannot be Merleau-Ponty's challenge to empirical psychology, namely, the legitimation of a "science" of the individual in intentional-ontological terms. On the contrary, the task is one of genealogical investigation which shows "the multiplicity of often minor processes, of different origin and scattered location, which overlap, repeat, or imitate one another, support one another, distinguish themselves from one another according to their domain of application, converge and gradually produce the blueprint of a general method."[15]

Chapter 7

REHABILITATING THE "I"

Susan Bordo and Mario Moussa

Many disciplines since the turn of the century have worked to undermine the sovereignty of the human subject. Philosophers from both the Continental and Anglo-American traditions have assailed the conceptual underpinnings of Cartesian subjectivity, and feminists have exposed the ways in which the seemingly disinterested rationality of the Western philosophical tradition is race- and gender-biased: for terms such as "Man" and "mind," feminists substitute "white males" and "phallocentric thinking." Sociologists and anthropologists have contributed to a general critique of subjectivity by revealing its place in a system of beliefs and symbols specific to Western culture. Historians, for their part, have questioned the importance of human agency; in many histories, the "great men" have been replaced by everyday objects, market forces and natural events. Likewise questioning the centrality of the individual subject, literary critics have proclaimed the death of the author, outraging and confounding the literate public by arguing for a kind of reading that banishes authorial intention from the text.

These intellectual critiques—varied, persistent—offer a difficult challenge to anyone still concerned to establish the autonomy or unity of the abstract subject. But perhaps they have been too successful. Or, better yet, it might be said they have lost a sense of their aim. At the start, the critiques were directed toward one particular understanding of the subject: the one framed by the philosophical-cultural tradition of the modern West. But, recently, countermodernist movements have begun to collapse under the weight of their own theories: in splintering the monolithic subject, they have unwittingly splintered themselves. The result is an ironic—and, it seems, unconscious—recapitulation of the very modernist ideas that motivated the critiques in the first place. Dissected by postmodern critics, the "I" has become a theoretical puzzle and, practically speaking, a distraction from the questions most worth asking today.

We argue, in the following sections, that the human subject amounts to far less than the transcendental source of thought and action, as indeed the various twentieth-century critiques have been at pains to show. In particular, three of those critiques—the historical, the linguistic, and the feminist—seem to us the most powerful, and we offer a review of their arguments. Given the vast amount of literature involved and the obvious space constraints of a single article, this review will be at once general and highly selective; we aim to describe contours rather than to provide extensive critical detail. We aim to show that, as convincing as they are, these arguments have had a destructive and probably unintended effect: the initial and crucial recognition that the universalistic pretensions of the subject cannot be sustained has recently given way to a paralyzing theoretical concern with doing justice to particularity and "difference." Not that theory itself is the problem—the difficulties seem to arise from a fascination with a certain understanding of theory. That understanding, we argue, is merely the newest configuration of the very Cartesian ideals—of epistemological adequacy, of unimpeachable method, of foundations—that poststructuralism and feminism have rightly called into question.

Finally, we will suggest that some historical perspective, a more practice-oriented approach to theory, and a recognition of voices that have been speaking outside the authorized scholarly discourse, can lead in the direction of a "rehabilitation" of the "I"—without entailing a return to the discredited, abstract subject. The contemporary critique of "the subject," in its most pointed and productive form, is of a *particular* historical conception of knowledge and human identity. The deconstruction of that conception, while it may mean "the end of philosophy" or "the death of the subject" to those identified with it, hardly spells nihilism to those who have resisted it, who have been excluded from it, who may embody other forms of knowing and being. Under such circumstances, those who declare the death of the "I" project their own loss onto "culture" at a time when others who have been historically marginalized are ready to begin doing and making a new philosophy for a changed and changing world. One form of subjectivity may be dead or dying, or at least it may have outlived its usefulness, but other forms of subjectivity need to be recognized, even created, and then refined as vehicles for effective action.

The Historicization of the Cartesian Father: Marx and After

Over a hundred years ago, Marx recognized that both the modern West's unique intellectual enterprise—what might be called the Baconian-Cartesian project—and the social order that produced it were undergoing significant changes, ones which promised to have consequences for the Subject. He went so far as to predict its very dissolution and, along with it, the end of philosophy. In the mid-1960s, Michel Foucault made a similar prediction, claiming (somewhat oracularly): "As the archaeology of our thought easily shows, man is an invention of recent date. And one perhaps nearing its end."[1] Of course, Marx and Foucault are both referring to a particular *kind* of subject or man: namely, the Cartesian. And many of the recent critiques of the Subject return to Descartes as their point of origin, as if by way of providing historical and biographical ballast for the strange metaphysical figure—the monolithic "I"—in the background of modernist thought.

In linking intellectual systems to social conditions, Marx established the boundaries for later critiques of subjectivity. From the standpoint of political conflict, Marx argued, traditional philosophical questions—including those about the nature of the self—are merely conceptual drapery hung over the structural tensions within bourgeois society. In his positivistic moods, alternatively, Marx considered philosophy the muddled expression of scientific problems. In either case, confusion stemmed from facts being ignored: "When we conceive of things . . . as they really are and happened," Marx wrote in *The German Ideology*, "every profound philosophical problem is resolved . . . quite simply into an empirical fact."[2] And the critical revelation of empirical fact also makes a step toward doing away with "the estranged essential reality of man," characterized by the "abstract enmity between sense and spirit."[3] In other words, the philosophical equation of rationality and human identity, with the body as their oddly inessential vehicle, grows out of a *social* condition—alienation. While the philosophical (and particularly the Cartesian) tradition has taken this product of estrangement to be universal human nature, positive communism—so Marx predicts—will overcome alienation and affirm the human being "in the objective world not only in the act of thinking, but with *all* his senses" (*MER*, 88).

With Foucault and other recent writers, the understanding of the human subject changes considerably, for the most part in the direction of malleability. Gone is anything like an "essential human reality," estranged or otherwise: the self is a construction. As Foucault said in 1983, looking back over his work: "My objective . . . has been to create a history of the different modes by which, in our culture, human beings are *made* subjects."[4] Beginning in the modern period, Foucault argues, innovative technologies of the body that applied a "constant coercion" to the activities of criminals and noncriminals alike began to shape a particular form of subjectivity.[5] He groups these modern technologies of the body under the heading of "discipline," a term designating a group of similar practices found in mental hospitals, schools, and penitentiaries, all of which exercise "punitive power" (*DP*, 29).

By means of a microphysics operating on the body—as Foucault says, by rendering it "docile"—this punitive power created the tablet of the modern "soul," on which the newly emergent intellectual disciplines began to write the analyses of such concepts as the psyche, subjectivity, personality, and consciousness (*DP*, 29). According to Foucault, it is Descartes who wrote the first pages, in the "anatomico-metaphysical register," about the modern subject (*DP*, 136). Contrary to Descartes' assumptions, however, the metaphysical subject, far from being "given" to anyone practicing philosophical self-analysis, appears at the intersection of various modern intellectual discourses about the self, on the one hand, and, on the other, practical strategies for pacifying the body. By looking "inside" himself, Descartes did not really discover a new metaphysical foundation for scientific knowledge; but, through the activity of constructing the New

Philosophy, he did help produce the "reality-reference" (as Foucault puts it) that has been taken as such (*DP*, 29). After Descartes, the subject ceased to be defined by ethical questions and exercises, as it was for the ancient Greeks and Romans; it became the pure subject of knowledge, with an uncertain relationship to the practical activities of everyday life.[6]

While seventeenth-century philosophy was moving *away* from the world of practical activities, it was also moving *toward* the "interior" of the self. As Stephen Toulmin argues, Descartes's style of philosophizing established a tradition that conceives of mental life as located somewhere inside the body, as if each person's thoughts, fantasies, and emotions were screened within a totally enclosed movie theater.[7] This theoretical picture of the inner life—a picture with appeal to philosophers and scientists even in the twentieth century—points to the deep differences between the modern Subject and earlier forms of the self. For the historian Norbert Elias, the modern Subject—the interiorized foundation of knowledge—owes its nature largely to the extreme self-restraint people found it necessary to exercise, in the "civilized" social intercourse of the West, from the Renaissance onward. Cartesian doubts regarding the reliability of human judgments about the world arise, Elias claims, from "the detachment of emotions from the objects of thought."[8] The origins of such detachment Elias traces back to the upper strata of Renaissance society, in which the warrior class was domesticated and eventually transformed into the sophisticates attached to, for example, Louis XIV's court. For this elite group, the wall of ingrained self-restraint between impulse and the social world assumes the character of an actually existing barrier. Hence the interiorized self:

> The uncertainty over the nature of "reality," which led Descartes to the conclusion that the only certainty was thought itself, is a good example of the reification of an emotive idea corresponding to a structural peculiarity of people at a certain stage of social development, and therefore of human self-consciousness. (*CS*, 253)

Tied to this experience of "interiority" (as Toulmin describes it) is a form of rationality designed to ensure survival in the elite social setting of the court; among its characteristics are a control of the affects and a finely tuned, calculating foresight. The resemblance between the self-conscious intellectual rationalism of the Enlightenment and court rationality is, Elias suggests, more than coincidental, as in the cases of Descartes, Leibniz, and Voltaire (CS, 113).[9]

For Foucault and Elias, "power" draws the dividing line between private and public, inner and outer. And as the forms and effectiveness of power change from century to century, so do those elusive notions "the inner life" and "subjectivity." Somewhere among the collections of everyday objects such as jewelry, furniture, prayer books, wall-hangings, undergarments, keys, and financial records, and the lengthy inventories of the social practices peculiar to the West, lies the forebearers of the modern subject—what might be called a "power-effect."[10] Feminist historians of the Subject would agree, but they would also argue that power relations cannot be understood without considering the organization of gender. Merchant, Easlea, Keller, Harding, and Bordo have argued, in different ways, that the detached, interiorized Cartesian subject represents a new construction of masculinity—new to the seventeenth century—and a changed relation to (the formerly "female," now mechanical) nature.[11]

All of these critiques agree that the Cartesian foundational subject grew out of particular sociocultural conditions. The "I think," far from being transcendental, had an historical birth and, presumably, will meet an historical demise. Is philosophy now witnessing the demise of this subject? Lacan, Derrida, and postmodern feminists seem to answer "Yes," and to these critiques we now turn.

Lost in Language

Like the historically minded writers, the critics of modern philosophy inspired by Saussurian linguistics—Lacan and Derrida foremost among them, together with their respective followers—have assailed the "given" foundational subject. The more exuberant of these critics celebrate multiple and mutating selves, elusive and contradictory selves, with the cacaphony rising from such a rabble drowning out the solitary Cartesian, who speaks of clarity, distinctness, and truth. As Derrida says, in a 1982 interview discussing the notion of sexual difference:

I would like to believe in the multiplicity of sexually marked voices. I would like to believe in the masses, [an] indeterminable number of blended voices, [a] mobile of non-identified sexual marks whose choreography can carry, divide, multiply the body of each "individual," whether he be classified as "man" or as "woman" according to the criteria of usage.[12]

In Derrida's kinetic vision, sexual identity, like the self, emerges out of language—a dynamic field of relations—and not out of some biological (or metaphysical) ground. If the Subject as analyzed by the historicist critique may be described as a "power-effect," then the linguistic critiques reveal it to be a "language-effect."

Lacan is explicit on this point. He claims that the psychoanalyst must attend to language, rather than to shadowy entities "deep within" the personality of the analysand. Even before there is a self—before it is possible to speak of an "I"—there must be a structure of relations, and specifically linguistic relations. Without being aware of it, Lacan suggests, the so-called human sciences are the study of these relations, whose patterns coalesce into the terms "human" and "subject," among many other related terms. Recent linguistics, whose field (according to Lacan) encompasses "the combinatory operation [of signs], functioning spontaneously, of itself, in a presubjective way," reveals what the human sciences are "really" about.[13] Like most critics of the modern Subject, Lacan returns to Descartes in order to demonstrate its (and Descartes's own) limitations. While Freud and Descartes begin from the same point—the subject of certainty, the cogito, the "I"—Lacan sidesteps it: he observes that Descartes can formulate the "I think" only "by *saying* it to us, implicitly—a fact he forgets" (*FFC*, 36). In other words, language, not the "I," reveals itself. But when the analyst encounters resistance, for example, what is it that resists, if not the subject? "The phrase *resistance of the subject*," Lacan writes by way of an answer, "too much implies the existence of a supposed ego and it is not certain whether [what resists] is something that we can justifiably call an ego" (*FFC*, 68). Lacan prefers the phrase *resistance of discourse*. His language-oriented psychoanalysis therefore volitilizes the self and, as Paul Ricoeur says of Lévi-Strauss's anthropology, results in a sort of Kantianism without the subject.

Derrida, for his part, takes the linguistic critique even further. Vestiges of empiricism remain in Lacan's writings, in that, despite the absence of a subject in any traditional metaphysical sense, at least the combinatory operation of signs provides a reliable focal point for the analyst. But whatever empirical certainty might be associated with linguistic structure dissolves when Derrida and others begin to address (in his words) "the structurality of structure."[14] With this, "everything became discourse, . . . that is to say, a system in which the central signified, the original or transcendental signified, is never absolutely present outside a system of differences" (WD, 280). If everything is discourse, then the subject no doubt disappears—as Lacan recognized—but so do notions such as unshakable truth, unity, and certainty into the bargain.

Derrida also returns to the Cartesian cogito. He finds that Descartes' notions of unity and certainty only hide their opposing, shadow-ideas. As usual, Derrida proceeds by means of a close textual reading—in this instance, a reading of Foucault's interpretation, in *Madness and Civilization*, of Descartes's *Meditations*. Far from succeeding in excluding madness from the discourse of rationality, as Foucault's interpretation would have it, Descartes, according to Derrida, actually enshrines madness within the *cogito;* given that he must speak, Descartes can do nothing else. "At bottom," Derrida says, "leaving in silence the problem of speech posed by the Cogito, Descartes seems to imply that thinking *and* saying what is clear and distinct are the same thing."[15] But the two are not the same: in "pronouncing" the *cogito*, Descartes inscribes it within a "system of deductions and protections," where self-identity cannot possibly exist, where indentity always presupposes an Other (madness, in this case) (WD, 59).

So for Derrida, as for Lacan, the Cartesian Subject disappears amid the corridors of language. And both would argue, each in his own way, that no foundational subject of any sort could possibly be found: owing to the instability of meaning and interpretation, any project that sets out to discover the truth of the self will end in failure; words inevitably combine together to form philosophical mazes that confound the search for essences, subjective or otherwise.

The Demystification of "the Human" and the Fragmentation of Identity: Feminism and the Social Critique of the Subject

The subject is not only an historical creation and a "language-effect"; it is also a powerful piece of ideology/mythology, which feminists in particular have been concerned to expose.[16] At the center of both the political and the epistemological conception of the subject since the seventeenth century stands abstract, universal "Man," the featureless bearer of "human" rights and responsibilities, the disembodied mirrorer of nature. For this conception, the particularities of human locatedness—race, class, gender, religion, geography, ethnicity, historical place—are so much obscuring detritus, which must be shook loose from the mirror of the mind if it is to attain impartial moral judgment or clear and distinct insight into the nature of things. Such unclouded and disinterested insight is possible for all persons (as Descartes most clearly articulated), given the right method—a method which will allow reason (or human powers of observation) to rise above the limitations of embodied perspective, to achieve what Thomas Nagel has called "the view from nowhere."[17]

Although Nietzsche was the first to mount a direct assault on the notion of perspectiveless thought, it was Marx who initially discerned its fault lines and forged the weapons of political and social analyses with which twentieth-century critics would thoroughly shatter it. "The Human," Marx insisted, is fragmented by history, and by class; for the dialectic of "pure reason" one must now substitute the history of ideologies, reflecting and sustaining the concrete historical interests of the dominant social class. The liberation movements of the nineteen-sixties and seventies added race and gender to class, completing a powerful modernist triumverate of demystifying and "locating" categories, exposing the myth of "the Human" and its pretensions to neutral perspective. The official stories of Western culture—of its philosophy, religion, literature, material history—now required radical reconstruction. Not only were vast areas of human experience unrepresented and marginalized, but what *had* been privileged in the story of Western culture now had to be seen as the products of historically situated individuals with very particular class, race, and gender interests. The imperial categories that had provided justification for those stories—"Reason," "Truth," "Human Nature," "Tradition"—were now displaced by the (historical, social) questions: *Whose* "truth"? *Whose* "nature"? *Whose* "tradition"?

Feminists set about demonstrating the gendered nature of dominant models of philosophical and ethical reason, scientific method, literary and artistic values, conceptions of history, and so forth. The male biases of "the Western intellectual tradition," they argued, operated both explicitly (in misogynist imagery and theory, lack of representation of women's experiences, and so forth) and *perspectivally* (in its styles of conceptualization, modes of reasoning and argumentation, ethical values and metaphysical assumptions). Feminists developed these insights in different ways, some attempting to connect the biases of various traditions and writers to the construction of male psychology and personality (to features of "masculinity"), others focusing on the unconscious gynophobia and phallocentrism—the repression of "the feminine," the privileging of "phallic" unity, stability, and mastery—that inform the deepest structures of the male-created symbolic order. (Examples of the first approach include Nancy Chodorow and Carol Gilligan; of the second, Dorothy Dinnerstein, Luce Irigaray, Hélène Cixous, and Julia Kristeva.[18] Despite significant differences, however, these feminist approaches were linked by a common project: the shattering of the myth of unity assumed by the "universal voice" of male culture, and the exposure of the female "Other" denied by that myth. For many feminists, too, the recovery of female alterity seemed to offer a route to the imagination of new cultural possibilities, to the reconstruction of science, ethics, literature, pedagogy, politics.[19]

At the same time, certain forces revealed fault lines fragmenting the unity of the "gendered human" as surely as gender had revealed the fragmentation within the apparent unity of "the Human." Some of these fractures have been exposed by the internal practice and politics of feminism; others, by feminism allied with "poststructuralist" theory.

Within the internal feminist conversation, as women of color and lesbians protested against the lack of representation of their experience in the prevailing discussions of gender,[20] feminists were forced to confront the biases and exclusionary aspects of their own narratives, and their universalizing assumptions about "male" and "female" reality. The central implication of such recognitions, for many feminists, was "practical": the urgency to shatter the institutional hegemonies that had allowed some women (chiefly white, heterosexual, academically affiliated) to make determinations about "reality" for all. Although this internal feminist critique had a theoretical dimension, it rarely (if ever) imagined that an answer to ethnocentrism, racism, and heterosexism was to be found in "correct" theory. Rather, on the most entrenched psychological and institutional levels, feminist self-definitions, social process, and political goals needed to be reconstructed. In the context of academia, this was seen as requiring, not only consciousness-raising on the part of individuals and groups, but extensive transformation of curricula, course reading lists, lecture series, student and faculty recruitment, tenure and publication criteria—all of which covertly perpetuate a predominantly white, heterosexual experience as normative, and exclude those who have a different story to tell.

More recently, these indigenous feminist concerns have undergone an infusion from poststructuralist thought,[21] a development that has led some feminists to the methodological rejection of gender as a coherent category of intellectual analysis. Nothing in the earlier critique had declared the theoretical illegitimacy of gender-generalization and abstraction. The myopia of prevailing conceptions of gender was attributed, rather, to the dynamics of racism and heterosexism—deep psychocultural currents that could not be cured by better theory. For "postmodern" feminists, on the other hand, talk about "male" and "female" realities is eschewed on theoretical grounds, and it is imagined that more adequate representations can avoid the distortions of past theorizing. So, for example, deconstructionist feminist Susan Suleiman urges feminist critics to "get beyond the number two" (the grid of gender) to explore "endless complication," and a "dizzying accumulation" of meanings.[22] In so doing, Suleiman suggests, feminists would allow their narratives to reflect more adequately the indeterminacy and instability of language, and avoid perpetuating a "phallogocentric" construction of reality: the bi-furcation of reality into binary elements, one of which is privi-leged, the other of which is conceived as inferior, derivative, the "other."

Other feminists, drawing more on the historicist wing of post-structuralist thought (e.g., Foucault, Lyotard), have found in the work of such writers a theoretical ground for feminist political concerns about the ethnocentrisms of gender theory, and the basis for more adequate conceptions of identity. Generalizations about "male" and "female" experience and reality, it is argued, inevitably and perniciously (no matter who makes them, or through what social process) "totalize": that is, create a false unity out of heterogeneous elements, relegating the submerged elements to marginality or invisibility. For gender is never experi-enced in "pure" or isolatable form, but constantly intersects with and is inflected by the multiple other "axes" that configure hu-man identities in historically particular and culturally specific ways. Feminists must therefore, so this argument goes, develop approaches to identity that will more adequately reflect its frag-mented nature: more "local" narratives concerned to explore multiple "axes" rather than propose "grand" theory, narratives which will treat gender "as one relevant strand among others, attending also to class, race, ethnicity, age, and sexual orien-tation."[23]

The Cartesian Subject: Alive and Well in Academia

These recent critiques fail to notice that the logic of difference, once set in motion, cannot be so easily satisfied. For the "strands" that constitute identity are endless, and no matter how "local" and circumscribed the object of analysis, or the number of "axes" attended to, some elements will be relegated to obscurity and invisibility. No method can protect against this, or against the just claims of a voice from the "margins," already speaking (or perhaps currently muted but awaiting the conditions for speak-ing) of what has been excluded, effaced, damaged.[24] Clinging to the imagination of a theoretical framework that will be adequate to the heterogeneity of identity and experience, postmoderns struggle against this recognition. They accept, even celebrate, the death of the abstract, universal subject—even, as in the case of feminist postmodernism, when central categories of feminist analysis are detonated in the bargain. But postmoderns (apparently without knowing it) are having a hard time relinquishing the epistemological fantasies of Cartesian Man: fantasies of an unimpeachable method, of adequate representations of reality, of an intellectual "turn" that will enable the critic to write the world newly, free of the prejudices of the past. The cultural critique of "the Human," having exposed the imperial "I" as a Wizard of Oz, and revealed the inescapably located and perspectival nature of human enterprise, ought to have delivered an unhealable wound to such fantasies. Yet they continue to be recycled.

The Cartesian subject and his fantasies still reign in academia, where "the race for [an authoritative] theory," as Barbara Christian argues, remains the privileged game in town, even (indeed especially) among those most critical of the "logocentrism" of Western culture.[25] Here academics perpetuate, in refurbished form, the intellectual hegemony of the theory-centered style, inaugurated by Descartes, that replaced the "practical" orientation of preceding styles of philosophy. Stephen Toulmin has pointed out how, beginning with Descartes, philosophers avoided issues that carried the taint of particularity: formal logic replaced rhetoric, for example, and the establishment of universal principles replaced debates concerning legal and medical practice.[26] Today, academics no longer assume the role of the transcendental "I" nor speak baldly of "universal principles." But they continue to convert the particular sins of the (largely white, male, and Western) culture of "modernity" into general problems of "discourse," "speech," and so forth; ironically, they constitute those problems as an authoritative theoretical discourse that legislates the ultimate terms of all discussion, much as the analytic language of Anglo-American philosophy was once the authoritative voice of all philosophical debate.

According to Christian, the result is as "totalizing" as the object of the critique. Consider that many postmodern writers, with inadvertent aptness, refer to their particular intellectual field simply as "theory"—the monolithic and colorless term serving to characterize the nature of their concerns.[27] Declaring the author dead, Christian says, "just when the literatures of peoples of color, black women, Latin Americans, and Africans began to move to 'the center'," the new "theory" is just as controlling of the world, just as "hegemonic as the world it attacks," just as oblivious to "difference" (the abstractness of that fashionable term speaks volumes here):

> [I]n their attempt to change the orientation of Western scholarship, they, as usual, concentrated on themselves and were not in the slightest interested in the worlds they had ignored or controlled. Again I was supposed to know *them*, while they were not at all interested in knowing *me*. Instead, they sought to "deconstruct" the traditions to which they belonged even as they used the same forms, style, and language of that tradition, forms that necessarily embody its values. . . . Increasingly, as *their* way, *their* terms, *their* approaches remained central and became the means by which one defined literary critics, many of my own peers who had previously been concentrating on dealing with the other side of the equation—the reclamation and discussion of past and *present* Third world literatures—were diverted into continually discussing the new literary theory. (*RT*, 72–73)

"Theory," with its need to avoid the "I," with its eagerness to celebrate the death of the "I," has only provided it with a new language: one that is in some ways more effectively exclusionary than the former language of transcendental philosophy.

Academic preference for the "theory-centered" style is also evident in various postmodern political theorists' desperate search for adequate theories of "resistance" and the "revolutionary subject." These theorists begin with the recognition that the Cartesian subject was primarily the site or foundation of knowledge—an "I" for which action was somehow incidental, even inessential. The problem with such an account of the subject, as this argument has it, is obvious: engagement in the social world through politics, love, or any other activity except knowing falls outside its limited territory. Later analyses of the "I," particularly among the Marxists and Freudians, helped to contextualize it within the realm of social activity, but at the same time new problems emerged. Marxist and psychoanalytic arguments concerning the subject, along with their respective "post-" forms, were hard pressed to explain the *active* subject: the subject who decides, say, to work toward political change. The new philosophical problem took the following form: if it is true that numerous social forces crisscross and shape the subject—if, as implied by the social scientific accounts of the subject, it exists only at the intersection of those forces—then little room exists for the human will. Hence the question of *agency* (a popular term among postmodern writers). This question, however, is more peculiar than what high-minded discussions about it might suggest.

The social movements of the sixties and seventies began to work for gender and racial equality without an adequate *theory* of resistance. And, given the inability of academics to come up with one, segregation and sexism would still be largely unquestioned practices today if a theory had actually been needed. Of course, there are those who would argue that the lack of adequate theory is responsible for the failure of contemporary social movements to successfully counter the forces of fragmentation and cooptation undermining them today. Bad theory or lack of theory is not the problem, however, but rather, among myriad social factors, an inability to maintain a flexible, skeptical "negativity" toward changing contexts and their dangers. As Foucault says, "everything is dangerous," and every new context demands that you reassess the "main danger" (*GE*, 232). This requires a "hyper and pessimistic activism," not an alliance with "correct" theory.

Marx's observation about the great events of history—that they occur the first time as tragedy, the second as farce—is sadly relevant in this connection. Only here philosophical arguments repeat themselves: the postmodern project of "theorizing resistance" represents a farcical return of Zeno's paradox. For Zeno, the problem was how to account for movement; for many postmoderns, it is how to account for political action. Of course, movement occurred no matter how much it puzzled the philosophers, and the same goes for action. Yet academics continue to write as though action is impossible without the adequate theory. In a recent book-length treatment of "agency," for example, Paul Smith turns to feminism as the movement that now holds the greatest promise of constructing a "political logic" of resistance.[28] In addition, he says, feminism has already succeeded in meeting the "theoretical demand" for the balance between its account of the (resisting) subject, on the one hand, and active political resistance, on the other. After a glance toward Jesse Jackson's Rainbow Coalition and the left-wing of the British Labour Party—the suggestion seems to be that Jackson, like other progressive activists, has assimilated the most trenchant postmodern political critiques into his organizational work—Smith compares his own argument to "a series of raids from a mobile base" (DS, 154).

Despite the martial imagery, the conception of postmodern theory as political action represents yet another philosophical recurrence. In this case, it is Descartes's impulse to construct an adequate theory of knowledge that has stepped back onto the stage. The costumes differ—grimy fatigues and an AK–47 have replaced the philosopher's bedclothes—but the need, even the demand for adequation remains. It is as if theory itself demanded a hearing. What the postmoderns fail to see is that acceding to such a demand (real or not) only perpetuates the project of modernism, which after all began with a desire to produce a theory authorizing the claims of one significant human activity: namely, that of knowing. So, while philosophy has turned its attention toward acting, it has not outgrown the desire for theoretical justification: for a *foundation*. The background of contemporary philosophical debate might well be "wars of liberation against neocolonialism" and other local political struggles—admittedly such events have influenced recent thinking about even the most abstract epistemological questions—but somehow, to judge from academic writing, the participants appear to be conflicting theories rather than real-life soldiers.[29]

Not that political theory is a contradiction in terms; not that philosophy can never, in good faith, be *engaged*. To borrow a description that Foucault applied to his own books, analyses of power that arise out of concrete struggles and do not indulge in self-defeating (quasi-)epistemological questions can function as "hand-grenades," interrupting and scattering dominant discursive practices. But, as Nietzsche told his fellow philosophers, "our task is and remains above all not to mistake ourselves for others."[30] Such a mistake is made by those contemporary theorists of the subject who balance such an unwieldly freight of theory and jargon on one arm, while at the same time gesturing with the other toward the political demonstrations taking place outside the windows of the seminar room. Postmodern theorists deceive themselves if they think they are attending to the problems of "otherness" and of "agency" when so many concrete others and actors are excluded from the conversation. Who or what, after all, are the postmodern critiques directed toward?

The problem of agency, which seems to occupy such a prominent place in postmodern discussions of subjectivity, misdirects the efforts of current critical thought.[31] Here again Foucault can be helpful. Is political action, or action of any sort, possible? This is not Foucault's question. But consider a question of a different order: What can be done to break up the discourse that has accreted on the walls of the prison? That, for instance, is Foucault's question in *Discipline and Punish*, and the book itself is his answer. But he was very clear that this "bookish act of participation," as he described his writing, was not a substitute for activism pure and simple.[32] "The essence of being radical is physical," he said. "The essence of being radical is the radicalness of existence itself" (*FL*, 191). For better or worse, Foucault was radical; he took part in political movements; he never asked whether action was possible. Any philosopher and, for that matter, any citizen can decide to take part in political movements—to demonstrate for gay rights (as Foucault did), to garner support for reproductive freedom (as feminists do), to organize action groups for the homeless (as artists and writers do). But those who ask whether political action is even possible will never have an effect on today's most pressing and timely issues.

To place the emphasis on the "physical," as Foucault does, is not to call into question theory in all its forms. Foucault did, it is true, make some extreme statements in his most radical moods that have led to many misunderstandings. "Reject theory and all forms of general discourse," was one of those statements, made in 1971,[33] but the trajectory of his work from *Madness and Civilization* until his death in 1984 shows that he was not advocating an anarchist trashing of rationality or theory itself. In a late interview, responding to the suggestion his work was antirationalist, he said that the various forms of rationality "rest upon a foundation of human practices and human faces; because they are made they can be unmade—of course, assuming we know how they were made."[34] Foucault should be taken literally when he refers to "human practices" and forms of rationality being "made" and possibly "unmade."

The concern with explicit practices is obvious in *Discipline and Punish*, for example, where Foucault discusses particular timetables (such as Leon Faucher's rules for the young Parisian prisoners) (*DP*, 6) and detailed methods for "making" soldiers (such as the ordinance of 1764) (*DP*, 135–36). The same goes for his later analyses of self-forming practices among the Greeks and Romans. As he stresses time and again, the "care of the self" was not merely an "attitude of consciousness or a form of attention," but also a "form of activity."[35] These self-forming practices constituted an important part of the day, much the way meditation, prayer, or even exercise does among other cultures and peoples in other times. Literally working upon the body, in explicit and often meticulous ways, the practices Foucault analyzed throughout his career (from the incarceration of the mad to the self-scrutiny of the Stoic) had a hand in creating the notions of rationality, truth, self-evidence and, most relevant here, subjectivity that define the boundaries of intellectual discourse. The possibility Foucault envisioned, and it is an exciting one, is that by exposing and then helping to dismantle (if necessary) those practices, intellectuals might help in the "formation of a political will," as he described it.[36]

So, far from calling for the rejection of theory, the rehabilitation of the "I," as we understand it, necessitates a turn toward specific practices. Such a move curbs the tendency of philosophical critique to veer toward the abstract and the fabrication of groundless or even destructive problems. Pierre Bourdieu, in *Outline of a Theory of Practice*, describes this tendency as "theoretical neutralization": theory, he says, can easily flatten out the particularities of practice and distort them so that they take on the guise of elements in a well-structured conceptual scheme, which has little to do with the practices themselves.[37]

Rehabilitating the "I": Notes on the Practice-oriented Recovery and Creation of Non-Cartesian Subjectivities

Writers who discern a "crisis" of rationality or philosophy, precipitated by the collapse of the Cartesian subject, betray a profoundly ahistorical bias. Ironically, both the anxiety and the celebration over the "death of the subject" represent an affirmation of Cartesianism, which accorded central importance to subjectivity (but only one limited form of it) in the exercise of rationality. Intellectual disciplines today do not face a choice between stark alternatives: between Cartesianism, on the one hand, with its metaphysical-epistemological foundation resting on a self-transparent, autonomous thinking subject; and, on the other hand, the postmodern "postsubjective" voice that seems to issue from a background of obscure terminology and notions, and that often seems to lack a stake in its claims or to be unable to stake a claim at all. On the contrary, the cultural history of the West demonstrates that, like Nietzsche's truths, old forms of subjectivity and rationality give way to new ones. Consider, for example, Lyotard's analysis of postmodern culture. Lyotard writes: "each of us [today] knows that our *self* does not amount to much," but from this he does not conclude that the self is useless or illusory or must be abandoned (however that might be done).[38] Instead, he locates the "postmodern self" in the information-saturated communication networks of postindustrial societies, where each person functions as recipient and sender of myriad diverse messages; the modernist project of "knowing the whole," of creating one philosophical metalanguage that would provide the epistemological foundation for all human knowledge, is finished, swamped by the profusion of recent technical languages (the language of the genetic code, new systems of musical notation, etc.). Having lost his "nostalgia" for the grand modern narratives of legitimation—and he encourages his readers to do the same—Lyotard still continues to discuss legitimation of a certain kind. Setting down *The Postmodern Condition,* a reader might well cry: "The Subject is dead. Long live subjects!"

If, however, there *is* a Subject that now must die, it is the imperial "I," the monolithic "I"—not the "I" itself, whatever it might be. The imperial "I" blithely speaks for all and presumes (as Paul Zweig put it) to "cast no shadow"; it is the "I" that refuses to accept the embodied, located, temporal nature of his or her experience and perspective. It is this "I," for example, that lesbian feminists and feminists of color exposed and took to task in their critiques of early gender theory; postmodern feminists should not conflate a theoretical embrace of "fragmented identities" with a conquering of that imperial "I" in themselves. The embrace of fragmentation by postmodern writers of all kinds serves to establish a kind of hegemony that, in theory, postmodernism opposes: the imperial "I," as we have argued, has simply begun speaking a different, but no less exclusionary language. But there are circumstances that do call for the use of an "I," that call for what might be termed "strategic generalizations"—and these need to be distinguished from totalizations, phallogocentric or otherwise. For a poststructuralist seeking "correctness"—seeking, that is, a theory cognizant of the heterogeneous, unstable nature of identity—general categories of social identity (race, class, gender) are simply effacing of difference; yet from the standpoint of a philosophy oriented toward practices—or, in that special sense, a practical philosophy—those categories remain vital.

Take the case of identity politics, for example. It requires such generalizations (e.g., the "black women" of the Combahee River Collective) at particular moments in its development; they are useful, "life-enhancing fictions" that enable the recognition of solidarity with others. General categories of social identity also continue to be essential to the ongoing exposure and analysis of the biases of white, male culture—biases that do not only reflect the particular historical situations of authors, but transhistorical configurations of race, class, and gender. (The "phallogocentrism" of Western metaphysics, for example, is the product of the overdetermined privilege—racial, class, and gender privilege—that has been characteristic of the social situations of the authors of our classical canon.) And, finally, the (epistemologically and politically) "correct" rejection of general categories of identity would return social critics, in practice, to the terrain of "the Human." For without such categories, the notions of social interest, location, and perspective—notions that give content and force to the critique of abstract humanism—are no longer "usable." They remain theoretically in force, while in practice critics are hobbled in making the general claims that drive them home. Most contemporary institutions have barely begun to absorb the message of "modernist" social criticism; surely it is too soon to let them off the hook via postmodern complexity and instability.

Generalizations about gender, race, and class also obscure and exclude. For a practical philosophy, however, such determinations cannot be made abstractly but must be decided in concrete situations. The central problem with the "totalizations" of white, middle-class feminists, for a practical philosophy, was not that they spoke of "female reality" (for there are contexts where gender-generalizations were and are still edifying and politically important), but that they presumed to do so hegemonically, without knowledge of women's lives different from their own, their desire to create a unified theory superseding the need to listen, look, and learn from the world outside what Minnie Bruce Pratt has called "the narrow circle of the self."

For postmodern intellectuals to declare "the death of the subject"—to proscribe, as it were, all forms of the "I"—is to imagine once again that the features of Cartesian Man constitute the profile of "the Human." Nevertheless, other forms of subjectivity—constructed around embodiment, limitation, pragmatic concerns, self-reflectiveness concerning one's biases, and so forth—are there at the "margins" of the philosophical tradition, waiting to be noticed. They are to be found in "recessive" strains in philosophy, in resistant figures such as Nietzsche and Montaigne, whose works are rich with insights that readers may only now be in a position to understand. And they are there in conceptions of identity that have developed through contemporary experiences of exclusion and resistance, such as Minnie Bruce Pratt's "autobiography" of her constantly evolving identities of "skin, blood, heart," changing shape in response to her changing situation and developing understanding of herself as wife, woman, white, lesbian.[39] These accounts point to non-Cartesian models of what it means to be an "I," and to speak with conviction without the fantasy of authority. Although it is beyond the scope of this essay to elaborate such models, we would like to end on a note suggestive of the directions they might take, by calling on some of those accounts. Many more, of course, could be added to these; our aim here is only to sound a note or two counter to the dominant Cartesian strain.

When Nietzsche writes, for example, "Everybody is farthest away—from himself," he is consciously stepping away from the Cartesian tradition of foundational, self-transparent subjectivity. Nonetheless, this does not lead him away from self-assertion and certainty. Nietzsche predicts his philosophers of the future will love truth, as all philosophers have loved it; but they will have the "good taste" to proclaim: "My judgment is *my* judgment."[40] As for certainty, Nietzsche understands the experience of it to be an essential aspect of holding any idea at all. New truths replace the old ones as they fall away.[41] The very ideas over which so many fights have been waged and that have caused so much pain may some day appear to be childrens' toys, but Nietzsche stops short of saying that some day human beings will have reached "maturity" and confront reality as it is, Truth or no Truth. Once "God" and "sin" have been abandoned, Nietzsche speculates, "perhaps 'the old' will then be in need of another toy and another pain—still children enough, eternal children!" (*BGE*, 57). Far from claiming it is possible to forego truth, Nietzsche seems to suggest that maturity involves taking truth seriously while, at the same time, *playing* with it like a toy: "One's maturity—consists in having found again the seriousness one had as a child, at play" (*BGE*, 94). Knowledge and the self may therefore have no metaphysical or transcendental foundation, but the knower and the actor *live* as though they do. And, it should be emphasized, Nietzsche argues they must live in that way; without the needed "life-enhancing fiction" (as he would put it) of a self, both knower and actor would slip into paralysis, as it seems so much "theory" already has.

Characteristically playful and subtle, Montaigne at the end of the sixteenth century reached a conclusion regarding the self much like Derrida's and Lacan's, but without their sometimes apocalyptic overtones:

> It is a thorny undertaking, and more so than it seems, to follow a movement so wandering as that of our mind, to penetrate the opaque depths of its innermost folds, to pick out and immobilize the innumerable flutterings that agitate it. . . . There is no *description* equal in difficulty, or certainly in usefulness, to the *description* of oneself. . . . The more I frequent myself and know myself, the more my deformity astonishes me, and the less I understand myself.[42]

Remembering Montaigne's urbanity and wit in the face of philosophy's limited power over language might well contribute to the rehabilitation of the "I," whose death notices, despite the avowed playfulness of postmodernism, are as solemn as peremptory.

Consider Derrida, for instance, who appears surprisingly mor-

alistic when he says of his work: "I do not select. The interpretations select themselves" (*DS*, 47). He sounds disingenuous,
forced, like an Evangelical for whom public avowals of commitment to Christian dogma overshadow true belief. And many
Derridians, like many postmodern feminists, manifest a similar
puritanical aversion to the "I." Ironically, by renouncing the
"I" so strictly, they are helping to perpetuate one of the most
significant elements of the Cartesian intellectual tradition: a tradition that created and sustained the pernicious fiction that a person could negate the accidents of individual existence and speak
with a purely philosophical voice. In Minnie Bruce Pratt's account,
on the other hand, the "I" is ubiquitously present, in all its instability and vulnerability. This "I" does not pretend to the impossible
ambition to "do justice" to difference; it does not imagine that the
"correct" theoretical discourse could ever enable the self to transcend ethnocentrism. Rather, Pratt realizes that confrontation
with "the narrow circle of the self" and what it has excluded is a
constant risk, even an inevitability. She dares to speak anyway, to
interact with "difference" (and not merely "theorize" it), and thus
allow it to put her in—to reveal to her—"her place":

> When I am trying to understand myself in relation to folks
> different from me, when there are discussions, conflicts
> about anti-Semitism and racism among women, criticisms,
> criticisms of me, and I get afraid; when, for instance, in a
> group discussion about race and class, I say I feel we have
> talked too much about race, not enough about class, and a
> woman of color asks me in anger and pain if I don't think
> her skin has something to do with class, and I get afraid;
> when, for instance, I say carelessly to my Jewish lover that
> there were no Jews where I grew up, and she begins to ask
> me: how do I know? do I hear what I'm saying? and I get
> afraid; when I feel my racing heart, breath, the tightening
> of my skin around me, literally defenses to protect my
> narrow circle, I try to say to myself: . . . Yes, that fear is
> there, but I will try to be at the edge between my fear and
> outside, on the edge at my skin, listening, asking what
> new thing will I hear, will I see, will I let myself feel,
> beyond the fear. (*ISBH*, 18)

Pratt's attempt to remain "at the edge" might be taken as a small-scale example of Foucault's hyperactivism.

Perhaps it is much too soon, then, to declare the death of the Cartesian "I." While critics may have killed the phallogocentric father "in theory," they continue to sustain him in practice. On the other hand, even if he were emitting his death-rattle, it would not signal the demise of the "I" itself. For all along, other "I"s have been speaking, writing, and acting—with or without theoretical authorization.

Chapter 8

CRITICAL EXCHANGES: THE SYMBOLIC AND QUESTIONS OF GENDER[1]

Judith Butler

Structuralist discourse tends to refer to the Law in the singular, accepting Lévi-Strauss's contention that there is a universal system of regulating exchange that characterizes all systems of kinship. According to *The Elementary Structures of Kinship,* the object of exchange that both consolidates and differentiates kinship relations is *women,* given as gifts from one patrilineal clan to another through the institution of marriage. The bride, the gift, the object of exchange constitutes "a sign and a value" that opens a channel of exchange that not only serves the *functional* purpose of facilitating trade, but performs the *symbolic* or *ritualistic* purpose of consolidating the internal bonds, the collective identity, of each clan.[2] In other words, the bride functions as a relational term between groups; she does not *have* an identity, and neither does she exchange one identity for another. She *reflects* masculine identities through being the site of their absence. Identity is the prerogative of the clan members, invariably male, who gain their identity through a repeated symbolic act of differentiation, that act being marriage. Patrilineality is secured only through the ritualistic expulsion of women and, reciprocally, the ritualistic importation of women, who not only secure the reproduction of the *paternal name* (the functional purpose), but who, by exchanging patronyms, effect a symbolic intercourse between clans of men. The woman in marriage is thus not an identity, but a relational term that both distinguishes and binds the various patrilineal claims to common but internally differentiated identity.

The structural systematicity of Lévi-Strauss's explanation of kinship relations presumes a universal logic that structures human relations. Although a number of questions can be raised about the presumptions of universality in Lévi-Strauss's work, (for example, in anthropologist Clifford Geertz's *Local Knowledge*), the question that concerns this inquiry is both (a) the place of identitarian assumptions in this universal logic, and (b) the relationship of that identitarian logic to the subordinate status of women within the cultural reality described within the terms of that logic. If the symbolic nature of exchange is its universally human character as well, and if that universal structure distributes "identity" to male persons and a subordinate and relational "negation" or *lack* to women, then to what extent does the redescription of cultural reality from the point of view of women require a displacement of the symbolic as such?

Lacanian psychoanalysis has been alternately defended and maligned by feminists who, in the first case, applaud the structuralist account of women's subordination cross-culturally or who, in the second place, fear in that description a reification of that very subordination. Significantly, Lacan's ambiguous status for feminists is related to the uncertainty over whether Lacan ought to be understood as a *structuralist*, suggesting an uncritical extension and application of Lévi-Strauss's system of the exchange of women to psychoanalytic theory, or whether he is a *post*structuralist who understands linguistic and cultural meaning to be a deferred indeterminancy within an open field of signification. Although Saussure understands the relationship of signifier and signified as arbitrary, he places this arbitrary relation within a necessarily complete linguistic system: all linguistic terms presuppose a linguistic totality of structures, the entirety of which is presupposed and implicitly recalled for any one term to signify. This quasi-Leibnizian view in which language figures as a systematic totality effectively suppresses the moment of difference between signifier and signified, domesticating that moment of arbitrariness within a totalizing field. The poststructuralist break with Saussure and with the identitarian structures of exchange found in Lévi-Strauss refuted the claims of totality and universality and the presumption of binary structural oppositions that implicitly operate to quell the insistent ambiguity and openness of linguistic and cultural meanings.[3] As a result, the discrepancy between signifier and signified becomes the operative and limitless *différance* of language, rendering all referentiality into a potentially limitless displacement.

Although Lacan accepts the universal and identitarian logic of the exchange of women, he nevertheless rejects the postulation of a linguistic totality, defended by both Saussure and Lévi-Strauss, that makes linguistic signification into an internal feature of an all-encompassing system.

The displacement of desire compelled by prohibition initiates a potentially limitless metonymic slide of signifiability. It is, of course, the *universalist* claim of the exchange of women that poses the question of structuralism's reification of women's subordination. If cultural identity is established through differentiation, then is the "difference" of this relation, in Hegelian fashion, one which simultaneously distinguishes and binds? In other words, is the differentiating moment of social exchange a bond, a unity between the terms that are simultaneously specified and individualized?[4] On an abstract level, this is an identity-in-difference, since both clans retain a similar identity: male, patriarchal, and patrilineal. And yet, they do bear different *names*, thus particularizing themselves within this more general masculine cultural identity. In effect, the relations between patrilineal clans is based in homosocial desire, a relationship between men which is, finally, about the bonds of men, but which takes place through the exchange and distribution of women.[5]

Significantly, the intellectual movement to reformulate and, indeed, to criticize Lévi-Strauss came in the wake of anti-Hegelianism in France. An occasional member of Alexandre Kojève's seminar, Lévi-Strauss was not wholly uninfluenced by Hegelian thinking. Moreover, in making its argument for the *arbitrary* nature of the sign, structural linguistics made use of Hegel's distinction in the *Logic* between the *symbol* (the inseparability of linguistic vehicle and meaning) and the *sign* (the arbitrary relation between linguistic vehicle and meaning).[5] Poststructuralism is thereby understood as anti-Hegelianism, not only because of the turn against historicism and the revisionist Marxist-Hegelianism of Kojève and Hyppolite, but because of the oppressive identitarian structures associated with Hegelian modes of thought. Whereas for Hegel the systematic totality of the social world was produced and reproduced through a cognitive and laboring subject, for Lévi-Strauss that systematic totality, conceived as a web of structures, made the subject into an effect of signification.

In *Tristes Tropique*, Lévi-Strauss sought to show, against Sartre and other existential Hegelians, that the structures of exchange, the relational modes, effectively *produced* social subjects, and that the relation between the linguistic agent and its meanings had to be fully inverted. The mistake of Sartrean existentialism as well as the Hegelian philosophy of the subject was to assume that there might be a subject who, prior to any relation, "enters into" a social relation as an in tact cognitive agent. The presupposition of the subject, whether in its Cartesian mode as a thinking subject, or in its Hegelian mode as a cognitive producer, misses the point that any and all positions of identity, of subjecthood, are constituted and specified through the differentiating binary oppositions of which they constitute one oppositional term. *The Elementary Structures of Kinship* sought to show, among other concerns, that for identity to be culturally intelligible and, hence, existent, there must first exist a set of differentiating binary relations or *structures* within which that identity can be located. Opposed to an existential point of view which conceives of a subject creating or entering into a set of social structures, where these structures are conceived as so many *external* relations, Lévi-Strauss insisted that the subject was produced only in and by the web of interrelated binary structures, indeed, as an *internal* feature of a specific set of complementary structures. This anthropological claim was confirmed by the linguistic insight that meaning takes place *not* as the consequence of a subjective intention, but rather in the relational exchange between the signifier and signified. The shift from understanding linguistic meaning as the consequence of an intention to a function of a relation challenged the humanist assumptions implicit in twentieth-century French readings of Descartes, Husserl, Sartre, Kojève, Hyppolite, and the Hegelian philosophy of the subject. But while it challenged Hegelian humanism (what some might consider Kojève's invention to begin with), the structuralist move nevertheless retains the postulates of systematic totality constituted by binary oppositions that are clearly similar to Hegel's. Among those oppositions which are said to be both binary and universally true is that which constitutes the universal subordination of women as a differentiating relation between men in omnipresent and external systems of patrilineality and patriarchy.

The effort to *historicize* the constitutive or genetic laws of structural anthropology have for the most part sought to find empirical evidence to refute the universalist claims of Lévi-Strauss and his followers. Although such a procedure may be sufficiently persuasive in some intellectual contexts, an historicizing critique must do more than often empirical evidence; it must account for what qualifies as "empirical"; it must ask how given objects within a given discursive field are *constituted* as empirical.[7] The structuralist would not object to such a question, secure in the knowledge that empirical objects are, in fact, constituted or generated by and within binary structures which precede them. But a more radical critique would replace a mechanics of the genetic formation of objects with a genealogy of precisely those discursive fields that permit such objects to come into being. For the critique of structuralism, the task is less to disprove the universality of certain objects of thought than to disprove the recurrent generative power of given structures. Hence, the claim of a universal relation of kinship which distributes identity and negation to men and women respectively needs to be challenged on at least two different levels. First, there is the question of what women "are," what sort of "identity" or "lack" they exhibit when they are, in fact, outside the bounds of the kinship lines that Lévi-Strauss claims to be universally applicable. Second, to what extent do disruptions within the frame of kinship subvert and displace its constitutive identitarian logic and offer either quite different structures of meaning or antistructures, sites of difference, that produce different configurations of gender?

The review of feminist reformulations and critical responses to the "exchange of women" that follows takes place through a reading of Lévi-Strauss as well as Lacan. In the course of reading these texts through the perspective of women who, within the terms of the text read, figure as its constitutive absence, lack, or object of exchange, the reader/critic presents the paradox of a negation that suddenly speaks, and speaks within a language that, by definition, presupposes its silence, the impossibility of its very speaking. Women as "sign" becomes a troublesome signifier only to displace the foundational oppositions of the structuralist system of linguistic and sexual exchange. The question of the possibility of a reading from the perspective of that exchange item leads, for some feminists, to a kind of writing that raises the question of a different language with a different set of presuppositions and possibilities.[8] The feminist critique of the symbolic, then, does not ask after a place within the language that has been described by structuralism. On the contrary, through the performative act of critical reading and writing, the feminist critique opens another space and time for language or another configuration of logic altogether. But does this alternative language succeed as an effective disruption of the patronymic law, or is it limited as a form of feminist critique? The consideration of this question suggests a feminist version of genealogical critique that exposes the narrative conventions of structuralist description as tacit strategies for restricting the cultural possibilities of gender relations through a preemptory invocation of the singular Law.

The Sexual Politics of Identitarian Logic

The history of structuralism is often thought to begin with the Prague School of linguistics, then appropriated by anthropology, and finally reapplied to the science of language through the psychoanalytic theory of Jacques Lacan.[9] In the course of structuralism's second meeting with language, the notion of the patronymic law, the law of the father, emerges as the (necessarily) repressive foundation of linguistic and cultural intelligibility. Lacan argues that kinship relations are first instituted through the repression of incest wherein the male infant is enjoined to become a subject through a primary differentiation from the mother. This *Ürverdrangung* permanently defers the *jouissance* or full pleasure associated with an (imagined) primary fusion with the maternal body. Hence, the repudiation of the mother effects the possibility of masculine individuation and the use of pronomial discriminations between siblings and parents that denote and institute a set of laws prohibiting incest. The differentiating capacity of language *is* the structure of kinship inscribed in the formation of infantile sexuality. As a consequence, the possibility of speech is understood to be a masculine prerogative acquired through the repudiation of an egoless, sexual fusion with the maternal body. To speak at all is first to inhabit a subject-position within language, which means "learning" the laws of kinship encoded in that language, a lesson forcefully taught, as it were, through the primary repression of the sexual dependency on the maternal body.

According to Lacan, women are enjoined to become a substitute object of desire, representing through displacement the maternal object as well as its prohibition, understood as the phallus, the law of the father which both exemplifies and prohibits the maternal figure of lost desire. As in *The Elementary Structures of Kinship*, women constitute the absence (*le manque*: the lack, the want), the differentiating negation, through which masculine identity is established. Masculine heterosexual desire is as much about the repudiation of the feminine, conceived as the repressed maternal body, as it is about the appropriation of the feminine as an impossible representation of the possibility of satisfaction. Of course, the possibility of *jouissance* would mean the dissolution of the masculine subject as such; hence, masculine desire perpetually founders on its own impossible project to enjoy a pleasure which would entail its own psychic death. The bodies of women become the site on which this ambivalence is played out. As in the description of the exchange of women, women become the "traveling sign" of masculine desire, the negative possibility of masculine identity as well as the everpresent threat of its demise.

Jacqueline Rose, a feminist theorist whose work is grounded in Lacanian psychoanalysis, emphasizes the *inefficacy* of the laws of kinship, the persistent failure of the incest taboo, and the laws which constitute unambiguous, polarized, and hierarchical sexual identities. According to Rose, the application of the rules of kinship invariably falter as a consequence of the force of unconscious resistance to any such effort to regulate sexuality into forms of cultural coherence. As a result, the incest taboo is perpetually destabilized by incestuous desire; sexual identity is always haunted by the "Other" it seeks to repress. For Rose, then, the Lacanian elaboration of the rules of kinship in the Oedipal domain entails a necessary exposure of the fragility of those rules. Rather than view the law of the father as unilaterally constituting sexuality, Rose insists that the unconscious not only partially escapes the law of the father, but perpetually contests its claims.[10]

The speech of the masculine subject lays claim to a self-transparency that persistently and unwittingly admits to its own opacity. The repudiation of maternal foundations is simultaneously a repudiation of the unconscious and those semantic possibilities that exceed the strictures of univocal and literal speech. Through the primary repression that constitutes this subject, the *materiality* of language is subordinated to the ideality it is said to express. Hence, the law which bars son from mother and institutes the differentiating meaning structures of culturally coherent speech is at once the law which separates sound from sense and privileges the ideality of meaning over its materiality. The fusion of sense and sound characteristic of poetic language (what is in structuralism the opposite of the symbolic, but which in Hegel and German Romanticism generally was considered the very meaning of the symbolic) is precisely what is excluded in the speech of the coherent subject, who not only subordinates the maternal body, but subordinates all materiality, including the materiality of language, to an ideal or essential set of meanings.

Julia Kristeva argues that the effects of this joint symbolic repression of the feminine and the poetic are bound to fail. For Kristeva, however, this failure does not result from the force of the unconscious per se, as it does for Rose, but from the maternal body as a source of alternative poetic significations that perpetually contest the hegemony of the paternal law and its allegiance to semantic idealities. Kristeva argues that the *symbolic* assumes a univocal, abstract, and potentially closed mode of signification that operates according to abstract and universalizable structures. The syntax of universalizable meanings implies that linguistic agents can operate within a symbolic authority that both exceeds and sanctions their own individual authority. In Lacanian terms, the language user within the symbolic participates in the phallus, although that system of universal authority is always more encompassing than any speaker who finds him/herself within its web or mobilized by its authority.

Accepting Lacan's psychoanalytic reformulation of the laws of kinship/language, Kristeva writes, "language as symbolic function constitutes itself at the cost of repressing instinctual drive and continuous relation with the mother."[11] Although Lacan subsequently concludes that any effort at speech or meaning outside the terms of the symbolic is nonsensical and unintelligible, Kristeva argues that *the semiotic* provides an alternative linguistic economy in which univocal and identitarian meanings are contested. The semiotic is "a mark of the working of drives," the materiality of language, its rhythms, tones, assonances, and poetic texture (*DL*, 136). This semiotic dimension is most clearly evident in certain kinds of high modernist art forms which take the sound-structures of language as their object and vehicle. This attunement of the variegated materiality of poetic language signifies the presence and, hence, incomplete repression of the primary instinctual relationship to the maternal body that is not yet repressed through the founding law that initiates the subject into symbolic speech.

According to Kristeva, the semiotic is invariably subordinate to the symbolic and constitutes only a temporary rupture of its seamless identitarian pretensions.[12] Moreover, the speaker of the semiotic may be either male or female as long as a primary and continuous relation to the maternal body is allowed to surface in language in defiance of symbolic strictures. The semiotic does not constitute a politics as such, but a temporary and disruptive poetic possibility that, precisely by virtue of its defiance of the symbolic, cannot be translated into an enduring linguistic, social, or political practice. Further, this is a temporary rebellion within language which is *bound to fail* and which concedes the ultimate supervening authority of the symbolic. Indeed, communicability remains the prerogative of symbolic speech and, hence, the order of kinship, the phallus.[13]

The same problem emerges in connection with Rose's claim that the nonidentitarian character of unconscious sexuality contests and subverts the pretensions within the symbolic to discrete and oppositional sexual identity. That binary relation is effectively subverted through recourse to a psychic principle of nonidentity that characterizes infantile sexuality prior to ego-formation and, indeed, destabilizes the seamless appearance of that ego in the various unintentional moves of its desire, action, and language. But here again, it remains crucial to ask whether this disruptive potential can translate into an effective and enduring practice, or whether it is destined to remain a temporary disruption which is always and only superseded by the symbolic. In other words, can the unconscious or the semiotic ever operate to displace the symbolic as such?

"When the Goods Get Together"—Or Feminist Challenges to the Structuralist System of Exchange

Although Rose and Kristeva elaborate Lacanian premises for the purposes of showing nonidentitarian possibilities of displacement within the Lacanian perspective, other feminist critics of Lacan, such as Luce Irigaray and Gayle Rubin, in very different ways, challenge both the universality and immutability of the paternal law as such. In 1974, the publication of Juliet Mitchell's *Psychoanalysis and Feminism* suggested a synthesis of Lacanian psychoanalysis with a Marxist critique of exchange relations. Relying on Engels's *The Origins of the Family, Private Property and the State*, Mitchell argued that the exchange of women, characterized by Lévi-Strauss, had a universal status as well as a particular social formation within capitalist societies. As suggested by Engels, women's bodies acquired an exchange-value (as opposed to a use-value) within capitalism, with the consequence that women's status as an unpaid domestic worker as well as the market value of her sexuality were part of the surplus-value mechanism of capitalism. But Engels suggested that the subordinate status of women within capitalism was a product of precapitalist social relations that had survived within the terms of capitalism. In trying to ascertain which "precapitalist" relations conditioned the subordinate status of women within capitalism, Juliet Mitchell found the structuralist analysis women as objects of exchange to fit the theoretical need to discover a system of patriarchy prior to capitalism. Mitchell further suggested that psychoanalysis showed the workings of this precapitalist mode of exchange in the production of psychic and sexual identity and disparity. Extending Engels's insight in *The Origins of the Family* that material relations encompassed not only relations of production, but also the social relations wherein the species itself is reproduced,[14] Mitchell turned to psychoanalysis to trace the remnants of the laws of kinship in the contemporary workings of incest taboo as well as its repressive construction of sexual identities in accord with a system of exchange based in gender disparity.

In an influential article, "The Traffic in Women: Notes on the 'Political Economy' of Sex," Gayle Rubin specified Mitchell's argument further: psychoanalysis gives feminists a way to understand the "reproduction" of gendered identities that come to desire the hierarchical positions they assume within social relations.[15] Rubin's departure from Lacanian psychoanalysis, however, is perhaps more significant than her reformulation. As a set of kinship relations that have survived and changed within capitalist societies, gender hierarchies, she argued, are capable of cultural reformulation and variability. In other words, kinship relations that require masculine dominance are, according to Rubin, hegemonic but not universal. In a departure from Lacanian theory, Rubin suggests that if the laws of gender hierarchy are inculcated through early childhood training, then child-rearing practices might eventually produce other gender formations or, she speculates, move culture beyond gender difference itself. Lacanian critics would no doubt respond that the constitutive law of the phallus cannot be displaced through the social practice of child-rearing. The laws of sexual difference, the hierarchical distribution of identity and lack, are instituted by language itself and, hence, structure in advance the very possibility of signification. Prior to any particular social practice, such as child-rearing, the child is, by virtue of the gendering entrance into language, already subject to those differentiating structures.

Rubin suggests, but does not elaborate, yet another way in which the symbolically instituted binary of gender hierarchy might be displaced. Gender, she argues, is a matter of both cultural identity (or nonidentity, if the gender is "woman"), and of heterosexual desire (TAW, 180). But what precisely is meant by this? If gender identity is established within a binary opposition in which "man" is a possible gender only to the extent that he is not woman, and woman is, in effect, the "not," the negative limit of masculine identity, then masculine heterosexual desire is precisely the differentiating operation of this binary in which identity assumes a masculine character, and nonidentity assumes a feminine one. Such a desire is both connection and repudiation, for only through that desire is identity elaborated as discrete and oppositional. Gender remains discrete, binary, and hierarchical to the extent that the differentiating mechanism of heterosexual desire remains intact. In the case of homosexuality or bisexuality, gender immediately loses its discreteness precisely because the binary opposition within which its identity is established no longer works as a description of this formation of sexuality. It is, of course, always possible to reduce bisexuality or homosexuality to the heterosexual matrix, claiming that the *psychic* positions of masculine and feminine are intact regardless of the anatomical appearance of two bodies of the same sex. But such a task is notoriously difficult, and the bulk of psychoanalytic theory tends to defend primary bisexuality and/or infantile polymorphous perversity over and against such a claim.

Although homosexuality and gender "indiscretion" is everywhere confirmed by Lacan as the structuring loss of the subject—the masculine infant *is* the maternal body prior to the founding prohibitive law, and the maternal body is the primary object of feminine desire as well as its identity—the symbolic realm of cultural intelligibility and legitimacy permits of homosexuality either as regression or psychosis or as a subordinate psychic moment within an explicitly heterosexual development. Just as Kristeva argued that poetic speech constitutes a domain of language that exceeds the bounds of the symbolic, so Rubin suggests a domain of sexuality and identity that defies the sanctioned standards of symbolic and cultural intelligibility.

If either or both of these fields of sexuality and language exceed the paternal law, can they offer a viable way to displace the symbolic as such?

In an article entitled, "When the Goods Get Together," French feminist Luce Irigaray ironically engages the central tropes of the structuralist account of kinship only to expose the masculine sexual economy that motivates and structures that description of the symbolic.[16] "Women, signs, goods, currency, all pass from one man to another or—so it is said—suffer the penalty of relapsing into the incestuous and exclusively endogamous ties that would paralyze all commerce" (*NFF,* 107). Because all exchange is between men, and only men can act as agents who perform such exchanges, Irigaray concludes that the "patriarchal" system of exchange is predicated on a male homosexual economy that is at once engaged, proliferated, and yet everywhere denied. The term "homosocial" perhaps better describes the unconsummated

145

and disavowed status of this sexual economy, but Irigaray clearly wants to underscore the repressed and celebrated nature of this connection in which women figure as absence or as the scene of a displaced and disavowed male homoerotic desire.

The *repressed* or disavowed status of this masculine homoerotic economy, however, is perhaps more important than Irigaray suggests. The law which facilitates exchange also institutes heterosexuality as a compulsory cultural form, and marriage as the guarantor of both the reproduction of the clan (progeny) and production of goods (trade). Although Irigaray, like Roland Barthes and occasionally Foucault, argues that sex for *pleasure* rather than reproduction is the ultimate subversion of the regulating norms of kinship, it seems that this notion of pleasure outside the reproductive law is itself constituted by the law as its negative limit. The prohibition of sexuality outside the terms of monogamous marriage effectively produces those sets of possibilities within culture. The structuralist paradox consists in rendering culturally unintelligible, i.e., outside the symbolic, precisely those cultural possibilities that become intelligible in order to be prohibited at all. In other words, the prohibition effectively *renders intelligible* precisely what it claims to be *outside* the domain of intelligibility. As Foucault suggests in the first volume of *The History of Sexuality* with respect to medical classification of homosexuality in the nineteenth century, prohibitions tend to delimit and demarcate a domain of cultural life, to give a name and identity, and, hence, unwittingly to mobilize precisely those cultural possibilities that are intended to be suppressed.[17]

Toward a Genealogical Critique of the Paternal Law

The forms of sexuality said to be "outside" the symbolic, which poststructuralist feminists identify as a locus of subversion are, in fact, constructions within the terms of that constitutive discourse, constructions of an "outside" that is nevertheless fully "inside," not a possibility beyond culture, but a concrete cultural possibility that is refused and redescribed as impossible. What remains "unthinkable" and "unsayable" within the terms of an existing cultural form is not necessarily what is excluded from the matrix of intelligibility within that form; on the contrary, the marginalized, not the excluded, is the cultural possibility that threatens the loss of sanctions. Not to have social recognition as an effective heterosexual is to lose one possible social identity, and perhaps to gain one that is radically less sanctioned. The "unthinkable" is thus fully within culture, but fully excluded from *dominant* culture. The theory which presumes bisexuality or homosexuality as the "before" of culture (as a regressive state) or as an "outside" (as prohibited and/or unintelligible) and then locates that "priority" as the source of a prediscursive subversion, effectively forbids from within the terms of culture the very subversion that it ambivalently defends and defends against. Indeed, in that case subversion becomes a futile gesture, or one entertained only in a derealized aesthetic mode which can never be translated into other cultural practices.

In the case of the incest taboo, we can acknowledge with Lacan that desire (as opposed to need) is instituted through that law, and that "intelligible" existence within the terms of the symbolic requires both the institutionalization of desire and its dissatisfaction, the necessary consequence of the repression of the *original* pleasure and need associated with the maternal body. This full pleasure that haunts desire as that which it can never attain is the irrecoverable fantasy of pleasure before the law.[18] Lacan is clear that pleasure before the law only recurs in the infinite phantasms of desire. But in what sense is the phantasm, itself forbidden from the literal recovery of an original pleasure, the effect or consequence of a fantasy of "originality" that may or may not correspond to a developmentally prior libidinal state? Indeed, to what extent is such a question decidable within the terms of Lacanian theory? A displacement or substitution can be understood as such only in relation to an original, one which in this case can never be recovered or known. This speculative origin is always seen from a retrospective position where it takes on the character of an ideal. And the sanctification of this pleasurable "beyond" is instituted through the invocation of a symbolic order that is essentially unchangeable.

Indeed, the drama of the symbolic, of the institution of sexual difference, ought to be read as a self-supporting signifying economy that wields power in the marking off of what can and cannot be thought within the terms of cultural intelligibility. Mobilizing the distinction between what is "before" and what is "during," what is "inside" and "outside" culture, is one way to construct artificial binaries that foreclose cultural possibilities from the start. The "order of appearances," the founding temporality of the account, as much as it contests narrative coherence by introducing the split into the subject, and the *fêlure* into desire, reinstitutes that coherence at the level of its temporal exposition. As a result, this narrative strategy, revolving around the distinction between an irrecoverable origin and a perpetually displaced present makes all effort at recovering that origin in the name of subversion inevitably belated.

Feminist theorists, in their critical reappropriations of Lacan, have isolated the prediscursive unconscious or a set of semiotic impulses as a locus of subversion or critical displacement. This has served the purpose of finding an "outside" to the mechanism of cultural construction that is not always already assimilated into the law of incest and the compulsory norm of heterosexuality. Hence, we have examined two different ways of establishing the unconscious and/or the semiotic as the source of a critical subversion, that of Julia Kristeva, and that of Jacqueline Rose. In the first instance, we saw that the semiotic, conceived as the "outside" to the paternal law is itself structured by that law. In the case of Rose, the problem is more difficult. And yet, the postulation of a psychic split or primary bisexuality which contests whatever "identity" is established remains a point of resistance to the consolidation of identity, but does not translate into an active political gesture. In other words, if libidinal multiplicity (Kristeva) or primary bisexuality (Rose) operate to contest the cultural fixity of identity, it is unclear whether this contestation can ever be more than a futile gesture which is always thwarted by the reemergence of that very law. In other words, can that locus of subversion, in either case, translate into a set of cultural possibilities, or is the notion of culture in these contexts too rigid to become transformed by the subversions which originate outside that field? Can there be a culturally enacted subversion, or is subversion, for these positions, permanently located outside culture itself?

There is, of course, the anthropological question of whether "culture" in the singular or "the law" exist at all. The pluralization of cultures and of kinship structures disputes the universality of structuralism's claims, but fails to interrogate critically the universalizing postulate as a specific cultural strategy of epistemological imperialism. Rubin suggests the progressive breakdown of kinship relations through modernization and the proliferation of sexual forms, but the implicit utopianism of her early position precludes an analysis of how modern forms of sexuality are effectively produced through the inadvertent generative power of the law (her later work, however, centers precisely on this claim).[19] And though Irigaray suggests that the patriarchal exchange relation is founded on a male homosexuality that it explicitly prohibits, her analysis only suggests the alternative cultural forms that effectively challenge the hegemony of the symbolic.

But one further possibility is offered by the fundamental duality of the paternal law as that which both prohibits and engenders the misnomer of the cultural "outside." One answer, it seems, is to deconstruct the spatial and temporal discursive conventions that theories based on the symbolic tend to maintain. Only by showing the "outside" of culture as an out-lawed cultural possibility, and the "before" of culture as a performative tactic, can we read the temporal and spatial conventions of structuralist discourse as the political tactics of prohibition that they are, and reread them as potential sites for generating subversion.

PART III
CULTURE

Chapter 9

Foundations and Cultural Studies

Gayatri Chakravorty Spivak

Deconstruction as I understand it is not exactly "nonfoundation-alist."[1] It is rather, among other things, a repeated staging of attention on the construction of foundations presupposed as self-evident. By this route, deconstruction offers for us a perpetually rehearsed critique of the European ethico-political universal. There is a profound historical irony in that this deconstructionist critique finds its most convincing layout among the detritus of the last wave of imperialism and the incessantly breaking surf of neocolonialism. In this essay, I will try to establish this thesis by looking at a recent Indian film within the current configuration of Transnational Culture Studies.

In this new field of Transnational Cultural Studies the difference and the relationship between academic and "revolutionary" practices in the interest of social change must constantly be kept in mind precisely in terms of the negotiability of foundations. The radical academic here, *when she is in the academy*, has to reckon that names like "Asian" or "African" (or indeed "American" or "British") have histories that are not anchored in identities but rather secure them. We cannot exchange as "truth," in the currency of the university, what might be immediate needs for identitarian collectivities. If academic and "revolutionary" practices do not bring each other to productive crisis, the power of the script has clearly passed elsewhere. There can be no universalist claims in the human sciences. This is most strikingly obvious in the case of establishing "marginality" as a subject-position in literary and cultural critique. The reader must accustom herself to starting from a particular situation and then to the ground shifting under her feet.

From what space is the artist speaking, in what space is a particular readership placing him or her? What does the audience expect to hear today?

The strategies and techniques of knowing and making distinctions (*pouvoir-savoir*) are not only evident in the great rationalized institutions of knowledge. They are also at work incessantly to create the foundations of "common sense."[2] Thus the radical academic cannot afford to ignore, for example, that in Britain in July of 1988 a section of underclass "Asians" was vigorously demanding to be recognized as different from underclass "blacks." This is where the long tradition of distinguishing between Africa and Asia in terms of kinship to Europe within European institutions of knowledge must be remembered by the academic, *in the same thought* before claiming any sort of identity based on a politically foundationalist revision of knowledge. To academics and cultural workers, eager to respond to documents of cultural value such as the film to be discussed in this essay, the speaker's identity must not be merely "Asian," with underclass differentiations left out of sight. Unless we continue to nurse the platitudinous conviction that the masses are necessarily identical with "the revolutionary vanguard," or conversely that, stepping into the university, "the truth has made us free," we must attend to the possibility of dissension among resistant groups and their imbrication with the history and burden of names. Identitarian foundationalism can be as dangerous as it is powerful, and the radical teacher in the university can hope to work, however indirectly, toward controlling the dangers by making them visible.

The name "Third World" can seem useful precisely because, for any metropolitan audience, it can cover over the unease of internal dissension. For many radical readers and viewers in the so-called First World, a certain solidarity seems to be invoked by identifying the artist as "Third World." (This is more the case in the United States, marking the difference between Britain as the central excolonial, and the United States as a central neocolonial power.)[3] Some sociologists have warned us against using the label "Third World," contaminated at birth by the new economic programs of neocolonialism.[4] And, indeed, in the discipline of sociology, in the decade spanning *The New International Division of Labour* and *The End of the Third World*, the genealogy of a culturalist use of that term seems rather shabby.[5] What need does it satisfy? It gives a proper name, and therefore, seemingly, a founding identity, to a generalized margin.

A word to name the margin. That is what the radical metropolitan readership most often wants to hear: a fully-fledged voice-consciousness from the margin. When a cultural identity is thrust upon an artist from a certain space because the center wants an identifiable margin, claims for marginality assure validation from the center. What is negotiated here is not even a "race or a social type" (as in the passage below) but an economic principle of identification through separation.

> The analysis of *Herkunft* [descent] often involves a consideration of race or social type. But the traits it attempts to identify are not the exclusive generic characteristics of an individual, a sentiment, or an idea, which permit us to qualify them as "Greek" or "English" [or "Third World"]; rather, it seeks the subtle, singular, and subindividual marks that might possibly intersect in them to form a network that is difficult to unravel.[6]

Less than a hundred years ago, in another area of the academic enterprise, namely archeology, the "Asian" was used to fix a center, not the margin: the *Urheimat* (the original home), the *Ursprache* (the original language). An interested separation between Africa and "Indo-European" Asia worked in the interest of imperialism. A transnational study of culture must combat these foundational distinctions as much as it must repeatedly unpack foundational identities, so that the political register does not masquerade as knowledge. Such a study can reveal the historical negotiability of founding identities: fifty, or seventy, or a hundred years ago, cultural artifacts produced by a middle-class caste-Hindu might well have been validated by a British audience as from an "Aryan," as it is today in the United States by way of the proper name "Third World."[7]

Deconstruction often attends to the staging of foundations by showing up a complicity between opposites. In that spirit, I am suggesting that there is not much more than a reversal of the erased name "Aryan" in the representation of the Indian as "third-world ethnic" *in an academic arena*. In the subindividual theatre of "utterances" that come to hand for giving shape to resistance, the discursive formation within which the reversal happens is still marked by nationalism.

In the literary-critical academic arena, the impulse for an organized study of the margins came, in the United States, from Edward Said's *Orientalism*.[8] Said's book was not a study of marginality, not even of marginalization. It was the study of the construction of an object, for investigation and control. The study of colonial discourse, directly released by work such as Said's, has, however, blossomed into a garden where the marginal can speak and be spoken, even spoken for. It is an important (and yet beleaguered) area of the discipline of literary criticism today.[9]

As this material begins to be absorbed into the discipline, the long-established but supple, heterogeneous, and hierarchical power-lines of the institutional "dissemination of knowledge" continue to determine and overdetermine their condition of representability. Here, at the moment of infiltration or insertion, sufficiently under threat by the custodians of a phantasmatically grounded High Western Culture, the greatest caution must be exercised.[10] The price of success must not compromise the enterprise irreparably. As teachers we are now involved in the construction of a new and ethnically founded object of investigation—"the Third World," "the marginal," etc.—for institutional validation and certification. One has only to analyze carefully the proliferating but carefully exclusivist "third-worldist" job descriptions to see the packaging at work. It is as if, in a certain way, we teachers are becoming complicitous in the perpetration of a "new orientalism."

> No "local centers," no pattern of transformation could function if, through a series of successive linkages [*enchainements successifs*], it were not eventually written into [*s'inscrivait*] an over-all strategy. . . . The [disciplinary] apparatus [*dispositif*], precisely to the extent that it [is] insular and heteromorphous with respect to the other power mechanisms, [is] used to support the great "manoeuvres."[11]

Let us attempt to read the possibility of our unwilling or unwitting perpetration of a "new Orientalism" as the inscription of an "overall strategy."

In the metropolitan countries, lines separate ethnic, gender, and class prejudice from indigenous cooperation with neocolonialism in the Third World proper. Arguments from culturalism, multiculturalism, ethnicity, and an overall racialization of resistance—however insulated and heteromorphous they might seem from and by contrast with the great narratives of the techniques of global economic control—can still work to obscure the separation between metropolis and periphery in the interests of the production of a homogenizing neocolonialist discourse. Today, the old ways of imperial adjudication and open systemic intervention cannot sustain unquestioned legitimacy. Neocolonialism fabricates allies by proposing a share of the center in a seemingly new way (not a rupture but a displacement): disciplinary support for the conviction of authentic and ethnically founded marginality by the (aspiring) elite.

"If a genealogical analysis of a scholar were made . . . his *Herkunft* would quickly divulge the official papers of the scribe and the pleadings of the lawyer—their father—in their apparently disinterested attention" (*LCP*, 147). Should we imagine ourselves free of this analysis? Should we not attempt also to "write the history of the present"?

As a result of a decade of the analysis of colonial discourse percolating into disciplinary pedagogy and its powerful adjuncts, and of the imbrication of techniques of knowledge with strategies of power, who claims marginality in the larger postcolonial field? What might this have to do with the old scenario of empowering a privileged group or a group susceptible to upward mobility as the authentic and ethnically and/or culturally founded inhabitants of the margin? Should we not cast a genealogical eye, over what we have spawned in literary criticism and the study of culture, in order to hold at bay the possibility of foundationalist dissension?

> One must not suppose that there exists a certain sphere of "marginality" that would be the legitimate concern of a free and disinterested scientific inquiry were it not the object of mechanisms of exclusion brought to bear by the economic or ideological requirements of power. If "marginality" is being constituted as an area of investigation, this is only because relations of power have established it as a possible object; and conversely, if power is able to take it as a

target, this is because techniques of knowledge [disciplinary regulations] were capable of switching it on [*investir*].[12] Between techniques of knowledge and strategies of power, there is no exteriority, even if they have specific roles *and are linked together on the basis of their difference*. . . . Not to look for who *has* the power in the order of marginality . . . and who *is* deprived of it. . . . But to look rather for the pattern of the modifications which the relationships of force imply by the very nature of their process. (*HS*, 98–99; emphasis and contextual modification added)

For such a pattern of modifications we can choose the name "postcolonial."

Global postcolonials can communicate with each other, to exchange, to establish sociality, because they have had access to the culture of imperialism. Shall we then assign to that culture a measure of "moral luck (to borrow Bernard Williams's phrase)"?[13] I have no doubt that the answer is "no." This impossible "no" to a structure, which one critiques yet inhabits intimately, is the deconstructive philosophical critique of precomprehended foundations, and the everyday here and now named "postcoloniality" is a case in point.[14]

Further, whatever the identitarian ethnicist claims of native or fundamental origin, the political claims that are most urgent in decolonized space are tacitly recognized as coded within the legacy of imperialism: nationhood, constitutionality, citizenship, democracy, even culturalism. Within the historical frame of exploration, colonization, decolonization, what is being effectively reclaimed today is a series of regulative political concepts, the supposedly authoritative narrative of the production of which was written elsewhere, in the social formations of Western Europe. They are being reclaimed, indeed claimed, as concept-metaphors for which no historically adequate foundation may be advanced from postcolonial space; yet that does not make the claims any less important. A concept-metaphor without an adequate referent is a catachresis. These claims for founding catachreses also make post-coloniality a deconstructive case.

The persistent critique of what one must inhabit, the persistent consolidation of claims to founding catachreses, involve an incessant recoding of diversified fields of value. Let us attempt to imagine "identity," so cherished a foothold, as a flash-point in this recoding of the circuitry.[15] Let us, at least for the moment, arrest the understandable need to found and diagnose the identity of the most deserving marginal. Let us also suspend the mood of self-congratulation as saviors of marginality. Let us peer, however blindly, into the constantly shifting and tangled network of the techniques of knowledge and the strategies of power, through the optic of the question of value. This is not an invitation to step into the sunlit arena where values are so broad that philosophers can wrangle about them with reference to imaginary societies, ethical universals, and cultural particularity. It is rather to follow Pierre Bourdieu's remark: "In the beginning is . . . the founding of value."[16]

In fact, Marx's use of the word "value" may be seen as catachrestic to the philosophical usage.[17] This amounts to saying that the appropriate definitions of value might be versions of the recoding of what Marx names "value."[18]

"Value" is the name of that "contentless and simple" (*inhaltlos und einfach*) thing by way of which Marx rewrote not mediation, but the possibility of the mediation that itself makes possible all exchange, all communication: sociality itself.[19] Marx's special concern is the appropriation of the human capacity to produce, not objects, nor anything tangible, but that simple contentless thing which is not pure form—the possibility of mediation (through coding) so that exchange and sociality can exist. Marx's point of entry is the economic coding of value, but the notion itself has a much suppler range. As Marx wrote to Engels, "the issue of the matter of value is too decisive for the whole book [what subsequently became the three volumes of *Capital* and the *Theories of Surplus Value*]."[20]

In the early seventies, the authors of *Anti-Oedipus* (Deleuze and Guattari) attempted to extend the range of the Marxian argument from value by applying it to the production and appropriation of value in affective and social rather than merely economic coding. Their appeal—against Althusser—was to read again the first chapter of *Capital*, where the talk is of value—the contentless originary thing of human production—before it gets fully coded into an economic system of equivalences and entailed social relations. Their suggestion was that, since capital decoded and deterritorialized the socius by releasing the abstract as such, capitalism must manage this crisis *via* many reterritorializations, among which the generalized psychoanalytic mode of production of affective value operates by way of a generalized systemic institution of equivalence, however spectacular in its complexity and discontinuity.

The codings of value in the cognitive-political sphere, through the discursive system of marginality, whether by way of psychoanalysis, culturalism, or economism, are still part of this crisis-management. I cannot, of course, suggest that there is a founded postcolonial space of "marginality" to be recovered on the other side of the incessant coding. "Marginality," as it is becoming part of the disciplinary-cultural parlance, is in fact the name of a certain constantly changing set of representations that is the condition and effect of it. It is coded in the currency of the equivalencies of knowledge. That currency measures the magnitude of value in the sphere of knowledge.

We cannot grasp value as such; it is a possibility for grasping, without content. But if we position ourselves *as identities* in terms of links in the chain of a value-coding, as if those links were persons and things, and then ground our practice on that positioning, we become part of the problem.[21]

Work in gendering in principle sees the socius as an affectively coded site of exchange and surplus. The simple contentless moment of value as it is gender-coded has historically led to the appropriation of the sexual differential, subtracted from, but represented as, the theoretical fiction of sexual identity. (Economically codable value is the differential subtracted from the theoretical fiction of use-value in the identity of production and consumption.)[22] Gayle Rubin's "The Traffic in Women: Notes on the 'Political Economy' of Sex" was a pathbreaking essay in the analysis of gender-coding.[23] To my knowledge, Kalpana Bardhan's writings on the status of Indian women is the only scholarly work in the frame of postcoloniality in the subaltern context, which shares the presupposition that gender determinacy is the coding of the value-differential allowing for the possibility of the exchange of affective value, negotiating "sexuality" rather than sexual identity.[24]

In the field of ethno-cultural politics, the postcolonial teacher can help to develop this vigilance rather than continue pathetically either to dramatize victimage or to assert a spurious identity.

She says "no" to the "moral luck" of the culture of imperialism, while recognizing that she must inhabit it, indeed invest it, to critique it.

(The specificity of "postcoloniality" understood in this way can help us to grasp that no historically [or philosophically] adequate claims can be produced in any space for the guiding words of political, military, economic, ideological emancipation and oppression. You take positions not in terms of the discovery of historical or philosophical grounds, but in terms of reversing, displacing, and seizing the apparatus of value-coding. This is what it means to say "the agenda of onto-cultural commitments is negotiable." In that sense "postcoloniality," far from being marginal, can show the irreducible margin in the center: We are always *after* the empire of reason, our claims to it always short of adequate. In the hands of identitarians, alas, this can lead to further claims of marginality. "We are all postcolonials. . . .")

Claims to catachreses from a space that one cannot not want to inhabit and yet must critique is, then, the deconstructive predicament of the postcolonial. My hope is that this sense will put a particular constraint upon the metropolitan marginal or indigenous elite not to produce a merely "antiquarian history" which seeks the continuities of soil, language, and urban life in which our present is rooted and which, "by cultivating in a delicate manner that which existed for all time, . . . tries to conserve for posterity the conditions under which we were born" (*LCP*, 162).

In this spirit, then, I will view *Genesis*, a film by Mrinal Sen.

Postcoloniality in general is not subsumable under the model of the revolutionary or resistant marginal in metropolitan space. If "Black Britain" or the "Rainbow Coalition" is taken as paradigmatic of, say, India or the new African nations, the emphasis falls on Britain or the United States as nation-states. In such an assumption, the aggressive use made by an earlier nationalism of the difference between culture and political power has now been reversed in political intent, the main agenda today being the explosion of the phantasmatic "whiteness" of the metropolitan nation. In a powerful recent essay, Tim Mitchell has suggested that the typical Orientalist attitude was "the world as exhibition."[25] The "new orientalism" views "the world as immigrant." To suggest that this reminder undervalues the struggle of the marginal in metropolitan space is meretricious. It simply recalls to mind that such a struggle cannot be made the unexamined referent for all postcoloniality without serious problems. No "two-way dialogue" in "the great currents of international cultural exchange" can afford to forget this. The struggle of the metropolitan migrant (including the violently diasporized) and the everyday of the postcolonial national are related but separate cases of rendering foundations catachrestic.

Thus an art film out of India (*Genesis*), or out of Mali (Cissé Souleymane's *Yeelen*) cannot resemble *Thé au harem d'Archimedes* (Mehdi Charef, French/Algerian). The last sequence of Allain Tanner's film *Une flamme dans le coeur*, placing Mercedes (the migrant Arab woman in Paris) in Cairo, attempts to stage this problematic.

Current postcolonial claims to sovereignty, constitutionality, self-determination, nationhood, citizenship, even culturalism as the names for the legacy of the European Enlightenment are catachrestical, their strategy a displacing and seizing of a coding of value. They show us the negotiable agenda of a cultural commitment to marginality, whereas ethnicist academic agendas often make a fetish of identity. The project, as always, is the recoding of value as the differential possibility of exchange and the channeling of surplus. Postcoloniality as agency can make visible that the basis of *all* serious ontological commitment is catachrestical, because negotiable through the information that identity is, *in the larger sense*, a text—a socio-semiotic labyrinth shading off into indefinite margins not fully accessible to the "individual." It can show that the alternative to Europe's long story—generally translated as "great narratives"—is not only short tales (*petits récits*), but tampering with the authority of storylines.[26] In *all* beginnings—a repetition, a signature:

> In order for the tethering to the source to occur, what must be retained is the absolute singularity of a signature-event and a signature-form. . . . But . . . a signature must have a repeatable, iterable form; it must be able to be detached from the present and singular intention of its production.[27]

The first sequence of the film, repeating the formula, "as always, yet once again," ends in a shot of recognizably North

Indian men and women, peasantry or the urban poor dressed in their best, lining up to be perfunctorily interrogated and put their thumbprints on a long scroll. As the voiceover intones: "As always, yet once again, they lost everything they had and became slaves again." In the manner of didactic allegories some signals are clear to some groups tied together by various value-codings (systems of representation) whose elements Sen manipulates with a certain panache. Indigenous radicals sense the pervasiveness and ubiquity of bonded labor as a mode of production.[28] India-fanciers perceive the famous Indian cyclical time. Slightly more knowledgeable Indians perhaps catch an ironic reference to Krishna's famous promise in the *Gita*: "I take on existence from eon to eon, for the rescue of the good and the destruction of the evil, in order to reestablish the Law."[29]

Some would notice an *in medias res* reference to the sequential narrative of the modes of production, a reminder of the young Marx's impatience with the question of origins, an impatience that was never given up: "If you ask about the creation of nature and of man, then you are abstracting from nature and man. . . . Do not think and do not ask me questions, for as soon as you think and you ask questions, your *abstraction* from the existence of nature and man has no meaning."[30]

In this articulation of history in terms of the mode of production of (economic) value, the "worker" is represented as collectively caught in the primitive signature (at its most proximate the thumbprint, the body's mark), the originary contract—the first codification/identification. Both of these things take on importance in the film's subsequent emphasis on the name of the father and its use of the radical counterfactual.

Since the title flashes on the screen only after this originary scene of repetition, it is also a staging of the preoriginary. The title itself has something to do with origins: GENESIS. It looks self-consciously solemn, in large letters by itself on the screen. The ethnographically savvy viewer would find it embarrassingly pre-postmodern, the metropolitan third-worldist would perhaps suppress the embarrassment because it is a third-world allegory of the birth of a nation—"genesis" does mean birth—which unfortunately misses the appropriate style of magical realism. The "nontheoretical" metropolitan third-worldist would prefer something more de Sica in style perhaps, like *Salaam Bombay* or Adoor

Gopalakrishnan's *Face to Face*, with its heavy contemporary cultural content, spelling out the fate of a Western theory in the context of the encroachment of industrial capitalism in rural India; or yet Sen's earlier films, where the super-realistic technique achieves obsessive brilliance by laying bare, for the most part, the workings of the urban lower middle class in west Bengal. The appropriate, indeed felicitous, viewer of the film, the participants in the active high-cultural life of New Delhi, would recognize that it taps a rather banal tourist genre, the recent spate of Indian films celebrating the local ethnic color of Rajasthan. This is a crude taxonomy, but it is still slightly more complex than First World/Third World, Eurocentric/marginal.

If we look at the coding of these positions, what leaves the viewer baffled could be Sen's assumed *agency* of reinscription rather than the marginality generally associated with the postcolonial seen as ethnic or victim. As the opening credits unroll, we notice that it is Sen's first collaborative film, with French and Belgian support. *Gandhi* had to pretend that its British and United States casting and production were not "part of the film." In my view, Sen uses the structural fact of international collaboration to put together a film as a postcolonial, not as a Bengali for Bengalis.

The postcolonial text is often the site of the renegotiation of the banal for its telescoping of "an infinity of traces, without . . . inventory."[31] When a so-called third-world text speaks a postcolonial (rather than nationalist) allegory, what lexicon is, after all, most readily to hand? It's the difference between, let us say, the hermeneutic reinterpretation of Freud and a look at the operation of "pop-psych" in society to see how it has become an allegorical lexicon: between fixing your glance at the thickness of signifiers and at the impoverishment of the referential.[32] In such a text the allegory works in bits and pieces, with something like a relationship with the postmodern habit of citing without authority. For a pedagogy that sees this operation as the mark of the fragmented postcolonial mode, the allegory can offer a persistent *parabasis* to the development of any continuous ethnocultural narrative *or* of a continuous reinscription.[33]

Genesis is the "original," not the translated, title of the film. Why should a mainland Indian film not appropriate English as one of its moments, without the usual coyness of magical or teratological realism? Generally, in diasporic English fiction written by people who have no active contact with the native languages, the only way in which these native languages are denoted is through the monstrous mockery of a transformed Standard English (the "foundation"), which reflects more the writer's lack of real access to the languages of the country. On Sen's screen, the English word is, and is not, a *sub*title when it flashes on. That at least is the postcolonial Indian's relationship to English—a (sub)titular relationship that does not derive from an authentic title to the language. At the origin is something like a subtitle, something like a footnote, something like a postscript, and postcoloniality can be its scrupulous paradigm.

Among other things, the film recodes the origin myth of the Bible. Why should the center of Hinduism not appropriate Judaeo-Christianity with the haphazard points of contact and non-coherent reinscription, appropriate to the postcolonial mode, *without* the heavy trappings of transcendentalism, unitarianism, and the nineteenth-century legitimizing projects, such as the Brahmo Samaj or the semitized Hinduism that masquerades as the "the real thing"? Post-colonial pedagogy must teach the overdetermined play of cultural value in the inscription of the socius. Such unacknowledged appropriative overdeterminations are the substance of contemporary globality. Think for instance of the appropriative weaving of the great "European" narratives of socialism and "Christianity" ("Christianity" is not quite European, in its *fons et origo*, either) with the "Asian" narratives of "Ethnicity" and "Islam" in the fact that the trans-Caucasian autonomous region of Nagorno-Karabakh, representing 5 percent of the territory of the Republic of Azerbaijan, is attempting to secede from its Muslim-majority base to form the 75 percent Christian-majority Artsakh Autonomous Republic of Armenia.[34]

A postcolonialist pedagogy, looking at the title *Genesis* on the screen, can help us acknowledge the overdeterminations. It can see *glassnost* and its attendant outbursts of subnationalisms in the Soviet periphery within the curious logic of postcoloniality, the graphic of catachrestic foundations. Postcolonialist pedagogy is a strike in the direction of undoing the division between proper (founded) and unfounded, by marking the claim to socialism among the claims to catachresis. The fact that socialism can never fully (adequately) succeed is what it has in common with everything. Only *after* that fact does one start to make choices. And, in its perpetually postponed yet persistent establishment, there "should be no room" for the persistent moment of totalitarianism. The apparent contemporary success of capitalism ("democracy") depends on a seemingly benevolent identitarian ignoring of the shifting mechanics of value-coding in the interest of the socially and nationally "representative concrete individual." A postcolonial pedagogy in the literary case can help undermine the prejudices attendant upon such benevolence (which would also fix a systemic "marginal") by suggesting that the word "catachresis" is a least no harder than expressions like "freedom of choice."[35]

Genesis is not a continuist rewriting of the Judaeo-Christian story as one episode in an eternal return by way of the celebrated Hindu cycles of time. When we come to the end of the film, we do not conclude that capitalism is just another turn of the wheel. On the other hand, the Hindu story (available from high myth to "folklore") of the ten consecutive incarnations, accompanied by various natural cataclysms, allows Sen to offer parallel descents for the two men and the one woman who are the central characters of the story, the two men's from a drought, the woman's from a murderous flood. (I was amazed to hear a foundationalist new-Orientalist reading of this killer flood as the fertility symbol associated with the female symbol!) The woman is not produced by man or men. They share the same story with a difference: natural (theirs, drought; hers, flood) and social (their occupation, weaving and farming; hers, has been wifing, mothering, sharing work). Nor is this a story of "primitive communism," for Marx arguably a "presupposition," a theoretical fiction.[36] The snake appears at least twice, as a sort of reminder of one revised patriarchal story line.

The film uses a banal tourist genre, recognizable by the felicitous viewer. I am not suggesting that teaching within the postcolonial field of value should ignore the culturally "felicitous" and the scholarly. Instead we must learn to recognize it as another moment in the differential negotiation of ontological commitment to the object of investigation, rather than the foundation for the perennially "true" reading. As teachers, we must make every effort to know the appropriate diagnosis (historically and in the present) and then speak of it as one case, rather than the self-identical authority.[37] This permits one not to be trapped by authority, to look at other codings, other constellations. Let us try out this coding on the space named "Rajasthan."

In *Kiss of the Spider Woman*, the use of early Hollywood technicolor at the end is carefully framed in diverse filmic idioms, so that we can adjust our look. In *Genesis*, the unframed yet noticeably regressive use of lyric space and the wide screen, unproblematic light, primary colors, can be seen as denoting "Desert." Yes, this *is* the desert area of Northwest India, but we are rather aggressively not in veridical space, grounded ground. The stones of the ruins move, to denote insubstantiality, and the sound of an anachronistic aeroplane is the response of a god created out of a skull before the dawn of serious technology. Northwest India pushes toward the desert of West Asia as the felicitous theatre of *Genesis*. No garden in the beginning, but a desert in the middle of history. (West Asia, the Middle East, itself reveals the catachrestical nature of absolute directional naming of parts of the globe. It can only exist as an absolute descriptive if Europe is presupposed as the center.) This is no particular place—negotiable as the desert area of Northwest India, pushing toward West Asia, but not quite West Asia; perhaps the very looseness of this reference questions the heavy, scholarly, period films, the benevolent antiracist films (sometimes the benevolent racist films, one can hardly tell the difference) that have been about the Bible story in its appropriate geographical context.

There is something of this loose-knit denotation of space in the language of the film as well. The film is made by an Indian whose native language is not Hindi, the national language. Do you see it now? To be in a new "nation" (itself catachrestical to the appropriate development of nations), speak *for* it, in a national language that is not one's mother tongue. But what is a mother tongue?

A mother tongue is a language with a history—in that sense it is "instituted"—before our birth and after our death, where patterns that can be filled with anyone's motivation have affirmed themselves. In this sense, it is "unmotivated" but not "capricious."[38] We learn it in a "natural" way and fill it once and for all with our own "intentions" and thus make it "our own" for the span of our life, and then leave it without intent—as unmotivated and uncapricious as we found it (without intent) when it found us—for its other users: "The 'unmotivatedness' of the sign requires a synthesis in which the completely other is announced as such—without any simplicity, any identity, and resemblance or continuity—within what is not it" (*OG*, 47).[39]

Thus, the seemingly absurd self-differential of a non-native speaker of a national language can be used to show that this *is* the name of the game, that the predicament of the film's verbal text is only an instantiated representation of how one is "at home" in a language. There is no effort in *Genesis* to produce the rich texture of "authentic" Hindi, nor its Beckettized skeleton. This is just the spare Hindi of a man slightly exiled from his national language. And as such, one notices its careful focusing.

The extreme edge of Hindi as the "national language" is a peculiar concoction with a heavily Sanskritized artificial idiom, whose most notable confection is the speech of the flight attendants on Indian airplanes. By contrast, Hindi as it is spoken and written is enriched by many Arabic and Persian loan-words ("loan-words" is itself—you guessed it, a catachrestical concept-metaphor. "Those French words which we are so proud of pronouncing accurately are themselves only blunders made by the Gallic lips which mispronounced Latin or Saxon, our language being merely a defective pronunciation of several others," said Proust's Marcel).[40] And, in Sen's predictable stock Hindi, the Arabic- and Persian-origin words are emphasized in an eerie light, adding, as it were, to that nonspecific desert aura, the cradle of genesis, Arabia and Persia, somewhere off the Gulf, real enough today as the site of imperialist inhumanity. These "loan-words" move history out of the methodological necessity of a presupposed origin. You will see what I mean if I list the three most important: *zarurat* (necessity), *huq* (right), and the most interesting to me, *khud muqtar*.

The subtitle translates this last expression as "self-reliant" or "independent." The trader keeps repeating this phrase with contempt to the weaver and the farmer, whom he exploits, as a kind of scornful reprimand: "You went to the market yourself, to check up on the price of what you're producing for me. You want to represent yourself. You want to be *khud muqtar*. The English "independent" gives the exchange too nationalist an aura. The actual phrase would be something more like "pleading your own case," and would underscore an everyday fact: in spite of efforts at Sanskritization, much of the language of legal procedure in India comes, understandably, from court Persian.

The aura of a place which is the semi-Japhetic desert, a semi-Japhetic language arranged by a non-native speaker; the perfect staging for *Genesis*. In the beginning is an impossible language marked with a star. Progress is made by way of the imagined identity of an original caught between two translations.[41]

The postcolonial teacher can actually renegotiate some of the deceptive "banality" of the film so as to insert the "Third World" into the text of value.

The film loosens the tight logic of progression of the mode of production narrative most movingly by taking a distance from the tough outdated comprehensive ambitious reasonableness of the Engelsian account of the origin of the family.[42] Rumor has it that the intellectuals of the majority-left party in Calcutta have said about this part of the film that Sen hadn't really understood his Engels. Again, the authority of the authoritative account, the appropriate reading, is invoked. We are caught in a much more overdetermined web than one might think—inappropriate use of Hindi, inappropriate use of Engels, India Tourist Board use of Rajasthan: and you think you're just watching an *Indian* film, you even want to just listen to the voice of the native.

> Far from being a category of resemblance, this origin [the Nietzschean *Herkunft* or descent] allows the sorting out of different traits; the [Indo-Europeans] imagined that they had finally accounted for their complexity by saying that they possessed a double soul. . . . they were simply trying to master the racial disorder from which they had formed themselves. (*LCP*, 145; "Indo-Europeans" substituted for "Germans")

Woman in *Genesis* marks the place of the radical counterfactual: the road not taken of an alternative history which will not allow the verification of a possible world by the actual one.[43] The two moments that I would like to discuss are in that sense not "true to history" but full of the possibility of pedagogic exactitude.

A work of art (I use this expression because I feel wary about our present tendency to avoid such old-fashioned phrases for no reason but to show that we are politically correct, although our presuppositions are in many ways unaltered) is a part of history and society, but its function is not to behave like "history" and "sociology" as disciplinary formations that secure foundations of knowledge about culture. My general argument, here as elsewhere, has been that, in terms of this characteristic, and as long as it does not itself become a totalizing masterword, art or the pedagogy of art can point at the ultimately catachrestic limits of being-human in the will to truth, life, or power. But with the resistance to the menace of catachresis (use or mention, mention as use) comes a tendency to dismiss such arguments as "nothing but" the aestheticization of the political (the assumption being, of course, that the veridical is *eo ipso* political).[44] I leave the suggestion aside, then, and look at the representation of the woman as the radical counterfactual in history.

Engels finds the origin of class exploitation within the sexual division of labor involved in the structure of support around the reproduction of society. Woman's labor-power, the power to produce children, was, according to Engels, fetishized into a relationship of dependence and subordination. Quite possibly, this Engelsian script has written Sen's woman as she suddenly appears on the screen in *Genesis*, for she is shown after the monogamian family. The Flood has killed her former husband and children. But, in *this* historical moment, in *this* text, in *this* "self-mediated birth," she negotiates reproduction as agent of production, able to articulate a position *against* the perversion of her agency.

In this counterfactual account, the woman points out the problem of the fetish-character of the commodity. In answer to her question ("does the weaver have the right [*huq*] to satisfy the need [*zarurat*] of the farmer for a new cloth?"), the distinction between productive consumption and individual consumption and the meaning of bondage as nonownership of the means of production emerges in the false haven. The trader lets the weaver weave a new cloth for his friend the farmer. This is not producing a use-value, but merely including the cloth as part of their real subsistence wage. But Sen represents another change in this moment inaugurated by the questioning of the curious woman (Eve in the "real" Genesis story). The trader gives the weaver money. The desert is inserted into the generalized commodity exchange.

Is this how it happened? Probably not. And certainly not according to most great narratives, anthropological or politico-economic. Yet why not? Women's story is not the substance of great narratives. But women are curious, they have a knack of asking the outsider's uncanny questions, even though they are not encouraged to take credit for what follows. Thus, here too the two men will tell her "you won't understand" when they go to a distant market with their money, although her curiosity produced the money.

The point is not to contradict Engels but rather to see the counterfactual presentation of the woman as the motor of "effective" history. It is perhaps not surprising that within the most touristic footage in the film Sen fabricates the emergence of the autonomous aesthetic moment. No knowledge of Indic aesthetics or ethnics is required to flesh out the bold strokes, which I tabulate below.

1. The possibility of autonomous representation as one of the gifts of generalized commodity exchange. The weaver opens the sequence with these words: in order to dream, all you need is money.

2. The framing of the aesthetic as such so that its production can be hidden. The two men unwillingly hide themselves until the woman, decorated with silver anklets, appears as an aesthetic object.

3. True to the autonomy of the aesthetic in this allegorical context, the aesthetic object is endowed with a hermetically represented subjectship. The woman sings, without subtitles. GENESIS in the beginning, in English (?) in the "original," marks postcolonial accessibility. Here, framed in the film, is a parody of culturalist art, inaccessible except to the authentic native; the audience of postcoloniality has no access to the authentic text. The song is in a Rajasthani dialect, ironically the only verbal marker that this is "Rajasthan." This most stunningly double-edged moment in the film is also a negotiation of a banality belonging to the internationally accessible idiom of a general "Indian" mass culture of long standing—the Bombay film industry: the woman breaking into a folk song. Unlike the rest of the film, which creates interesting collages of musical idioms, this lilting singing voice is autonomous and unaccompanied. There is also an interesting manipulation of gazes here.

4. As the sequence cuts to a scene at the well, the wordless tune infects the noise of the pulley. Labor is aestheticized.

Aesthetic objectification and commodity exchange bring out the supplement of sexual possessiveness that was implicit in the text. The two men are individualized by jealousy. If we must quote Engels, the here and now of the film (preceded by all those cycles of disaster) is clearly post-lapsarian:

> Monogamy does not by any means make its appearance in history as the reconciliation of man and woman, still less as the highest form of such reconciliation. On the contrary, it appears as the subjection of one sex by the other, as the proclamation of a conflict between the sexes entirely unknown hitherto in prehistoric times. . . . The first class antagonism which appears in history coincides with the development of the antagonism between man and woman in monogamian marriage, and the first class oppression with that of the female sex by the male. (*OF*, 74–75)

The film is not an origin story, but a story of "once again, once again." What we are watching here is not "first class oppression," but the discontinuity between developed class oppression and gender oppression. The woman has shared class oppression with the weaver and the farmer. The men join the merchant, their master, in the role of gender oppressor. Neither truth to Engels nor truth to Rajasthani kinship patterns is needed here, although both help in creating the aura of fields of meaning. Again, postcoloniality is a mode of existence whose importance and fragility would be destroyed by techniques of specialist knowledge as they work with strategies of power. If the radical academic wants to get a grasp on how the agency of the postcolonial is being obliterated in order to inscribe him and her as marginals, she has a two-step to learn. Culture Studies must use, and yet actively frame and resist, the temptation to freeze into specialisms. It must, at all costs, retain its skill as a strategy that works on cases with shifting identities.

"The overthrow of mother right was the *world-historic defeat of the female sex*. . . . In order to guarantee the fidelity of the wife, that is, the paternity of the children, the woman is placed in the man's absolute power" (*OF*, 68–69).

The woman in the film is finally pregnant. The men are obsessed by the question of paternity. In the spare dialogue, a point is made that does not apply only to the "Third World" or "the marginal"; the point is that the real issue in the overthrow of mother right is not merely ownership but control. The woman is the subject of knowledge; she *knows* the name of the father in the most literal way. This scandalous power is modified and shifted into "a strange reversal": power is consolidated *in* the name of the father and the woman is reduced to the figure who cannot know. Again counterfactually, the woman is given the right to answer the question of the name of the father and of mother right:

She: *I* am the one to tell you?
He (the farmer): Then who else can?
He (the weaver): It's my child, isn't it?
She: Why are you asking me?
He: Who else shall I ask?
She: Ask yourself. Ask your friend.

When the question of right (*huq*) is posed, she answers in terms of the men's need (*zarurat*). In the simple language of affective exchange she speaks mother right. This, too, is counterfactual, for it has little in common with the heavily coded exchange-system of matriarchal societies.

She: What difference will it make who the father is?
He: Who has the right over it?
She: I don't know who has the right over it. I accepted you both. In three we were one. Now you talk of rights, you want to be master. The enemy is not outside, but in. This child is mine.

This moment does not belong in the accounting of history, and the men do not get her point. "Our first sin was to call her a whore," they mutter. The admission has, strictly speaking, no consequence. The eruption of jealousy, the enmity between the comrades, the defeat of the female sex seem to mark a moment of rupture. The tempo speeds up. This disaster is neither drought nor flood, but a quick succession of colonial wars: on camels, with bombs; succeeded by neocolonialism, "development"—a bulldozer.

In a completely unexpected final freeze-frame, what comes up from below is a Caterpillar bulldozer. You see the word "CATER-

PILLAR" on its nose and, again, it is not a subtitle; like GENESIS, it is a word that the postcolonial understands. The innumerable links between capitalism and patriarchy are not spelled out. The film ends with the immediately recognizable banality of the phallus—the angle of the shot focuses attention on the erect pipe so that you don't even know that it's quite a bulldozer. The subtitle becomes part of the text again, and the catachresis is brutally shifted into the literality of the present struggle.

Let us imagine a contrast between this bulldozer and the bulldozer in *Sammy and Rosie Get Laid*, so textualized that it can work as a rich symbol. In Sen the lexicon is resolutely and precariously "outside." Pedagogy here must try to retrench from that outside the fragmented semiotic of an overdetermining globality, which must not be retranslated into the autonomy of the art object or its status as ethnic evidence, the particular voice of the marginal. Our agency must not be reinscribed through the benevolence of the discipline.

Not all "postcolonial" texts have to look like *Genesis*. In fact, I do not know what the paradigmatic postcolonial stylistic production would be. At any rate, these pages are as much about a postcolonial style of pedagogy, attending to catachreses at the origin, as about the look of a postcolonial text.[45]

We must, however, attend to taxonomic talk of paradigms and such, for "no 'local center,' no 'pattern of transformation' could function if, through a series of sequences, it did not eventually enter into an over-all strategy" (*HS*, 99). Yet this attention cannot be our end and goal. We must arrest the emergence of disciplinary currency by keeping our eye on the double (multiple and irregular) movement of the local *and* the overall.

In chapter 1 of *Capital* Marx speaks of four forms of value: the simple, the total or expanded, the general, and money.

The "simple" form of value (20 yards of linen = 1 coat) is heuristic or accidental. The "general," where all value is economically expressed in terms of *one* commodity, is on its way to the money form. The second form—"the total or expanded"—is where "z commodity $A = u$ commodity B or v commodity C or $= w$ commodity D or $= x$ commodity E or $=$ etc." (*Cap*, 156).

In the Western European mid-nineteenth century, Marx felt that the most appropriate object of investigation for an emancipatory critique was capital. In the analysis of capital (traffic in economic value-coding), which releases the abstract as such, both capitalist and critical activist must use the most logical form of value (general and then money) as his tool. This lesson cannot be ignored. But in the analysis of contemporary capital*ism* in the broadest sense, taking patriarchy (traffic in affective value-coding) and neocolonialism (traffic in epistemic-cognitive-politi-cal-institutional value-coding) into account, it is "the total or expanded form of value": where "the series of [the] representa-tions [of value] never comes to an end"; which "is a motley mosaic of disparate and unconnected expressions"; where the endless series of expressions are all different from each other; and where "the totality has no single, unified form of appear-ance"—that is what Foucault, or Deleuze, or indeed, implicitly, Gayle Rubin choose as their analytical field (*Cap*, 156–157). "We must conceive discourse as a series of discontinuous segments whose tactical function is neither uniform nor stable" (*HS*, 100).

Rubin, Deleuze, and Guattari seem to know their relationship to Marx. Kalpana Bardhan, like Sen, although necessarily in a different form, gives us the ingredients for an expanded analysis from within the generalist position (adhering to the importance of the general or money form). From a staunchly humanist-structuralist position, Rubin's work is in some ways most excit-ing, because she comes to the threshold of the total expanded form (which she calls, somewhat metaphorically, "political economy").

As for Marx's and Foucault's apparently opposed claims for their methodological choices, the only *useful* way to read them is as determined by their objects of investigation.[46] Thus, in the economic sphere, "the total or expanded form" is "defective" as a form of analysis (Marx). And, in the cognitive-political sphere "it is a question of orienting ourselves to a conception of power which *replaces* the privilege of the law with the viewpoint of the stake [*enjeu*]" (*HS*, 102; emphasis added; and *Cap*, 156). I have tried to flesh out their relationship by reading the production of "marginality" as a taxonomic diagnosis in our trade, and by suggesting that, here and now, "postcoloniality" may serve as the name for a strategy that repeatedly undoes the seeming opposition, as well as for the systole and diastole between the longing to found and its persistent critique.

175

Chapter 10

Grund and Abgrund: Questioning Poetic Foundations in Heidegger and Celan

James Hatley

For Heidegger, the question of the poem is far more than the question of its species or of its particular province within a philosophical taxonomy. As Heidegger himself argues, "the reflection upon what *art* is, is entirely and decisively determined only by the question about *Being*."[1] The poem, as the preeminent work of art (at least for Heidegger), is particularly implicated in such a claim. The poem, insofar as it is led to question the Being of beings, allows various entities to come forth *as themselves*, i.e., to emerge no longer as the objects of this or that use but *as* themselves, as beings whose Being is at issue.

Because the artwork serves as the opening up of a clearing in which the entities of the world emerge *as themselves*, Heidegger argues that the artwork must be characterized as a primordial setting into work of truth (*OWA*, 81). Such a claim attacks the philosophical distinction (as old as Plato and especially important since the Enlightenment) between aesthetics and epistemology. The poem's truth does not presume that things have already been determined and that one must now search for their most clear and distinct representation. The artwork is not a re-presentation of things according to their substance and accidents or their form and matter. Nor is the artwork the subjective arrangement of an objective truth, one which would seek to give the beauty of an entity apart from its reality. The artwork is itself an inauguration of truth as it is situated in the ongoing process of history, and gives the ground for beings in their very showing-forth into appearance. The poem first indicates the very nature of truth, insofar as it "first clears the openness of the open into which it (i.e. the entity) comes forth" (*OWA*, 62). The poem acts as a de-concealing of beings. The truth grounded in the poem in this manner acquires disturbing implications for traditional philosophical thinking.

One such implication is found in Heidegger's claim, first made in 1935, that "art is history in the essential sense, in that it grounds history" (*OWA*, 77). In grounding history, the poem gives the essential shape of existence and so of the possibilities which experience might take. The most essential impetus of history is no longer left to the working out of grand laws, or to the contingent necessity of everyday, mechanical causes and effects, but comes as a gift of the poem, of its capability to allow entities to arise from out of the depths of their Being, a depth that does not yield to the inquiries of a mind which would simply represent what a being is.

In claiming the artwork as the ground of history, Heidegger is brought to pose again the question of what ground implies. In seeking to frame this question, to give it its proper measure, he turns in his essay on *The Origin of the Work of Art*, presented in 1935 and first published in 1956, to the principle of "earth," *die Erde*, which is defined in his analysis of the artwork as embodied in the Greek temple. "Earth" serves as that trope in which Heidegger's text establishes the depth and scope of ground. It is, so to speak, the grounding of ground. Heidegger's derivation of this trope ultimately limits the way in which the artwork's role in the formation of the historical, even of history "in its most essential sense," can be thought. I will argue that in his emphasis upon the ontological sense of ground, of its articulation of the Being of beings, Heidegger remains incapable of adequately accounting for the particularity of those beings who suffer injustice in the ongoing drama of history. In order to better understand the nature of Heidegger's own argument, this paper begins with a consideration of his rethinking of grounding, especially as it is developed in "The Origin of the Work of Art." The paper then turns to the poetry of Paul Celan for an alternative reading of "earth" in relation to the grounding of the artwork, a reading in which the Hebraic sense of *Ameth*, of truth as *Treue*, as loyalty, comes to play a prominent role in the poem's articulation of history.

Heidegger's Bestowal of Being

After discounting the notion that the artwork is essentially a beautiful representation, Heidegger turns to the task of reading the truth of the artwork as deconcealment. To this end, Heidegger chooses a specific work to serve as an example for the discussion of the artwork as such. The work chosen is a Greek temple, which according to Heidegger, "portrays nothing" (*OWA*, 41) and so serves as a telling counterexample to the received conception that art necessarily involves representation. Heidegger's choice privileges immediately the Greek temple as the locus where the truth of the artwork as such will arise. The description of the temple moves the reader to experience the temple as a gathering of the various entities in the area of the temple into a landscape in which the invisible space of air above is made visible, in which "tree and grass, eagle and bull, snake and cricket first enter into their distinctive shapes and thus come to appear as what they are" (*OWA*, 42). Not only animals and space but human history and culture are drawn into appearance by the temple's gathering around itself "the unity of those paths and relations in which birth and death, disaster and blessing, victory and disgrace, endurance and decline acquire the shape of destiny [*Geschick*] for human beings" (*OWA*, 42).[2] In the figure of the temple, history is no longer thought of as "a sequence in time of events" but as "the transporting of a people into its appointed task as entrance into that people's endowment" (*OWA*, 77).

The Greek temple's gathering of things into appearance culminates in antiquity's recognition of *phusis* as that process of each entity's "rising and emerging in itself" (*OWA*, 42). As an opening into the illumination of entities in their Being, *phusis* brings not only the various entities and their world into a distinctive appearing but also "clears and illuminates that on which man bases his dwelling," that is, *die Erde*, the earth. The earth as ground is not to be confused with the notion of mere matter, or of a mere solidity upon which the world and its diverse entities might find

178

a static foundation. "Earth is that whence the arising brings back and shelters everything that arises without violation. In the things that arise earth is present as the sheltering agent" (*OWA*, 42). Earth, as ground, not only supports the arising of things into appearance but also "shelters" such arising. In such sheltering, the process of deconcealing is given an opposing movement, one in which what arises is brought back into the ground, into concealment. The entities brought into unconcealment through the artwork maintain what Pöggeler terms "an opposition of presence," i.e., their clarity is sheltered in a darkening, a withholding, that is essential to their Being.[3]

The articulation of the Being of beings in the sheltering withdrawal of earth finds its voice in Heidegger's summoning of a Greek temple into the text of his argument. But what is the reason, the ground, for this choice of artwork? The sudden appearance of a temple, carrying with it the vague rumors of old gods and the scent of a Mediterranean breeze, is, one could say, poetic. The reader succumbs to its rightness without being moved to question its inherent necessity. But in a philosophical mood, one must persist to question why Heidegger chooses precisely this example.

His answer might be that this temple's necessity arises from its nearness to the historical origin of the thought of *phusis* and of truth as such. As a result the artwork looms at the very horizon of our historical awareness as a work that still gathers the thingliness of things relatively undisturbed by the paradigms of representation. The work nature of the artwork can come into view here unencumbered by the weight of represented things. Here, truth can appear relatively free from the distortions of the metaphysical tradition, in which the force of truth has been weakened by the insistence that it is the fashioning of an appropriate representation of the thing, an insistence that ultimately leads to the technological stance of the modern period. For such a period things are no longer thingly but serve as a standing resource at the disposal of an unbridled will.

The temple functions to restore a possibility to thinking that has been nearly lost, as a corrective to a history that goes astray, that forgets the wonder implied in the question of Being as it was found in the earliest Greek experience of world and its grounding. Thus, the introduction of the temple does not stem from a poetical whimsy on Heidegger's part. Standing at the origin of the history of Being, it serves to give the modern reader a yet unthought access to the earth, to that upon which "man bases his dwelling."

But earth itself does not show forth, at least not as earth. It is the "essentially self-secluding" (*OWA*, 47). The "matter" of the earth continually withdraws from any attempt to make it appear. In the play, in the intertwining of appearance and disappearance, earth is precisely that which already has always disappeared. But its disappearance can only be thought of as the countermovement to appearance. *Its withdrawal makes possible the showing forth of things as things.* In such a showing forth a people finds "its appointed task," its "endowment," its history.

With the introduction of earth, Heidegger goes beyond that account of world found in *Being and Time*, in which "the for-the-sake-of in which the world is grounded as environment is thought one-sidedly in terms of the understanding (of humans) which projects significance" (*HPT*, 168). The *pragmata* of *Sein und Zeit*, things-as-equipment, now gives way to a diversity of beings whose appearing is caught up within *phusis*, within a process of granting and withholding in which those entities granted within the artwork remain fixed within an essential mystery, an inexhaustible excess which resists a definitive unveiling.

The introduction of earth as that which in withdrawing shelters the Being of beings also extends Heidegger's earlier account of ground, especially as it was developed in *Vom Wesen Des Grundes*.[4] There he argues that the question of ground—i.e., "Why are there beings rather than nothing?"—inevitably leads to the insight that no ground is possible for ground itself. "Freedom" is named as the "ground of grounds," insofar as the essential ground grounds beings in a movement of "*Überschwung und Entzug*," of "excess and withdrawal" (*WG*, 170, 71). In such a movement ground shows itself to be "a transcendental and essential characteristic of Being itself" (*WG*, 169). As freedom, Ground is also *Ab-Grund*, abyss. Since ground is itself without ground, it challenges humans in every moment to move beyond entities "in order that humans might be able to understand themselves first of all out of this elevation (*Erhöhung*) as abyss (*Ab-Grund*" (*WG*, 172). Such a movement beyond entities confronts humans with the question of Being. In the inauguration of such a question, humans find their essence as a freedom, i.e., as a "transcendence swinging beyond into possibility" (*WG*, 175). The opening up of *Grund* into *Ab-Grund* is now thematized in *The Origin* as a sheltering of beings (rather than only of human beings) which withdraws. In both cases, withdrawal, as a loss of normality, of everydayness, allows beings to waver and shimmer beyond themselves. In such shimmering is announced a fecundity of Being, an essential excess which always exceeds. In the words of Pöggeler, "the Nothing (i.e., that which cannot appear as something, that which grounds but is not grounded) is . . . the self withdrawing and concealing as what accords and shelters inexhaustibility" (*HPT*, 173).

But the praxis of technological thinking seeks in every moment to make all things transparent to thinking, i.e., to unveil their Being in an exhaustive description of their essence, of what can be represented about them. The Being of the thing comes to reside in the thinking of its epistemological determination. For such a thinking, the resistance of the earth to appearance becomes impossible, since such a resistance cannot be understood in a representation of a thing. The modern era threatens to utterly forget the earth. To remember the earth, one must turn to the artwork, which not only describes things but inaugurates a world of diverse entities and so moves the earth into a spaciousness, an opening, whereby the earth can appear as the self-secluding. The work then sets world and earth into an intimate unity based upon the striving of opposite inclinations, of *Überschwung und Entzug*.

By moving to the Greek temple and so to the earth which serves as its ground, Heidegger has readopted the ancient dialectics of Heraclitus in a daring reinterpretation of its logic of strife. Heidegger speaks of the striving between earth and world as mediated through the work as both a conflict and an intimacy. The work encourages this strife so as to encourage the complicity of each member of the opposition with the other. Here is found no final transformation of earth into world, no bringing of the hidden into absolute appearance. Rather, the drawing into appearance is intimately resisted at every step as the earth withdraws into its seclusion. In this strife a ground is given, not as a fixed and stable point of reference but as an oscillation, an exchange between figure and earth in the opening of a world achieved by the work.

But the difference and togetherness of earth and world as articulated in the figuration, the trope, of the work is not simply a universal principle, set forth in a fixed logic of strife that, once articulated, gives us the essential nature of ground. Ground is itself the result of an originary strife that cannot be stilled. Ground does not stay fixed within itself but rather discloses, lets appear. Heidegger notes as much when he states that world "is the self-disclosing openness of the broad paths of the simple and essential decisions in the destiny of an historical people" (*OWA*, 48). The world is not merely a system of disclosure—rather it comes from the "the simple and essential decisions" made in "the destiny of a historical people." Insofar as the world is involved in the decisions of a people to meet their destiny, the world is not merely the outcome of some mechanical or otherwise predeter-mined structure of openness which would gather the earth into the gestalt of a world. In fact, the world is never gestalt but the opening whereby a gestalt, a figure, can come into appearance. In this manner the world is said to be historical. The earth's "spontaneous forthcoming" is only spontaneous and forthcom-ing insofar as people build works which set the world into play against its ground, its earth. The ground then for the world is not simply the earth as such but the trinitarian logic of earth, work, and world which in their interplay come historically into the open, which is an epochal, a provisional, rather than eternal unity of their strife. Only in such a structuring of deconcealment, drawn provisionally from the example of a Greek temple, can the earth come to *ground* a world.

But might not some other work than the temple of Greek antiquity be chosen to situate the question of Being in our time? Heidegger's account in 1935 of the intimate strife between earth and world seems inappropriate, a nostalgic dream in the face of a world whose gathering of beings-into-a-showing-forth will shortly find its most characteristic figure in the crematoriums of Auschwitz. Rather than turning to the limit at the very beginning of the history of Being, what is to come of the earth if we turn to the other limit, in which a historical epoch threatens to enact its own annihilation of world even as it places that world upon the "ground" of the so-called fatherland, of a so-called people's sacred soil?

Celan's Bestowal of Loss

The building of temples is not possible in exile. For the Jew of the diaspora, a temple-dweller who has found him or herself transformed into a nomad by the catastrophes of history, the gathering of earth into world has failed to provide a temple sufficient to the God who would dwell within it. The temple is now always elsewhere, always already torn down, leveled to the bare ground and then rebuilt with the hands of other peoples, of other histories, and even, of other gods.[5]

The temple, like the Jew, is in exile. Its essence is no longer to be found in its past but in its future. The temple beckons as that which is yet to be built, yet to be grounded, a utopic boundary at the farthest edge of historical expectations. Confronted with the transiency of the temple after its second destruction in 69 C.E., the rabbinical tradition transformed the building of the temple into the temple of a book. For the Jew, there remained no building opening up the spaces above it, gathering the figures of behemoth and leviathan, ostrich and eagle into their true shapes. As Alan Mintz has argued:

> The temple was destroyed but the text remained. . . . The text, in sum, was the ground on which the grave issues raised by the Destruction had to be joined. . . . The only possible response to catastrophe was reading. . . . The Book of Lamentations . . . had somehow to be made to yield explanation, consolation, and reconciliation.[6]

Such explanation, consolation and reconciliation was afforded in the insight that the building of the temple must await a future yet to come, a messianic era thought in terms of an ethical perfection, a dedication to justice.

But with Auschwitz there was a rebuilding of the temple and a transformation of the book. Rebuilding, not in the sense of a reconfirmation of whatever it might have been to have had a temple in Jerusalem, but rather the building of the temple as antitemple, in the figure of a concentration camp who murdered and burned its victims. Accompanying this inversion of the temple was the inversion of its symbols: in the death camps wickedness did not "vanish like smoke" but the bodies of Jewish families piled into the crematoriums did.[7] The very rite of sacrifice, the chief ritual practiced in a temple, was itself horribly perverted. Blasphemy is too light, too easy a word to characterize the inversion accomplished in Auschwitz. Even the word "inversion" seems embarrassing and shameful. The death camps are not so much an inversion as they are the erasure of temple, whether that be of the Greek temple amidst the landscape of 400 B.C.E., or of the Jewish temple of the book. In the shadow of this erasure of the temple (does an erasure leave a shadow?), the contemporary artist, insofar as he or she comes to articulate the historicality of our times, must, to use Heidegger's words, call the earth into spaciousness so that the world's worlding might open up the appearance of things such as they are.

But how can an antitemple be used to call upon the earth, the self-secluding, the sheltering? The *Ab-Grund* of Auschwitz is no longer the excess of Being over beings that characterizes the Heideggerian notion of *Ab-Grund*. In the modern era, *Ab-Grund* has come to name the possibility of a nothingness in which all of history might disappear as its peoples are exterminated. The *Ab-Grund* of Auschwitz sheltered no one. Instead, its depths hid the shame of corpses reduced to facelessness.[8] But in such depths and such earth Paul Celan's poems seek to root the dimensions of their time, to articulate the history of this epoch. Like those rabbis who lived in the wake of the second temple's destruction, Celan seeks to initiate history in terms of the demand for justice, a demand which he founds in the experience of vocative address.

In "Radix, Matrix"[9] the themes of exile, earth, ground and the historical situation after Auschwitz boil up from subterranean depths laden with the threatening memories of repressed horrors:

> Wie man zum Stein spricht, wie
> du,
> mir vom Abgrund her, von
> einer Heimat her Ver-
> schwisterte, Zu-
> geschleuderte, du,

du mir vorzeiten,
du mir im Nichts einer Nacht,
du in der Aber-Nacht Be-
gegnete, du
Aber-du—:

As one speaks to stone, like
you,
from the chasm, from
a home become a
sister to me, hurled
towards me, you,
you that long ago
you in the nothingness of a night,
you in the multi-night encountered, you
multi-you—:

The title, composed of two Latin words—*radix, matrix*—can be roughly translated as "root, mother soil." The words suggest the fecundity of earth, its power to press things into being, to hold their roots in place, to nourish their growth through time. But the first stanza of the poem counters this expectation with a studied indirection. Something occurs but no independent sentence seems to be carried in its wake. Instead one only hears a list of adverbial constraints: "*Like* a man speaks to stone, *like* / you / from the chasm, from / a home." The poem speaks, perhaps, "like a man speaks to a stone," its first image expressing vaguely a countermovement to the gesture of fecundity implied in the poem's title. But this speaking to stone is also like a speaking to a "you." Thus, the poem is not only a gathering of stone into some figure but also the addressing of someone else, someone outside of the speaker or author of this poem. The identity of this you is complicated, overdetermined. It is eventually appealed to as a "multi-you," a "not-you," an "*Aber-du.*"[10] The speaking to this *Aber-du* is somehow already fruitless—in his or her presence (or absence?) the poem speaks like one "speaks to stone." This address is both invoked and immediately frustrated as a major trope of the poem. The almost hypnotic repetition of "du" throughout the stanza signals, as well, a certain obsession in the one who speaks, as if the *du* will not appear or cannot hear.

By the third line there is already the negation of the security offered in a "mother soil" by the figures of the "chasm," whose German equivalent *"Abgrund"* is even more suggestive, since it literally names a lack of ground as such. *Abgrund* is immediately made equivalent to home. And all three, the you, the chasm, and the home are "sistered" to the poet and hurled at him as well. In sistering and hurling is a confusing mixture of violence and tenderness, of freely-given exchange and compelled inter-course. Following upon this ambiguous image is an appeal to time, to the "long ago," which is characterized sinisterly as the "nothingness of a night," then as a "multi-night" in which the "multi-you" is encountered.

The paratactic organization of this stanza makes any para-phrase of it difficult. The fragmentary nature of the syntax hurls itself at the reader too and forces the reader to struggle to put these words into some relationship that is more settled. But each attempt is frustrated by the lack of a final "ground" against which to measure the poet's saying. Not only is the internal organization of this relative clause disjointed, but it seems to be missing its main clause. The sentence itself has been shifted to the background, where it labors mysteriously and unheard against that which is able to come to articulation. The reader awaits throughout the poem some confirmation of the completed sentence which might serve to ground these disparate images and to bring them into some meaningful relationship.

What has come to articulation in the poem's initial moment is itself withheld, even as it is articulated. The you is unnamed and remains unidentified. The poem's remembrance of its "you" is repeatedly occluded—it comes by way of a stonelike speech, dense, silent, unyielding, broken into fragments, perhaps bear-ing no fruit at all, since its ground is "no-ground," "chasm," and its address moves toward a past vaguely alluded to as the "nothingness of a night." The promise of the poem's title is puzzling here. The disturbed syntax coupled with the promiscu-ous mingling of both reassuring and hostile images stop us short. What is at issue here?

This question is at least partially answered in the third and fourth verses:

> Wer,
> wer wars, jenes
> Geschlecht, jenes gemordete, jenes
> schwarz in den Himmel stehende:
> Rute und Hode—?
>
> (Wurzel.
> Wurzel Abrahams. Wurzel Jesse. Niemandes
> Wurzel—o
> unser.)
>
> Who,
> who was it, that
> lineage, the murdered, that looms
> black into the sky:
> rod and bulb—?
>
> (Root.
> Abraham's root. Jesse's root. No one's
> root—O
> ours.)

The poem reaches its interrogative moment: "Who, / who was it, that / lineage, the murdered, that looms / black into the sky?" In the question lurks a terrible hint toward its answer. The murdered who "loom black into the sky" can be none other than the Jews exterminated in the Holocaust as their bodies consumed in fire rose in columns of smoke into the air, just as smoke once rose from the temple in Jerusalem. This oblivion of holy sacrifice can only be remembered through indirection, through veiled questions, through the symbolic allusion to the final identity of the slaughtered in the fifth verse, bracketed from the rest of the poem, added as the most tentative of afterthoughts—(Root / Abraham's root. Jesse's root. No one's / root—O / ours.)." The latin *radix* of the title becomes here the German *Wurzel* which serves as a reference to the Jewish experience of its own lineage. *Radix* as "root" is enveloped in that which is ground and implies the planting of fields and the harvesting of grain. *Radix* means as well the foundation or origin. Finally it comes to mean the parentage of the Jewish people, the linking of generations together through "rod and bulb," which is perhaps more accurately translated from the German as "penis and testicle." Here we

187

observe the historical declension of Abraham, Jesse, and No One: Abraham as the father of the Jewish race, Jesse as symbolically the Christ, and finally No One as the effaced millions of the concentration camps. In three names, the destiny of three epochs. In the last name, the destiny of ours, "o unser."

But what sort of question has this poem asked and what has its answer brought into the world? We remember our earlier discussion of Heidegger—the work opens up a world in which is given "the self disclosing openness of the broad paths of the simple and essential decisions in the destiny of an historical people." It is such disclosure that will bring the earth into a "spontaneous forthcoming," that will enact the strife of earth and world in their reciprocal intimacy, that will allow the things of the world to stand out in their figures, their gestalts, against the secretive withdrawal of the earth. The work gathers world into worlding. Its impetus, as we have noted earlier, is, for Heidegger, the *Seinsfrage* itself, the questioning of the Being of beings.

Celan's question, while it seeks to initiate a new epoch, must confront a disturbance threatening to undo the very fabric of history, one in which the other who inhabits history, the "you" to which every poem comes to speak, is swallowed up into the hell of extermination, of *Vernichtung*. Here the question of appearing and disappearing also carries weight, but the effect of disappearing is thought differently than in the question of Being. The you, obliterated in the *Vernichtungslager*, no longer stands forth. His or her extermination weighs upon those who survive as an ethical question, a question of why there was evil instead of good, an evil so disturbing that history itself might finally disappear in its wake. To this question, the culminating verses of "Radix, Matrix" seek some answer, some sign, beyond the hell of Auschwitz:

> Ja,
> wie man zum Stein spricht, wie
> du
> mit meinen Händen dorthin
> und in Nichts greifst, so
> ist, was hier ist:

auch dieser
Fruchtboden klafft
dieses Hinab
ist die eine der wild-
blühenden Kronen.

Yes,
as one speaks to stone, as
you
with my hands grope into there,
and into nothing, such
is what is here:

this fertile
soil too gapes
this going down
is one of the
crests growing wild.

In the fifth verse of the poem, the poet finds his hand grasping so deeply that it "gropes into there, / and into nothing." The "you," however, gropes with the writing hand of the poet and not simply the poet him or herself. The confusion of the you with the I is startling; whatever the individuality of the poet might be, he or she is opened up to the grasp, the address of this other, this you. The confusion acts as a counterweight to an earlier time, mentioned in the second verse, when the "you" stepped "across the field, alone." Given the question of the third verse, this you, wandering in exile across the field (a profound contrast to the Nazi propaganda image of the devoted German *Bauer* plowing the field in the sweat of his brow), can be identified as a Jew of the Holocaust wandering to his or her destruction— she or he can also be identified with Celan's own mother who died while interred in a work camp. In its achievement, the poem now brings the loss of the other, this you, the erased root, the no one, into the field of the poem itself.

But is to bring the loss of the you into the poem the same as to bring the you itself into the poem? Indeed, can the you ever be named as an "itself," figured as a "being?" Or is our only recourse to the "you" in an address? In address the definite or indefinite article is removed from the pronoun: not *the* you or *a* you but *you*. The effect is startling: we switch from a discursive to a vocative mode. We no longer speak about but rather speak toward. The poems, the "noems" (*"Gedicht, Genicht"*) of *The No One's Rose* dwell in the mode of address, of speaking toward. The one spoken to is often doubly absent from the writer— absent because he or she can only read the poem retrospectively in order to hear its address and more profoundly absent because he or she is often, if not always, allusively identified with the murdered victims of the death camps. The poems of this collection speak simultaneously to both reader and the murdered. In the compression of many you's into the you of address, the *Aber-du*, the overdetermined you, draws us into close companionship with those who have died. The dedication of *The No One's Rose* to Ossip Mandelstamm, a Russian Jew who disappeared in the wastes of Siberia after the Russian revolution, adds yet another possibility for the you of the poem's address. The God of the Psalms or of the Kabbalah might be addressed as well. The victims of Auschwitz, a lost Russian poet, the absent divinity, the reader of the poem are all possible recipients of the poem's offer for conversation.

But the you never speaks for him or herself. The poem listens, gives every chance for the possibility of exchange, but the "you" hovers beyond the possibility of actual conversation. The poem records the address toward a you and the waiting for its answer. What the poem can never record is the answer itself.

Thus, the poem speaks "as one who speaks to stone," that is, as one speaks to one who will not answer, as one speaks to a tombstone. But the poem has achieved a complex expectation which reaches out toward a you that is both determined and beyond the reach of the poem or its poet. In the poem's waiting for the you, an opening is achieved in which the addressed you can act through its absence. Thus, the poet finds the you claiming his own hand.

This hand of confused identities becomes the hand which writes the poem and so grasps "into there, into the nothing." What is this "there" or "nothing"? It is at least the repressed memory of the Crystal Night, *die Aber-Nacht*. It is also the poem itself, the "noem" as Celan has termed it in another poem, which traces out the absence, the withdrawal, the loss of the other as

190

the only mark the other brings into the poem. The poem's title speaks of mothering, of nurturing and of root, of foundation and origin. But the grasping of the poem toward its origin is the writing hand of the poet as it searches out a personal contact with the you who comes only as a certain restraint, a waiting, a silence that takes the poet's hand from himself and then extends its grasp into "nothing."

At this crucial moment, the syntax of the poem turns—what appeared to be a set of fragmented adverbial constraints now lead into the main clause of a sentence: "*As* one speaks to stone . . . *so* is what is here:". In this turn, the poem finds its ground, its measure, but one which remains caught within the loss which the hand of the poet bestows: "this fertile / soil too gapes." The you remains unarticulated, will not grow within the soil, the matrix of the poem. Instead of a root reaching up toward the surface, the open, the *radix* becomes a "going down." The poem ends in the mystery of the withdrawal of the you, in the loss of the poet and the poem's fathering and mothering, in the destruction of the poet and the poem's lineage. In the poem's speaking, the soil of Celan's own lineage, his progenitors and offspring sink away. Yet with this withdrawal the poem is also given as "one of the crests growing wild." In the very abyss into which the poem is addressed, Celan finds a positive turn, an unexpected affirmation. But is this affirmation merely willed, a moment of poetic bad faith in the face of crippling loss? In what manner can Celan's poems open up upon the abyss of extermination and yet blossom, as he states in "Psalm:" "with our pistil soul-bright, / with our stamen heaven-ravaged, / our corolla red / with the crimson word which we sang / over, O over / the thorn"?[11]

Conclusion

The question of "Radix, Matrix": "*Wer wars*," "Who was it, this lineage, this murdered one, this black one standing in the Heaven: rod and testicle?" leads inevitably toward address and toward the withdrawal of the other as the root, the mother soil of the poem. That this other cannot appear, that he or she has been silenced in the crematoria of Auschwitz, leads the poem to struggle to remember what cannot speak for itself. Thus, the poem alludes to "the long ago, the nothing of a night," of *Kristal Nacht*, when Christians shattered the crystal tableware of Jews and ransacked and burned the Synagogues of Germany. In directing itself toward its ground, its lineage, the poem commemorates not the establishment of a temple but its destruction. The authority with which the poem calls into the "night" in which temples burned has been shattered by the very history which it addresses. The erased shadow of the "you" looms in the shadow of the death camps, which everywhere trouble the poem's symbolism and figuration without once having overtly entered into the poem. And yet the poem resists despair, it speaks of itself as a "crest growing wild."

In some respects Heidegger's account of the poem as the grounding of history is not so far from Celan's troubled address of the other. Like Heidegger, Celan fights the technological obsessions of a world in which the meaning of beings is to be articulated in what can be represented of them. Both philosopher and poet resist that light of modern intellect that would pierce into the heart of all things and find out once and for all their true shapes. Both understand the course of history to be filled with missteps, with disasters, whose depths elude all human efforts to exhaust their pain and significance. A Heideggerian could argue that Celan's notion of loss simply marks the withdrawal of Being into *lethe*, into forgetfulness, but one which bestows Being to beings in yet another epochal showing-forth of entities as world. The Celanian other, this "you," would be the figure which would draw the world and earth into intimate strife and resist the reduction of all entities to standing-reserve, to *Ge-stell*.[12] Here is where Celan would locate the open, that in which "the extraordinary [is] thrust to the surface and the long familiar thrust down" (*OWA*, 66).

But address of the other is *not* the same as the address of Being. Being remains, in Heidegger's account, forever anonymous, without the qualities of responsibility or passion. One might argue that in Being Heidegger has isolated the *mysterium tremendum* of traditional theology and developed its implications without reference to personhood, i.e., to the particularity of a being whose identity arises *only* in his or her responsibility to and desire for other particular identities. The Being which lurks in the Heideggerian grounding of history is an indeterminate excess, "an over-flowing, an endowing, a bestowal" (*OWA*, 75). Heidegger is always quick to emphasize that the question of Being is never of this or that particular being, not even of God as a being, but of Being.[13] In such a context, the question of Being inevitably becomes the question of how various beings are veiled and unveiled, of how their Being is brought into articulation, no matter how subtle and shadow-filled the play of such articulation might be.

Like other discourses in which beings, entities, are discussed in relation to their truth, Heidegger's discourse is most often limited to the third person. Address, even as it emerges in the later writings of Heidegger, is not treated in the vocative mode.[14] Insofar as Heidegger raises the question of Being as undermining the assertive mode of normal philosophical discourse, his work moves toward a radical appreciation of the historicality of any artwork and of the destiny it opens for human beings. But Heidegger's preference, perhaps obsession, with the question of Being and with the Greek conceptions of *phusis* and truth leads him to neglect the implications of the vocative mode in poetic utterance. Heidegger's characterization of a prerepresentational art in which truth and beauty are entwined within the same root forgets the depth of loss and alienation which resound in the thinking of history as an ethical and political event. There are historical moments in which human monstrosity exceeds the dimensions of the painful and gore-filled beauty of a tragic insight. In such moments, it is not enough that beings *are*, that they show-forth in their historical destiny.

Instead of an epochal horizon welling up from the excess of Being over beings, Celan draws our attention to the insufficiency of any world horizon to articulate adequately the particularity of individuals and their communities. Writing, for Celan, challenges the heroism, the epic vitality, of a world-horizon through the powerlessness of the vocative. Destiny, which has never led to the unmitigated triumph of a culture, has led regularly to its catastrophe; the vocative, by calling out to those who have been irredeemably lost, marks the limit of the healing powers of Being, and in fact, calls any such assertion of its healing power *into question*. While the later Heidegger reacts with increasing emphasis against the devastation (*Verwüstung*) of modern history and awaits the arrival of "the gods," of a new dispensation of Being,[15] Celan's poem points out that even the arrival of such gods will not excuse the murder of millions of human beings, nor restore their lives.

Rather than in the difference between Being and beings, the Celanian poem situates itself in the disjunction between the poets's "having called out" to the murdered and the silence of the murdered in the face of such address. As the articulation of that disjunction, the vocative address to this murdered *you* serves as a *Mal*, a "once-having-been," which marks (as a monument marks a tomb) the death of another as an ethical event, one in which is given the particular loss, one beyond restitution, which the death of the other bestows. Such a loss cannot be taken up into the play of excess which characterizes the withdrawal of beings into their Being.[16] Heidegger's thought remains embarrassed by that sense of negation thought as *Vernichtung*, as extermination. The suffering and slaughter of the innocent marks the shame of Being and neither its playfulness nor its epochal vitality.

Such loss need not, however, leave us without hope. The avoidance of catastrophe and the search for consolation in the face of catastrophe, rather than the achievement of a world-horizon encompassing all beings, becomes the ethical work through which a people finds its historical vocation. In this work is the recognition that truth must be thought not as the appearance of what a being *is* (nor of the non-appearance which supports this appearance), but rather as *Emeth*, i.e., as the faithfulness, the loyalty, one owes to the other, to the "you" of his or her address.[17] The Celanian poem, rather than giving a figure, a *Gestalt*, which establishes the world as the possibility for human showing-forth, is seen as that "place, where all tropes and metaphors are led to absurdity," i.e. to that impossible "place" at the very culmination of history in which the rabbinical demand for "true" justice would have been fulfilled.[18] By announcing this impossible goal as the necessary culmination of history, the poem becomes a "crest growing wild" that announces the ultimate resistence of the murdered to their murderers. Such a resistence calls out for justice, for an ending to that history in which mass murder and a multitude of other violences are perpetrated by one human upon another in the hope that a given world-horizon might come to dominate all beings. The *"Toposforschung"* of the poem can only find its "place" in *"U-topie,"* that ethical destination, no matter how impossible, toward which history is called. It is there that the temple might be built for the first time.

Chapter 11

GENEROSITY AND FORGETTING IN THE HISTORY OF BEING: MERLEAU-PONTY AND NIETZSCHE

Galen A. Johnson

> Everything happens, according to Bergson, as if man encountered at the roots of his constituted being a generosity which is not a compromise with the adversity of the world and which is on his side against it.
> —Merleau-Ponty, *In Praise of Philosophy*[1]

To question history: What shall we mean by such an interrogation? What shall we ask? With what authority do we ask, we who are historical beings? Do we mean to set ourselves apart from historical life, to turn it over in the hollow of our hand? To whom do we address our question—historians, philosophers, poets, soldiers—beings of time, beings within history? Speech and writing are historical events, yet this speech and this writing seem to want time stopped up, to catch time up short and to forget our selves. Does forgetting have a history? Does self-forgetting: the meditative trance? Does silence have a history: the absent stare, the absence of an answer, the absence of a question? Does death have a history? "Time is the way offered to all that will be to be no longer. It is the *Invitation to die*, for every phrase to decompose in the explicative and total concordance, to consummate the speech of adoration addressed to *Sigè* the Abyss" (*sigè* = silence).[2]

History is questioned while it is lived: we are historical beings but it is not ourselves from whom we wish to hear. We are historical, but we are not history. We do not seek our speech and our thought but a Speech and a Thought that have us. We wish to question this history, history itself. This is the history of Being. Does it speak?

In his last writings, Merleau-Ponty wrote of a "vertical history" (VI, 183, 186, 223; *VI*, 237, 240, 276), of a "vertical past" (VI, 244; *VI*, 297), of a "vertical present,"[3] and said that "all verticality comes from the vertical Being" (VI, 234; *VI*, 287). This is a mystery we have handled the way a child handles explosives.[4] Vertical Being is an explosion (dehiscence) within which nature and spirit are "simultaneous" (S, 177, 179; *S*, 223, 226), past and future are a "cohesion" (PriP, 187; *OE*, 85) in a "primordial historicity" that is a "single present" (PriP, 161; *OE*, 13). Here the whole of human history is "stationary" and "we cannot establish a hierarchy of civilizations or speak of progress" because the very first moment "went to the farthest reach of the future" (PriP, 190; *OE*, 92).

To question history we may begin from Merleau-Ponty's oracular remarks regarding vertical history and vertical Being. Our interrogation must be indirect, by way of listening and silence, yet by way of language and writing. Our interrogation leads through the history of philosophy and nonphilosophy. It leads through some texts of Merleau-Ponty and Nietzsche, and Merleau-Ponty's thoughts pertaining to forgetting, reversibility, circularity, silence, and abyss.

Vertical Time

At the beginning of the linkage between history and ontology, historicity and Being—so evident in Hegel, Marx, Heidegger, and Merleau-Ponty—the historicity of life, thought, and Being was a critique of the *cogito* as an Archimedean point for knowledge or value. In *Phenomenology of Perception*, Merleau-Ponty contended (against Husserl) that every accepted "self-evidence" (*Evidenz*) is but a resting place in the search for foundations, every certainty but the opening to a further doubt, because behind every explicit cognitive judgment lies a historically given, unreflective background of implicit judgments. Behind Descartes's explicit doubt and discovery of the *cogito* are implicit scholastic doctrines of substance and personality. Behind even this reduced verbal *cogito* humming with words lies an inherited tacit *cogito* sedimented in our bodily style of gestures and habits that are our orientation toward the world. "To sum up," Merleau-Ponty wrote, "we are restoring to the *cogito* a temporal thickness."[5]

If the critique of the *cogito* was made in the name of the embodied subject's historical life, it was also made in the name of the most ordinary understanding of historical time. Our most celebrated philosophers of history, particularly Hegel and Marx, framed their philosophies within the most ordinary chronological, linear conceptions of time.[6] At best they offered us a dialectical conception of historical time still dependent upon seriality, still framed by the teleological conception of progress toward the "end of history." The notion of vertical history that Merleau-Ponty developed in his last writings is, in the first instance, a critique of the teleological conception of historical progress, of the *Endstiftung*. In "Eye and Mind," Merleau-Ponty wrote: "For if we cannot establish a hierarchy of civilizations or speak of progress—neither in painting nor in anything else that matters—it is not because some fate holds us back; it is, rather, because the very first painting in some sense went to the farthest reach of the future" (PriP, 190; *OE*, 92). The first paintings in the Lascaux caves of the French Périgord were sufficient to show us that the meanings of history do not lie in front of us in a future, they were sufficient to show us that each human symbolic expression enriches, enlightens, deepens, confirms, exalts, and recreates our everyday life together. There is no world-historical progress. There are new and renewed lightings of our dwelling with mortals on the earth under the sky. To say otherwise is retrospective illusion. To say otherwise is prospective hubris.

Against linear seriality, vertical time refers us to a variety of experiences that have as their inner structure losing oneself to the object. Some are quite mundane: we cannot take our eyes off flowing water, fire, moving trains. Some are extraordinary: joy, euphoria, fascination, infatuation, of course mystical intuition, perhaps artistic creation. We feel melted into the universe, and though the experience of self-negation is not pure or total, we experience the isolated presence of the *world*, its pure "being-there." The flow of time is stopped up. Experiences like these are within the "good narcissism" Merleau-Ponty spoke of, "not to see in the outside, as the others see it, the contour of a body one inhabits, but especially to be seen by the outside, to exist within it, to emigrate into it, to be seduced, captivated, alienated by the phantom, so that the seer and the visible reciprocate one another and we no longer know which sees and which is seen" (VI, 139; VI, 183). The meanings and depths of such experiences are not plumbed by referring to backward and forward temporal references, they are understood by referring to the magnetism of the world.

Merleau-Ponty's emphasis upon the vertical moment in his late writings is akin to Proust's attention to "privileged moments" and to Sartre's account of fascination and the doctrine of the moment: "at this privileged moment there was nothing else but the world."[7] References to Proust are threaded throughout the last chapter of *The Visible and the Invisible*. "No one has gone further than Proust in fixing the relations between the visible and the invisible," Merleau-Ponty wrote, "in describing an idea that is not the contrary of the sensible, that is its lining and its depth" (VI, 149; VI, 195). As to Sartre, Merleau-Ponty wrote that "what I call the *vertical* is what Sartre calls existence" (VI, 271; VI, 325). Vertical being is *simply being there*, it is the *il y a* (there is). It is a transversal *ecstasis*, though Sartre was wrong to say that it is a nothingness, and wrong to limit it to for-itself being. Sartre said there is an infinite number of realities inhabited by negation in their inner structure. He called them *negatités* (BN, 55). We would like to say there are realities inhabited by affirmation. The history of Being is the generous explosion of body and soul, nature and spirit, earth and sky. The history of cultural expression is intensifying, deepening astonishment (wonder) in the face of the "there is."

Such a stress was nearly absent from *Phenomenology of Perception*, found only tucked into the folds of the paragraphs and pages. Throughout the book, Merleau-Ponty was cautious about reducing the human subject to any one of its aspects or activities. He used predicate adjectives: the human being is embodied, is sexual, is mortal. Not so when Merleau-Ponty arrived at the chapter on temporality. "I am myself time. . . . We must understand time as the subject and the subject as time" (PhP, 421, 422; PP, 481, 483). Here is an identity relation. History is the structure that subsumes all other structures. To say embodied is to say historical; to say sexual is to say historical; to say mortal is to say historical. And to say historical is to describe a presence that is situated amidst temporal sediments that are given not made, to describe a presence whose meaning refers us to a past. Even Merleau-Ponty's account of *ecstasis* in that work succeeded only in absorbing transcendence within immanence.[8] Yet no philosophy of Being and human being, no general account of time, can be complete without recognizing our deepening astonishment in the face of the "there is," without allowing the possibility of self-expansive, self-forgetting moments.[9]

Forgetting

Body as recollection and repetition of historical existence, earth and sky as meaningful places marked out in the world: all this is praise of memory.[10] All this is consonant with a philosophy of history as recovery and archaeology, and with our majority tradition from Plato to Husserl that has longed for restoration of memory. From Plato to Husserl, forgetting has been viewed as a negative force, a destructive power to be overcome by the philosophy of recovery. Forgetting *is* destructive. It steals upon us, and in this unwanted form, its fruits are ignorance, senility, paralysis, loss of speech, loss of self-identity. These diseases have names: amnesia, aphasia, Alzheimer's. Yet healthful forgetting is also the invitation to presence. Merleau-Ponty was fond of citing Cézanne's quest for the "world's instant: "A minute in the world's life passes! to paint it in its reality! and forget everything for that. To become that minute, to be the sensitive plate, . . . give the image of what we see, forgetting everything that has appeared before our time" (PriP, 169; *OE*, 35).[11] Forgetting is also the invitation to sleep, and the doorway to our dreams. There is an interpenetration of presence and healthful forgetting. Vertical history requires rehabilitation of this forgetting.

Merleau-Ponty's first philosophical essay in 1935, on the subject of Scheler and Nietzsche's typology of *ressentiment*, discussed the central role of long memory in the formation of rancor. It praised our release from its destructive fruits: revenge, hatred, and envy.[12] Zarathustra spoke of the curative power of forgetting:

"a gruesome sight is a person single-mindedly obsessed by a wrong."[13] He possesses a killing poison like the tarantula. Zarathustra will never dance the tarantella,[14] the passionate folk dance popularly supposed to be a remedy against the bite of the tarantula. "Whoever cannot settle on the threshold of *the moment*," Nietzsche wrote, "forgetful of the whole past, whoever is incapable of standing on a point like a goddess of victory without vertigo or fear, will never know what happiness is, and worse yet, will never do anything to make others happy."[15] The metamorphosis of the spirit as told by Zarathustra unfolded from camel, to lion, to child—two forgetful beasts and a baby.

It is all well and good to praise healthful forgetting. It is another matter entirely to determine the essence of forgetting. In *Nietzsche and Philosophy*, Gilles Deleuze comments: "Psychology's mistake was to treat forgetting as a negative determination, not to discover its active and positive character."[16] In *Spurs*, Derrida entered the following remarks concerning Nietzsche's aphorism, "I have forgotten my umbrella": "In its current representation forgetting easily assumes the appearance of a simple lacuna, a lack, uncertainty. It is habitual to consider that to forget, to be forgetful, is exclusively 'to omit'. . . . We are still far from determining the essence of forgetting."[17] What is forgetting such that it has these curative powers? "Time heals all wounds": Why? Can a phenomenology of embodied time-consciousness accomodate forgetting?

Although Husserl's phenomenology of time-consciousness as well as his philosophy of history developed in *The Crisis of European Sciences* guided Merleau-Ponty's *Phenomenology of Perception*, forgetting is unexplained. Husserl's thought foundered on the question of forgetting. Perhaps the *aporia* is clearest in *The Origin of Geometry*, where there developed a deep ambivalence pertaining to the *crisis* of European sciences. If Husserl did not admit forgetting into the history of science and philosophy, there could be no cultural *crisis*. However, admitting forgetting opened up the possibility of a new kind of crisis, a deep ontological and epistemic crisis, not only a temporary forgetting of meaning (*Sinn*) as a form of human blindness, but the permanent oblivion of meaning (*Sinn*) and absolutization of nothingness. Derrida drew our attention to this ambivalence in his *Introduction* to Husserl's *Origin of Geometry*.[18] Is there any sense in which Husserl seriously meant that truth "appears" at a moment in history, implying the risk that it might "disappear"? Though Husserl characterized the cultural crisis as forgetting the originating meaning (*Sinn*) of signs handed down in texts,[19] it appears that for Husserl's philosophy of time-consciousness there could be no forgetting, even within the history of consciousness. All present judgments and perceptions sink down into retention and memory, and are therefore always available to retrieval. Past clings to presence.

In *The Visible and the Invisible* (in a "Working Note" dated May 1959 and titled "Transcendence—*forgetting*—time") Merleau-Ponty discussed Husserl's phenomenology of internal time-consciousness and the 1905 diagram of the sedimentation of retentions within living presence. It was this diagram that Merleau-Ponty had repeated in *Phenomenology of Perception* "*après Husserl*" (PhP, 417; *PP*, 477). This working note from May 1959 criticizes Husserl's time-diagram. It is therefore Merleau-Ponty's self-criticism of his own time-diagram and a presentation of historical sedimentation in the *Phenomenology*. Merleau-Ponty comments:

> The description of retention in Husserl (and that of subjectivity as time, of the absolute flux, of the pre-intentional retention) is a start, but leaves open the question: whence comes the "shrinking" of the temporal perspective, the passage of the remote retentions into the horizon, the forgetting? . . . Husserl's diagram is dependent on the convention that one can represent the series of nows by points on a line. (VI, 194–95; *VI*, 248)

How shall we understand the structure of forgetting? To characterize it as awareness of absence, nothingness, or void cannot be avoided. "I cannot remember; I forget": this is the absence of an intentional object, or better, absence *as* intentional object. Where there was once something, there is nothing; it is elsewhere.

Merleau-Ponty's note analyzes and criticizes three customary efforts to understand these experiences. (1) Forgetting is not the destruction of psychic *material*, the effacement of a corporeal trace (engram) in my brain, for among other things, memory is not only about objects and images, but a memorial field as organized and meaningful, and meanings are not given as "objective occultation." (It would be interesting to know if this criticism of physiological theories of forgetting would correspondingly apply to "tactile memory" and the tracings of past perceptions on, for example, the surface of our skin.) (2) Forgetting is not a part of a present-past system of coordinates, in which a new segment of the present descending from the future requires a corresponding segment of the past to become more remote, as Husserl's time-diagram suggests, for there are remote retentions that are not forgotten as they "recede" in memory. Besides, there is no objective "segment" of present that descends from the future. (3) Forgetting is not sheer annihilation, the "negintuition" of sheer nothingness; for the intuition of nothingness *as elsewhere* is the intuition of something *as difference*, as "behind," beyond, far-off, that is, the intuition of transcendence.

A solution to the essence of forgetting lies precisely in understanding this ontological difference or transcendence. Merleau-Ponty's fundamental model for understanding the subject-object relation in perception was the reversibility relation. My left hand touches my right even as it is touched by the right, and this relation of touching/being touched can be, in the next instant, reversed. What would it mean to say that vision is similarly reversible? It does not mean that absurdity, that the trees and things I see also see me in return. Rather, in seeing objects, they reflect back to me an image of myself. Inanimate things do so only feebly, thus the confrontation with living beings, finally with other people is the decisive advent for the reversibility of seeing/being seen. Yet even within the reversibility of subject and object, for-itself and in-itself, my differentiation from things is preserved, the things, the others, escape me. "There is no coinciding of the seer with the visible. But each borrows from the other, takes from or encroaches upon the other, intersects with the other, is in chiasm with the other" (VI, 261; *VI*, 314). There is not synthesis, there is encroachment. Perception is contact with differentiation. In touching, my hand is touched, but the touching is not coincident with being touched. In seeing, I am seen, but the seeing is differentiated from being seen. There is contact because there is reversibility, but there is also difference. When the difference is removed, as when my eye grows too close to the object, there is blurring, then blindness. With my eyes too close, there is loss of the visual field, loss of a horizon to ground a figure. Vision is contact that includes differentiation; loss of vision is contact without differentiation. If there be continuity of gradations from vision to memory image to remembering, as Merleau-Ponty believed with Bergson and Husserl, then remembering is contact with the past that includes differentiation; forgetting is contact without differentation.

Two passages from Merleau-Ponty's note on forgetting might make this experience somewhat clearer. His positive account of forgetting begins from this:

> Understand that the *Gestalt* is already transcendence . . . the present itself is not an absolute coincidence without transcendence, but partial coincidence, because it has horizons and would not be without them—the present, also, is ungraspable from close-up, in the forceps of attention, it is an encompassing. (VI, 195; *VI*, 248–49)

Forgetting is not the phenomenon of the past receding. To speak in terms of temporal flow, the past "grows closer" to presence, becoming undifferentiated from it, thereby blurring, thereby disappearing from memory. The things we do to help us remember are efforts to reestablish difference and articulation, to reestablish a field—retracing our steps, returning to the place where it happened, recalling associated items in the visual field.

Struggle as we might to remember the face of one we love who is absent from us, the features fade. We find ourselves resorting to a photograph to remember, a photograph that freezes the living face which, at the beginning, was so inadequate. Now we travel to see him. As the miles go by and we approach the place where he lives, the features of his face come back to life and into focus again.

It is easy to multiply examples. Try as I might to remember the name of that restaurant in a city where I used to live, I cannot. I forget. It seems strange. It has only been a few years, and I had so many happy evenings there. But when I return to the city and begin to feel my way through the streets and neighborhood; before I come upon it, I know the name. Charley's. Newberry Street. The horizon for a field has been restored, and with it articulation and memory.

Merleau-Ponty's final paragraph on forgetting contains these remarks:

> Understand perception as differentiation, forgetting as undifferentiation. The fact that one no longer sees the memory = not a destruction of a psychic *material* which would be *the* sensible, but its disarticulation which makes there be no longer a *separation [écart], a relief*. This is the night of forgetting. . . . It is *that separation [écart]*, first of all that is the perceptual meaning. (VI, 197; *VI*, 250)

Forgetting is the disarticulation of past from presence, the closing up of separation (*écart*). Sartre thought that time healed because it separates present from past. He wrote: "Time gnaws and wears away; it separates; it flies. And by virtue of separation—by separating us from our pain or from the object of our pain—time cures" (*BN*, 188). Our analysis reveals the opposite. The closing up of separation is the curative power of forgetting, enabling us to forget our past and concentrate all our powers on this moment, enabling me to forget my past which is to forget my self and stand outside myself and see, really see.

If disarticulation of intentional object from its field is the structure of forgetting, we can also see that Heidegger was right to speak of forgetting *the present*. An essential structure of the "inauthentic they" is an awaiting of "moments" in which they "are already forgotten as they glide by."[20] Merleau-Ponty's note wonders about this in parentheses: "There are fragments 'perceived' just now, that disappear (have they been perceived? And what exactly is the relation between the perceived and the *imperceived*?)" (VI, 195; *VI*, 248). Expecting you not to smoke, I do not see the ashtray on your desk. Expecting an important letter midday, I do not hear what you are saying to me. Expecting my brother at the train station, I anxiously search the crowd. Stupidly I do not see my wife though apparently I look right at her. Later she laughs at me. All these are ways of being distracted, forgetting to look, forgetting the present. They are disarticulations of a world. You live with the woman you love all your life, Cézanne said, and never really see her. "I am beginning to see," said Brigge in the *Notebook*. "It still goes badly, but I am making the most of my time."

Reversibility, Circularity, and Silence

What is the ontological import of all this? Are the absences in our intentional field—things present, things past—real absences, with an ontological weight of their own not supported by my consciousness? For an ontology of fullness and generosity in which the visible and invisible are ultimate terms, is there the night of absolute forgetting and absolute nothingness? It is one thing to praise healthful forgetting, it is something else to reflect on the essence of forgetting, and it is another matter entirely to measure the ontological import of forgetting.

We cannot take considerations of ontological time in relation to verticality very far here. The questions are too vast, involving us in general reflections on the reality of absent intentional objects, the reality of the past, its reversibility and irreversibility, its determination of presence and future. We will only undertake some reflections on the end of the dialogue between Merleau-Ponty and Nietzsche pertaining to vertical history by way of the question of circularity.

If we did not know Merleau-Ponty had been reading Nietzsche, we might read over Nietzsche's words without noticing them in the fourth and last chapter of *The Visible and Invisible* called "The Intertwining—The Chiasm": "What there is then are . . . things we could not dream of seeing 'all naked' because the gaze itself envelops them, clothes them with its own flesh" (VI, 131; VI, 173). Nietzsche's well-known words are found in the Preface to *The Gay Science*: "Today we consider it a matter of decency not to wish to see everything naked, or to be present at everything, or to understand and "know" everything. One should have more respect for the bashfulness with which nature has hidden behind riddles and irridescent uncertainties."[21] Merleau-Ponty quoted this passage and offered a commentary on it in the notes for his last course called "Philosophy and Non-Philosophy Since Hegel." At the end of *The Gay Science* (as prelude to *Zarathustra*), Nietzsche announces the enigma of the "eternal return of the same" under the heading "The greatest weight": "This life as you now live it and have lived it, you will have to live once more and innumerable times more. . . . The eternal hourglass of existence is turned upside down again and again, and you with it, speck of dust."[22]

Vertical history is critique of progress and *Endstiftung*. Vertical history is exaltation of the moment. Vertical history is praise of the curative power of forgetting. Vertical history is a critique of all remnants of a serial understanding of historical time that do not accomodate the fissures, interruptions, discontinuities, and gaps essential to a general account of our experience. Is vertical history another name for the eternal circulatory of time?

The images are manifestly different. Verticality is not a circle. It is a shaft, a column, a monument, the lightning that rends the sky. It would appear that vertical time should best be related to Nietzsche through his discussion in *The Use and Abuse of History* of "monumental history."[23] Images and pictures, however, often bear a second look. From the side of Nietzsche's image of the circle, in one of the best known presentations of the eternal recurrence (in a passage from *Thus Spoke Zarathustra* called "Of the Vision and the Riddle"), Nietzsche describes eternal recurrence as a gateway called "Moment" where the eternal past meets the eternal present:

> "Behold this gateway, dwarf!" I continued. "It has two faces. Two paths meet here; no one has yet followed either to its end. This long lane stretches back for an eternity. And the long lane out there, that is another eternity. They contradict each other, these two paths; they offend each other face to face; and it is here at this gateway that they come together. The name of the gateway is inscribed above: 'Moment.' "[24]

Now a gateway is an image of verticality. The name of the gateway of vertical time is the intensity of the "moment" in which past and present are a "cohesion," the same for Nietzsche as for Merleau-Ponty. Through this image, Nietzsche has added to the "psychological dimension" of intensified, vertical time the "metaphysical dimension" of the circular path of time. How far are we from Merleau-Ponty's own description of the visible and the invisible as a circular reversibility with depth: "If one wants metaphors, . . . the body sensed and the body sentient are as the obverse and the reverse, or again, as two segments of one sole circular course which goes above from left to right and below from right to left, but which is one sole movement in its two phases" (VI, 138; *VI*, 182).

Staying with the images briefly, if I may, from Merleau-Ponty's side we have a "Working Note" from February 1959 titled "History of Being." The note covers less than four pages and the words "circle" or "circularity" occur fully seven times. The circle is applied to Merleau-Ponty's own presentation of the history of philosophy projected for *The Visible and the Invisible*, and to the history of wild Being which that philosophy is about (VI, 177–78; *VI*, 213). To the image of the circularity of thought and Being, Merleau-Ponty adds the image of "levels" (*niveaux*) or "layers" (*couches*) (VI, 178; *VI*, 232). This results in a picture of the history of Being as a circular winding or coiling up like a spring, images of vertical Being which appear in the published text of *The Visible and the Invisible* (cf. VI, 140; *VI*, 185). We also find the repetition of circular imagery (VI, 143; *VI*, 188). Moreover, Merleau-Ponty ended his working note on the history of Being by explicitly mentioning Nietzsche's enigmatic formulation of the eternal return (from *Beyond Good and Evil*) with the three consecutive Latin nominatives: *circulus vitiosus deus* (vicious circle god?).[25]

Perhaps these parallels between Merleau-Ponty's images and Nietzsche's give us reason to take the possibility of a Nietzschean reading of vertical time more seriously. However, they will do little more until we add concepts to the images. The doctrine of the eternal return of the Same occurs in Nietzsche's texts in three forms. Based on *Will to Power*, Nietzsche meant the eternal return as a scientific or cosmological hypothesis about the inevitable recurrence of material formations in physical space-time. More often it is a psychological or existential doctrine regarding willing our fate and living dangerously and ecstatically. On the third reading, it is the ontology intended to undermine all remnants of a serial understanding of time. Most importantly, circular recurrence totally undermines the doctrine of absolute beginning from a first cause (*causa sui*, God), likewise of an absolute end (*telos*, *Endstiftung*). The eternal return of the Same is thus wedded to the madman's proclamation of the death of God and Zarathustra's teaching of the abyss. Being is an unending, cyclic repetition without foundation, grounded in nothing. Human being is a rope stretched over an abyss.

There are congenial aspects of this ontology for Merleau-Ponty's ontology of vertical Being and the meaning of vertical time. Eternal recurrence would help us see how past and present might be, in Merleau-Ponty's words, "simultaneous," "instantaneous," "a single cohesion," for things past would be repeated as they "come around again" within the present moment. Furthermore, the infinite circle of time undermines seriality in a way consistent with Merleau-Ponty's skepticism about an absolute beginning or ending. His skepticism about Hegel, Marx, or Husserl's absolute *telos* was there in his texts from *Phenomenology of Perception* forward. Yet he had seemed unwilling to part with that last remnant of seriality, the search for origins. He was mesmerized by the quest for the "first word," as for the "first expression" in gesture or painting. In fact, the very meaning of phenomenology is connected with the search for origins, and Husserl repeatedly described himself as an "absolute beginner." Nevertheless, if he had not divested himself of *Ursprungphilosophie* in the *Phenomenology of Perception*, the search for absolute origins is certainly gone from the interrogative, indirect ontology of *The Visible and the Invisible*. There remains a conceptual space for the idea of origin, but the indirect ontology circles around origins. One moment is as appropriate a beginning for thought as any other because all are "simultaneous," and each momentary part is a whole part.[26] This text could not be clearer: "For me it is no longer a question of origins, or limits, nor of a series of events going to a first cause, but one sole explosion of Being which is forever" (VI, 265; *VI*, 318). This is a fairly frank, unembarrassed use of the term "forever" (also "eternal") from the author who wrote in the *Phenomenology* of "the hypocritical feeling for eternity" (PhP, 423; *PP*, 484).

In spite of these congenialities that prompt us to place vertical history in proximity to eternal return, there are crucial respects in which we are here confronted with a proximity at a distance between Nietzschean circularity and Merleau-Ponty's doctrine of reversibility. I will bring into focus two points of significant contrast.

We should first ask what Nietzsche meant by eternal recurrence of "the Same." The question poses a somewhat familiar dilemma. If the doctrine means the recurrence of exact, literal sameness, then there is no way of noticing or identifying it as a re-occurrence. There must be at least numerical difference. On the other hand, if the doctrine means recognizable recurrence, it cannot mean the recurrence of the exact, literal "same" but of

"the same again," which is to say the same with a difference.[27]
The only point that we need to settle is that Merleau-Ponty's
ontology of vertical Being and philosophy of vertical history want
no part of any exact, literal "Same" when it speaks of a "single
cohesion" of things past/things present, and their reversibility.
Merleau-Ponty's ontology is a monism. Visibility requires contact
of seer and seen. They must be of one tissue. Yet such a monism
preserves divergence within the sensible, and divergence between the sensible and the intelligible. This is its genius. Visibility
requires the distance of articulation. Without it, there is no visual
field, no seeing, first blurring, then blindness. That is why all of
Merleau-Ponty's metaphors and images for the one element that
he named "Flesh" are cases of doubling: inside and outside,
obverse and reverse, left and right, a hand in a glove, two leaves,
two laps overlapping, a two-sided strait. If circularity, then con-
centric circles. If circularity, then layers of circles. This ontological
difference within vision has allowed us to say something meaningful about the essence of forgetting. To preserve the difference,
we have noted that Merleau-Ponty's circular images for Being
were augmented by an image of layers, resulting in a winding
coil, or spring. It is not altogether clear that Nietzsche's account
of "the Same" eradicates ontological difference, but where it
does, visibility is lost, forgetting is lost, and with them, a host of
other realities like dialogue, writing, generosity, compassion,
and justice that depend upon "the two."

When past blurs with presence in a "single cohesion," there
can be no question of the recurrence of an exact, literally same
past. Here the past is present, the "past again" and with a difference. *Signs* is the only text in which Merleau-Ponty worked out
concretely what this means for the history of thought. He referred to the "secondary truths" of the classics—the writings of
Descartes or Marx—that bear "an expressive power that exceeds
their statements and propositions" (S, 11; S, 16). Today no one
takes them literally, he said, yet they call forth new echoes and
reveal new shinings. There is no absolute forgetting. When we
forget, when we lay down to die, though separation (*écart*) may
close up within our consciousness and body, the ontological
difference within the reversibility of Being remains fundamental.
The closing up of the past from presence (as forgetting) is never
total. Though you and I may forget, no one, nothing is forgotten

in the coiling up of Being. "In short, nothing (or rather non-being) is hollow and not a *hole*. . . . The negintuition of nothingness is to be rejected because nothingness also is always *elsewhere* (VI, 196; *VI*, 249–50).

By these reflections on the ontological difference we arrive at the distance between Merleau-Ponty and Nietzsche pertaining to abyss, reflected in the last paragraph of Merleau-Ponty's note on the "history of Being" explicitly mentioning eternal recurrence. Referring to the circularity within his indirect interrogation of thought and Being, he wrote: "This reversal itself—*circulus vitiosus deus*—is not hesitation, bad faith and bad dialectic, but return to *Sigè* the abyss" (VI, 179; *VI*, 233). Abyss has a name. The name was given by Paul Claudel in a tour de force at the end of *Art Poétique*: "Time is the way offered to all that will be to be no longer. It is the *Invitation to die*, for every phrase to decompose in the explicative and total concordance, to consummate the speech of adoration addressed to *Sigè* the Abyss."[28]

There is a kind of silence within language—the pauses, what might have been said otherwise, what is not said. There is also a postlinguistic silence. After the tumult of words, the turbulence of philosophy and myth well-spoken, there is the spent, meditative rest. Among the relics remaining from the celebration of the Dionysian mysteries is a marble base upon which there was once a statue of Agripinilla, priestess of the second century A.D. sacred college (*thiasos*) devoted to the Bacchic mysteries at Torre Nova in Italy. The base, now housed at the Metropolitan Museum in New York, bears an inscription—the names and functions of the members of that Dionysian sacred college. At the very end of the inscription are the names of twenty-three men and women classified as *seigetai*. This plural of *sigè*, a usage hitherto unknown, means either "those who impose silence" or "those who are silent." Archaeologists conclude, from the humble place accorded the *seigetai* at the bottom of the list, that the second is the more probable meaning. They must have formed a class of novitiates of both sexes who were obliged to remain mute for a given length of time, to show themselves capable of keeping the secrets to be later confided to them.[29]

Incredible noise-making of cymbals, flutes, and drums announced Dionysus and accompanied him. Homer introduced Dionysus as Bromios, the roarer.[30] However, there is nothing that reveals the meaning of Dionysus so well as the counterpart to this din, the deathlike silence into which it suddenly changes. Wild uproar and numbed silence, different forms of that nameless intensity which shatters all composure. After the ecstatic, deafening pandemonium, then peace and fullness. The Bacchic maenad (madwoman) frightens us with her rigid, speechless stare, snake coiling itself around her windswept hair. For so she is painted on the inside of a cup from 490 B.C. Greece (Brygos school). "In short," Merleau-Ponty wrote, "language speaks and the voices of painting are the voices of silence" (S, 81; *S*, 101).

The force of this name *Sigè* situates abyss not within the visible itself, Being itself, but somewhere in the chiasmatic relation between the sensible and the intelligible. Word is the transfiguration of flesh, it is the world become more transparent and ideal. Yet silence haunts speech and prevents coincidence of the sensible and the intelligible, of *logos* and *phusis*. This silence is not nothing, but a positive reality within language and after language that gives birth to meaning. It is circumscribed by the edges and contours of language, what is said, the words that are chosen, the tonalities that express a style. Its name is not Sysiphus, it is *Sigè*. It is a matter of decency not to seek to see everything naked. Abyss is not nothing (S, 15; *S*, 21), because abyss has edges and contours even if no bottom (S, 21; *S*, 29). Nothingness is not absolute, it is parasitic upon Being as emptiness upon fullness, as adversity upon generosity. The outlook Merleau-Ponty attributed to Bergson may be taken as his own, dare we say as our own: "Everything happens, according to Bergson, as if man encountered at the roots of his constituted being a generosity which is not a compromise with the adversity of the world and which is on his side against it" (IPP, 26–27; *EP*, 33).

212

Chapter 12

TENOCHTITLÁN

Alphonso Lingis

Of course, we were there already, in Honduras, where they are filling cargo ships with pineapples, coffee, fine tobaccos for us; in Kalimantan where they are streaming to the port of Balikpapan to fill the oil tankers that will fuel those ships, in the dunes of Morocco where they are shoveling phosphates, on the beaches of Malaysia where they are scooping up tin for us, in Zimbabwe where they are digging in pits under machine guns for the diamonds for our throats, in Irian Jaya where they are mining the uranium for our thermonuclear arsenals. But we don't just stay home and wait for the doorbell to ring. We ourselves go there, to them. We go to Acapulco, to Jamaica, to Rio, to Tangier, to Fiji, to Pattaya. No problems with planning, jet package tours; they are one of the most important developments in the economies of former colonies in those continents since our last world war. In many of the smaller of these new nations the majority of the resident population consists of busboys, waitresses, gardeners, and tour-bus operators. Certainly we do not go to Acapulco to look into our investments there; one is on vacation. One does not go to poke around in the hamlets of a backwater of the civilized world; one stays in a Hyatt or an Intercontinental. We would no go there to find something for ourselves in the Aztec civilization swept into dust four hundred years ago. One goes to the Anthropological Museum in downtown Mexico City—or one did, until two years ago when the key pieces were dispersed in the unsolved robbery. In the past twenty years enterprising bands of men have located most of the Maya sites in what is left of the Yucatan jungles and dislodged their notable carvings with crow bars and cut them with power saws into pieces of the size

213

to decorate our living rooms; they are to be seen in Austin, Nice, Kuwait. In 1840 United States Ambassador John Stevens personally bought the entire Maya city of Copán for fifty dollars. In Acapulco one bronzes one's skin, one swims, waterskies, goes parasailing, scuba diving, and shopping. One encounters the locals; the best-looking young creoles and mestizos and Indians, groomed, liveried, who bring cocktails and cocaine and themselves. In Pattaya the tourist season coincides with the dry season; there is for five months a resident population of fifty-five thousand prostitutes. But prostitute is too harsh and misleading a term for those upcountry adolescents who provide the sole subsistence for whole families during the five-months drought. The airline hostesses are the geisha girls of these decades, and it is their affability, their availability, their graces and their slang the country girls try to learn and imitate in their untrained and touching ways.

We ship back ourselves. They bought us, with all their bananas and uranium and diamonds. But we are not another commodity in the global economy. What, after all, can they do with us, but garland, feed, and massage us? The term prostitute decidedly belongs to an obsolete vocabulary. We have not sold them ourselves for money. For we have become values. That is, money.

The streets, like the roads of old country towns, were narrow and tree-lined, but on either side there were ten-foot-high stone walls with two or three electronically operated doors cut in them on each block. There were no cars parked in the streets, and no one walking in them. There were no shops, no sidewalk stalls of newspapers or soft drinks. Inquiring several times from the armed police at corners, I found the street and the number; I pushed the buzzer and identified myself on the intercom. The lawyer himself opened the door for me. He had known our mutual acquaintance from the States for years; they had first met, he said, on the beach, at Cancun. He invited me to pull my car inside his compound; a hundred cars a day are stolen in this city, he said with a smile, and yours is new and beautiful. He beckoned me into his marble-floored home, introduced me to his wife, also a lawyer. We sat in the salon; a maid put margaritas and hors d'oeuvres on the onyx table before us. When he built this house, the lawyer explained, Tlalpan was a village on the south of the city, but already selected, for its clean air at the base of the Ajusco volcano, for subsidiary residences of the viceroys at the beginning of the colonial period. Now many movie actors and actresses had come here, and lived in palaces I did not see behind those walls. There was also an ultra-modern medical center reserved for senior government officials. It is decorated, the lawyer's wife said, with frescos by Siqueiros, Chavez Morado, and Nishizawa. The lawyer and his wife had both decided to retire two years earlier. Since then they had been traveling, to the States, to France, Spain, and Italy, to Japan, Singapore, Hong Kong, Australia. The lawyer's wife asked me about Kathmandu, I also described Bali and Bangkok. We had another margarita and then another. The conversation flowed easily, one odd place after another got mentioned, mused over. We got up to go contemplate an African mask over the fireplace, a Chinese Buddha in the hall, an Australian boomerang. We went at random from one continent to another, savoring the names of new places to go to. The heat of the afternoon passed; the lawyer's wife suggested a ride. The driver pulled out the lawyer's car; we drove through San Angel where there was an occasional wrought-iron spiked gate through which we caught glimpses into colonial gardens. We drove to Coyoacán, got out of the car to visit the remaining out-building of Cortés's palace. On the site of Cortés's main palace, a Dominican church had been built; the lawyer and his wife had been married there. Inside benediction was concluding; we knelt as the priest swung the monstrance, a four-foot-wide gold sun, over us, *Dominus vobiscum*. We walked over to see a building said to be the palace of la Malinche, the Aztec girl who had traded her nation for Cortés's affections, and the house where Leon Trotsky was assassinated.

We returned to Tlalpan; we drove through the gates of a wall that extended across the whole block; this had been the home of a surgeon the lawyer had known since childhood, and who had lived here with his wife and one son. The building extended the full length of the compound wall; before it were gardens with sleeping swans and peafowl. The owners had sold the mansion with all its furnishing to a restauranteur and had moved to the Costa del Sol in Spain. Inside, the walls were decorated with huge portraits of horses. We ordered margaritas and hors d'oeuvres; the waiter brought three silver dishes with oily inch-long eel fry, white termites's eggs, and *gusanos de maguey*, finger-sized segmented worms that are found in the maguey plants from whose white milk-sap the Aztecs, and today the *campesinos*, derive a fermented drink called *pulque*. The waiter showed me how to fold the wiry little eels into a tortilla with guacamole and piquant sauce. Then we had steak, cut, the waiter assured us, from bulls killed in the *corrida* the day before.

The lawyer refused me the honor of paying the bill. The pleasure was all theirs, he said, the pleasure of my company—how much I knew, how much I had seen. Back in his compound, the driver parked the lawyer's car and I unlocked mine. We embraced; how easily we had come to know and love one another. Then the lawyer went inside and returned to give me a blade of carved obsidian, which as a boy he had himself found at Teotihuacán in the weeds and rubble of ruins and which an archaeologist had dated for him as belonging to the second half of the first century B.C. The Aztecs believed that the pyramid of the sun at Teotihuacán was built by the vanished Toltecs at the beginning of their cosmic era, that of the Fifth Sun, which Aztec astrologers and priests had predicted was to come to an end in the year Nahui ollin. It was in the year Nahui ollin that Hernando Cortés landed on the beach of Chalchuihcuecan, which he renamed Vera Cruz.

Between 1521 and 1533 Spanish conquistadors and missionaries put an end to all the great civilizations of America. Of the Aztec, Mixtec, Zapotec, Pipil, Maya, and Inca cities, their social order, their science, their gods, writes Bernal Díaz del Castillo in his *True History of the Conquest of New Spain* "all . . . is overthrown and destroyed; nothing is left standing."[1] Pope Alexander VI, who had granted to the Catholic monarchs of Spain and Portugal the lands of all the heathens of the world, issued papal bulls granting plenary indulgences in advance for all sins committed in the Conquest. The superiority of the new Christian dispensation did not lie in its horror of war and human sacrifice; the conquistadors conquered because their wars were more treacherous and their massacres more wanton. The superiority lay in that the Christian conquistadors brought love to the worshipers of Quetzalcoatl.

That is, money. Although Tenochtitlán, built on the crater lake of an enormous dead volcano, was an immense market, the Aztecs, the Egret People, did not know money. The wealth arrived as tributes and gifts, and was distributed by prestations and barter. Gold was used to plate the walls of temples; there were no gold coins in Tenochtitlán.

Tributes made, gifts given, impose claims on the substance of the receiver. A regime of gifts is a regime of debts; it is the most demanding economic order, this has been understood since Marcel Mauss's *The Gift (Essai sur le don)* of 1923. It is the economy of the most rigorous reciprocity. Each gift proffered requires the return of the equivalent. In the economy of gifts man became man, that is, Nietzsche explained in the second essay of *The Genealogy of Morals*, the evaluator. The herd animal learned to calculate, to reckon, to appraise, he learned to remember, he became rational. He learned his own worth. The self-domesticated animal, a productive organism with use-value, became an exchange-value.

Money introduces a factor of nonreciprocity. One receives something useful, and one renders in return artifacts without utilizable properties. There is immediate discharge of indebtedness. One arises as a person, free to choose and to give. A value unto oneself. Burridge writes,

> Working against the narrow and rigorous moral
> discriminations of Subsistence economies—where love
> cannot be developed as a value in itself though its
> semblances are enforced—money vitiates strict reciprocities
> and differentiates given roles and statuses so as to provide
> options impossible in situations where *giving = receiving*.
> . . . Handling money, thinking about and "being thought"
> and constrained by it, vitiates firm dyadic relationships and
> makes possible the perception of oneself as a unitary being
> ranged against other unitary beings. The opportunity is
> presented to become and to be singular.[2]

When Cortés forced Moctezuma Xocoyotzin to take him to the summit of the Uitzilopochtli pyramid, the charnel-house stench of the blood-soaked priests of the war god filled him with revulsion. He prevailed upon Moctezuma to erect images of Jesus Universal Redeemer and of the Virgin Mother on the same summits as these demons. Yet the knights of Cortés certainly made no objection to the slaughter of captives and noncombatants, nor did their priests, who established the Inquisition in Mexico six years after the fall of Tenochtitlán. The Mesoamericanists today calculate the population of Mexico upon the arrival of Cortés variously between nine and twenty-five million; but all agree that it was reduced to one million during the first sixty years of the Conquest.

The Aztec civilization is singled out in revulsion for having made of human sacrifice a religious ritual. Díaz identifies Uitzilo-pochtli, the Hummingbird of the Left, with Satan, since, without promise of any afterlife, the supreme religious act of his worshippers is human sacrifice. Only brave soldiers killed in battle or sacrificed were promised a return to the earth as hummingbirds, whose plumage was woven into the quivering raiment of the Aztec ceremonial officials. Díaz recognizes here a religion of the most perverted form, utterly alien to any gospel, any kind of salvation.

Yet the conquistadors were not liberal Protestants assembling on Sundays for the purpose of listening to a moral exhortation; Catholic Christianity is a religion entirely centered on sacrifice. The redemption of an earth dammed since Adam's sin was wrought by deity becoming human in order to be led to sacrifice. Each Sunday the Catholic community assembles before an altar at which that sacrifice is not commemorated, but really reenacted. If each Christian is not actually enjoined to carry a cross to a gibbet in his turn, that is not because the sacrifice of the Son of Man freed mankind from any destination to be sacrificed; to the contrary, he simply must not put his sacrifice alongside that of Jesus. The Christian life can consist only in a real participation in the redemptive act of the Christ. "With Christ I am nailed to the cross. It is now no longer I that live, but Christ lives in me" (Galatians 2:19). To be a Christian is to make each moment, each act, each thought, each perception of one's existence a sacrifice. Not simply in partial and intermittent acts of mortification, which would compensate for acts of indulgence, but in a total putting to death of the flesh and of the world.

The Aztec religion did not require quantitatively more human sacrifice than did the Christian. It was the purpose of this sacrifice that differed. Jesus died for our redemption. In the Eden God created, nothing was wanting in the waters above and the waters below, in the skies and on the dry land; the only vice was man—more exactly, woman. Humankind corrupted itself, and against it several times the waters rose again over the dry land in a decreation, from which, for the sake of Noah, of Jonah, of ten just men in Ninevah, of Abraham, a remnant was spared. Paul recognized in Jesus a new Adam; the old mankind must now perish entirely. "For we know that our old self has been crucified with him, in order that the body of sin may be destroyed, that we may no longer be slaves to sin; for he who is dead is acquitted of sin" (Romans 6:6–7). The remnant saved by Jesus is not cleansed but reborn, in the waters from which all skies, dry land, fishes and flying things, creeping and crawling things once came. The new life is destined not for this now corrupted world but for the new Eden, and for immortality. Through mortification of his whole nature, the Christian accedes to definitive deathlessness.

On the pyramids of Tenochtitlán, sacrifice had nothing to do with human guilt or with human salvation, or with any attainment of deathlessness through death. The Aztec religion was a religion not of eternity but of time. All the deities were units of time. Each day had its deity, each day was a deity, a deity was a day. If the Mexica calculated astronomical events four billion years back and eclipses and comets to come a billion years hence, if they calculated the Venus year to fourteen seconds to what is today considered exact, if their calendar was more accurate than the one in our use, this astronomy and this mathematics was not of religious application—it was theology and of the most pressing cosmic urgency. For as each god has its day, each polyhedron of deities and each table has its time. Every fifty-two years all the orbits reach an equilibrium; the Aztecs could find nothing in all their nocturnal searching of the immense stretches of nothingness between the stars that would guarantee that this stasis could not continue indefinitely, and all motion, all life come to an end. It would then be necessary that motion be liberated, that it not be contained within the beings that move themselves. The Aztecs poured forth their blood in order to give movement to the most remote astral deities, suspended for a night in the voids.

At the great ceremony of Cuahuitlehua, all children of the Egret People born within the past year were taken to the temple of Tlaloc to be blessed; there the priests drew blood from the ear lobes of the infant girls and from the genitals of the infant boys.

Adults regularly drew blood from their earlobes, tongues, thighs, upper arms, chests, or genitals. Each day in the palaces the nobles pierced their ears, their nipples, their penises and testicles with *maguey* thorns in order that blood would flow to the heavens. The Aztec imperial order did not, like a Roman empire, extend its administration ever further over subject societies and economies; it existed to drain ever greater multitudes of blood-sacrifices toward the pyramids of the sun that the Aztecs erected upon the earth—that monster with yawning jaws that swallow the setting sun, the remains of the dead, and sacrificed victims. A youth destined to have no children—the sacrificial victim—arrayed as a god, ascended the pyramid to the heavens: man arrayed as the absolute value, absolute as that which does not exchange what belongs to him for anything he, or his children sacrificed with him, could receive in return. The Dominican theologian Bartolomé de las Casas writes:

> The Nations that offered human sacrifice to their gods,
> misled idolaters that they were, showed the lofty idea that
> they had of the excellence of divinity, the value of their
> gods, and how noble, how exalted was their veneration of
> divinity. They consequently demonstrated that they
> possessed, better than other nations, natural reflection,
> uprightness of speech and judgment of reason; better than
> others they used their understanding. And in religiousness
> they surpassed all other nations, for the most religious
> nations of the world are those that offer in sacrifice their
> own children.[3]

The conquistadors and the monks brought love to the Mexica. The Aztecs, Bernal Díaz reports dismally, were sodomists, as were the Mayas of Cape Catoche, the Cempoalans, the Xocotlans, the Tlascalans. Sodomy was their religion; in the very first Indian prayer-house he and his companions came upon on the Mexican coast, Díaz reports finding idols of baked clay, very ugly, which seemed to represent Indians committing sodomy with one another (*THCS*, 19). Of the Indians of whom the conquistadors had any knowledge, the only nonsodomist was Moctezuma II himself, despite his gastronomic taste for the flesh of young boys. It was this, rather than his gullibility and his elegant manners, that commanded the respect of the conquistadors. Cortés assigned a Spanish page to him to test him, and found him incorruptible. When they stabbed him to kill him, Moctezuma requested Catholic baptism. The priest, occupied breaking through the walls of the palace in search of treasure, did not come; Moctezuma died without the Catholic redemption. Today he is worshiped as a God in San Cristóbal and Cuaxtla.

The sodomy Bernal Díaz perceived is not contemporary homosexuality, nor that of Greek classicism and renaissance humanism. Sodomy, determined in the juridic discourse, civic and canonical, of Christendom, is conceptualized not as a nature, but as an act, a transgression of positive law, human and natural. It issues, then, not from an unconscious compulsion but from an intellect that conceives the law and a will that determines to defy it; it derives from libertinage and not from sensualism. Sodomy is the use of the erected male organ not to direct the germ for the propagation of the species, nor to give pleasure to the partner, but to gore the partner and release the germ of the race in its excrement. It is directed against the human species as such, is the act that isolates, that singularizes absolutely. Not simply unnatural, according to the ideology of perversion and degeneration of the modern period, which explains it positively by a fault in nature, explains it by nature—sodomy is antinatural, satanic. It does not only invert the natural finality of organs by which we came to exist, but attacks the natural genus directly, and the imperative to maintain the genus which every positive law, every universal, must presuppose. It is the last limit of outrage under the eyes of the monotheist god, God the Father, absolutized formula for the normative as well as unengendered principle of all generation. Positively, sodomy is the act in which Luciferian sovereignty is constituted and resides. It is the absolute, unmotivated and unjustifiable, position of the one alone in his kind, the monster. This singular, singularizing, act can only be incessantly repeated, rending the monotheist time of universal generation, that of God the Father, conjuring up a cosmic theatre without order or sanction in which trajectories of time rush to their dissipation.

When Cortés burnt his ships before advancing upon Tenochtitlán, when they were but four hundred slashing their way through the enraged Aztec citadel, what maintained the epic resolve in the conquistadors was their horror at falling into the hands of these sodomists and being sacrificed on the altars of their demons thirsty for the blood of the human species. "It must seem very strange to my readers," Bernal Díaz writes,

> that I should have suffered from this unaccustomed terror. For I had taken part in many battles, from the time when I made the voyage of discovery with Francisco Hernandez de Cordoba till the defeat of our army on the causeway under Alvarado. But up to that time when I saw the cruel deaths inflicted on our comrades before our very eyes, I had never felt such fear as I did in these last battles. . . . I must say that when I saw my comrades dragged up each day to the altar, and their chest struck open and their palpitating hearts drawn out, and when I saw the arms and legs of these sixty-two men cut off and eaten, I feared that one day or another they would do the same to me. (*THCS*, 407, 408)

Certainly it was not the painfulness of the Aztec sacrifice as compared to the burning under slow fires that Cortés preferred (and which the Inquisition sanctioned, since this method of execution does not produce the shedding of blood, which would risk making the death of heretics an image of the shedding of the redemptive blood of Jesus) that so horrified conquistador Bernal Díaz—but the monstrous and sodomist cause for which there was sacrifice.

Bernal Díaz knew that the Aztec priests daily let their own blood flow forth to their gods, and that the sacrificed victims, drawn from courts everywhere in the Aztec empire—whom he perceived, through empirical induction from the idols he had seen at every stage of the advance toward Tenochtitlán rather than through knowledge of Aztec sexual legislation, to be sodomists—were treated as incarnations of the gods and climbed willingly the calvary of the Aztec pyramids. If Cuauhtemoc destined Cortés for sacrifice on the altar of Uitzilopochtli, the Hummingbird of the Left, it is because he perceived him as Quetzalcoatl. What then would be a sodomist who sacrificed himself? Aztec sacrifice was not at all for our salvation, for the salvation of the Mexica, the people of Anahuac, The One World, or of the human species. Its purpose was cosmic and not anthropocentric: with the dagger of volcanic obsidian the human blood is released for the sake of the cosmic order; or more exactly, in order that the diurnal gods rise and fall, that the divine trajectories of time rush to their extinction. The blood that makes our bodies move themselves is released from them in order that time and not the stasis of eternity be. The apparition of the human species, and the reproduction of a human politico-economic order, are not guaranteed by a cosmic order, but are sacrificed to move the cosmic trajectories to their expiration. This religion assigns to man the most exorbitant destiny ever conceived in any system of thought. A destiny that would be fulfilled by those whose existence has broken with that of *Homo politicus, Homo oeconomicus*, an existence no longer a subject of, and a value in, reproduction and production. The Aztec destiny invokes a human existence that is no longer commanded by a nature that maintains itself—no longer commanded by universals (incarnated in the individual in the form of the instinct to reproduce the species) nor by self-regenerating compulsions of one's own sensuous nature. The Aztec sacrificial offering is an existence that realizes absolute singularity.

In Christendom, sacrifice is required by original sin. The concept of a sin of which we are all guilty because we are Adam's children is not really the epistemological short-circuit produced where the juridic concept of guilt was wired into the biological idea of heredity. Sin is not the ethical-juridical concept of guilt, which is elaborated in the theory of voluntariness in Aristotle's *Nicomachean Ethics*. Ethical culpability is imputed to the will and is coextensive with consciousness. Consciousness is not the measure of sinfulness; one's sin exceeds the measure of consciousness, as all the anguish of Job argues, and the sinner must first pray to know his sin. The notion of sin, schematized as exile, retains what was essential in the archaic notion of stain—evil as a state. The element of act that puts one in the state of sin is not the transgression as such, transgression of a positive law of the order in which one has been domesticated, but is rather a turning away, an existential conversion from God out of which all transgressions issue. The concept of original sin finds the origin of this act in the conscious choice of the individual but in the individual as participant in the history of a people.

The theological rationality of the concept of intrinsic sinfulness is formulated in St. Augustine of Hippo. Paul, in the Epistle to the Romans, had spoken of the inner mystery of iniquity: "For

I know that in me, that is, in my flesh, no good dwells, because to wish is within my power, but I do not find the strength to accomplish what is good. For I do not the good that I wish, but the evil that I do not wish, that I perform" (7:18–20). The flesh, in Paul, is not a concept related to the Aristotelian physics of the hylomorphic composition of our substance; it is the emblem of the opacity of a will that does not effect itself. For Augustine, the tale of Genesis, which does not isolate an individual faculty of choice but depicts a collusion of male and female natures that issues in the tasting of the fruit of the tree of the knowledge of good and evil and the radical corruption of human nature, is not simply a parable of Semitic patriachical legislation. This fateful complicity of man and woman is identified as carnal concupiscence, which violates Eden and is impossible in a divinely ordained cosmos. In an Eden, the will in mind which views the goodness of creation conducts the will in sensuous nature; orgasm occurs when the will in sensuous nature sinks into itself and the will in mind collapses. The supreme pleasure of orgasm is supreme not simply in quantitative degree but in that it is most fully our own; our will actively participates in and wills this collapse of will. Orgasm is then not just the exemplary, or the most compulsive instance of the will not effecting itself; it is the realization of sin as a state—original sin as originating sinfulness, a state where the will does not perform the good because it wills its nullity. The turning, the existential exile involved in the originating sinfulness is a turning toward nullity; it is also, for each of us, our primary way of participating in the history of a people. Our sinfulness is not a property, like racial color or specific morphology, that would be transmitted in the conjunction of sperm with ovum; it is an antiproperty, it is the willed defection of will in which we are conceived and conceive.

The Christ eternally engendered by our Creator then became incarnate, entered into this flesh of nullity, in order to be put to death, in order to put to death the nullity of flesh. He became flesh in order to be sacrificed, and in order to put to death with his death carnal concupiscent humanity. In the time of Noah, of Jonah, of Abraham, the Creator did not hesitate to engulf the material world in order to put carnal man to death; in Jesus, the Creator of the material world is himself put to death in order that his creation no longer conceive and reproduce in sin, in order that through the death of carnal nature mankind accede to death-lessness.

The Christian lives in the image and likeness of God, in the imitation of God; he procreates as God creates, as the Virgin Mary conceived, without orgasm. He reproduces human life in an act of making of his carnal nature a sacrificial offering.

Augustine's theology does not devalue man's carnal nature but values it absolutely in the divine economy of Redemption. In the economy of sin, in giving himself the supreme pleasure of orgasm, man ever augments his debt, which cannot be paid out of the nothingness of will that concupiscence engenders. In the sublime economy of Redemption, the substance whose use-value is null, the carnal, nature willing its own nullity of will, becomes the measure of the exchange-value of all goods of use-value. The value of concupiscence is no longer measured by the new, but equally concupiscent life, it produces. The value of our carnal substance is measured by the infinite value of the flesh of God sacrificed to redeem it, by the infinite series of earthly goods to be sacrificed for its unending mortification. It is the money of the city of God.

There is an inner economy in the man that participates in political economy, the economy of the polis, in the City of Man and in the City of God. By reason of his organism, Man is *Homo Oeconomicus*. Also by reason of the economy of the polis, the infant becomes an organism.

An infant is tubes disconnected, corpuscle full of yolk ejected from the fluid reservoir of the womb, gasping, gulping free air, pumping, circulating fluids. The disconnected tubes are open to multiple couplings, multiple usages. A mouth is a coupling that draws in fluid, but can also slobber or vomit it out forcibly, that babbles or cries, can pout, smile, spit, and kiss. From the first, the coupling that draws in sustenance, in which the infant vitality knows itself in maintaining itself, also produces an excess, foam, slaver, in which it produces and knows itself as an erotogenic surface, in immediate tangency with another surface it also knows erotogenically. The coupling is not only consuming, of sustenance, but productive, of pleasure, shared, spread. The anus is an orifice that ejects the segments of flow, but also holds them in, ejects vapors, noise, can pout, be coaxed, refuses, defiles, and defies. And spreads its excesses, producing a warm and viscous surface, and surface effects of pleasure. The excrement is waste and gratuity, and gift, the archetypal gift, which is a transfer without recompense not of one's possessions, but of oneself.

But the infant is domesticated; the home (*oikos*) is an economy (*oikonomia*). Maternal love has its price. The infant resources are not to be given freely, spread around on all the surfaces; they are to be retained, covered up, privatized, constituted into private property, in order to be then given not freely, but in exchange. The golden baby feces are to be exchanged for the maternal love on the installment plan. Elementary form of exchange-value; trope—metaphor. The libido is economized, human commerce begins. An economy begins to code the circulations in the infant tubes, begins to organize an organism.

The outside agitator seduces the infant with the lure of primitive communism; he is induced to retain his resources to give them over in exchange for the sustenance of the other, earthmother who holds back only to give more abundantly. Yet what she gives she values, gratifications that indebt him: How pleased Mummy is! Come sit by Mummy! Mummy will give you some sweets! For him to transform into golden feces that will have to be put out for exchange in turn.

The baby learns how to give himself no longer; he holds back for this transaction, holds back in this transaction. He puts out his liquid assets now, builds up hard assets in the cloacal vaults for the next transaction. After much badgering and coaxing, he wryly gets off the potty after having left only some visibly fraudulent measure of what he had to give. Soon he will be only giving his word, leaving his signature. This is the extended form of exchange-value; trope—metonymy. The organism becomes representational, an expressive system. An indefinitely extended system of equivalencies, offered in exchange for representatives of the indefinitely deferred absolute of gratification, love.

The grammar of the servile organization of a society proceeds in the trope of metonymy; a man is evaluated as equivalent to any of an open series of others, equivalent and interchangeable with just anyone, as anyone with him; servility is this evaluation of being completely dispensable. Servility is transformed into serfdom when the whole indefinite series of individuals are measured in terms of one individual in whom the absolute of gratification is realized, set up as the standard of value. Feudalism is constituted in a grammar that proceeds in the trope of synecdoche.

When does the inner servile economy of infancy get reorganized into a feudal economy? The change in the superstructure is prepared by developments in the infrastructure: the libidinal production is shifted from anal to penile material. The penis, a detachable appendage, which appears as a sort of exterior prolongation of the column of feces felt hardening within, acquires the value of the gold of feces. The orgasmic release, Freud wrote, is not only the most intensely productive of pleasure; it is for all our organs the inner diagram of their pleasure. Their use-value for the production of pleasure is measured by it.

But for the moment—for years yet—the infant does not realize the market value of his own resources. No buyer for jism turns up; by himself the child discovers the pleasures of wasting his seed; he smears this liquid currency around, he produces a surface of waste again, and surface effects of pleasure. He adheres to this viscous pleasure, wills this waste, this nullity; his will actively participates in and wills this collapse of domestic will. He would like to seduce the mother into this potlatch economy.

But these developments are being watched. The other intervenes. The father claims proprietary rights over the mother, interdicts masturbation. The paternal word is not indicative, informative, but imperative; it is prohibition, it is law. The law is jealous of the feudal principality constituting itself in the filial organism. The son is sentenced to castrate himself, that is, excise his penis as an organ for the production of pleasure, take it definitively out of anyone's reach.

The child laughs at the paternal threat, empirically most frequently formulated in the name of the father by the mother, even as she fondles him. He will take the paternal word seriously the day he discovers the castration of the mother. In horror he learns that the mother has already been mutilated.

At the same time he comes to realize the chance he is. He comes to understand that he has been pulled forth from that gaping wound between her thighs; he comes to understand that he is the organ of which she has been castrated. He comes to understand why all this time she has been holding him close to herself, fondling him, drooling over him. He recognizes reflected in her eyes something he has not touched, nor felt touched by her: the phallus, absent organ severed from her, separated from him, not even an image he sees in her eyes, only a floating mirage before them, or a sign sought by them. He formulates the project of making himself be that phallus of which his mother has been deprived, in order to hold on himself to her narcissist love. He sets out to identify himself wholly with this phallic phantasm. He understands that her solicitude for his needs reduces him to servility and parasitism; he understands that she satisfies his needs in order to frustrate the demand for gratuitous devotion and love that his infancy put on her. He will exchange all his infantile needs for the phallic contours, phenomenal form of void, that he parades before her as an insatiable sign, appeal and demand. This total investment of himself in the phallus makes it possible for him to effect the castration of a part of him, his penis as immediate pleasure-object, as the paternal word demanded, as well as the polymorphously perverse erotogenic surface production about it. The filial organism is organized as an economy of fetishized commodities.

The phallus is the primary fetish, the structure of every fetish. It is the absent part, the part only signaled, signified in the concupiscent eyes of the other; put in place of the whole. It is the phantasmal substance, of no use-value for the production of erotogenic pleasure, for which all carnal surfaces utilizable for the production of pleasure are exchanged—the carnal form of money. A meaning of the filial organism constituted in the trope of irony.

Money begets money. In order to obey the paternal law, in order to be able to realize his self-castration, the child has constituted himself as a phallic fetish. The father had renounced his own presence as an erotogenic surface laid out before the infantile contact, in order to figure before the child with the force of his word, as law. It is as word, as law, that the father becomes father for the son. The word of the father becomes incarnate in the son in order to castrate the penis through which the infantile substance is squandered, to put this production of nullity, this collapse of domestic will, to death. He puts it to death with his own death, with the excoriation of his own flesh craving for erotogenic contact with his son through which he arose as law, absolute measure of value. The father became incarnate in the son in order to be sacrificed and in order to put infancy to death with his death.

In internalizing the paternal law as the law of his inner libidinal economy, in engendering a superego, the child engenders his own father, puts himself in the place of the father. When now the son of the father comes to the other, the mother and her successors, with his penis, they will no longer meet in the market of a primitive communism, bartering for immediate gratification. They now meet in a monetary economy where nonreciprocity—love—is at stake. Inhabited by the mystical body of the father, the son does not now exchange his phallic value for penile gratification; rather, his real penis is now put in the place of the phallus, becomes a phallic metaphor, an imperative sign demanding subjection from the other. He uses it not to obtain immediate gratification, but to demand absolute love. For the care, the ministrations, the pleasures he demands, he does not give the equivalent in return: the woman must content herself with the child he engenders, and which he claims as his. This phallic metaphor reproduces itself; the son inhabited by the law uses his penis to produce an infant to castrate in turn in the name of the father. His law, his death, will enter into the flesh of his son, transubstantiating that flesh into value by excoriation of its erotogenic surface productivity. Phallic value is the obverse of erotogenic use-value; it is measured by the quantity of goods of use-value which are exchanged for it. The paternal economy fathers organisms, carnal money.

The sodomist in the eyes of Bernal Díaz perceiving the high priests of the Mayas, the Compoalans, the Xocotlans, the Tlascalans, and the Aztecs, is one that erects his real penis in the place of the ideal phallus and uses it to disembowel paternity and execrate infancy. Human sacrifice, common to the principal cultures of Mesoamerica—Olmec, Maya, Zapotec, Mixtec, Huastec, Totanac, Toltec, and Aztec—had accelerated in algebraic inverse-Malthus proportions. The Aztec world had to maintain a continual state of war, which was waged neither for political domination, territorial conquest, nor plunder, but for the sake of constituting brave and noble men as sacrificial stock. The conquistadors and their priests learned that when, in 1487, Auitzotzin dedicated the pyramid of Uitzilopochtli in Tenochtitlán, twenty thousand human beings were sacrificed. The Aztec order, sovereign, sumptuous, and frail as its lord Uitzilopochtli, the Hummingbird of the Left, succeeded the Toltecs, whose pacific deity Quetzalcoatl, the Plumed Serpent, had gone beyond the seas to the east. Moctezuma Xocoyotzin held himself in readiness to sacrifice resolutely the entire Aztec world upon his return. In the perception of Quetzalcoatl Hernando Cortés, the Aztec world had become a vast sodomist infernal machine turning for the damnation and annihilation of mankind. Hernando Cortés hurled himself against it, worshipping the Son of Man, driven by his sense of the value of man and of gold.

The sodomist perversion, perhaps like every perversion, is a perversion of the rationale of economy; the exchange can no longer continue by way of compensations. The sodomist phantasm, put in the place of the possible utility of the human organism, does not have the phenomenal form of value, exchange-value; it is an unevaluatable value. The perversity lies in the inexchangability of this phantasm. Recognizing a sodomist in the Aztec, Bernal Díaz recognizes a sovereign singularity, a cosmos severed from every genus; an exterminating angel, an angel in St. Thomas Aquinas's eidetic definition, alone in his species, unreproducing and without kin; an individual that exhausts the species, that comes to be in laying waste to the species. But what he, craving salvation, redemption, and gold, could not understand is that the supreme act on the pyramid of Uitzilopochtli was the sacrifice of his sovereignty in order that the gods exist, that the trajectories of time run their course. We should not say: that the cosmos turn, for precisely there was not, without blood, an order that would maintain the terrible dispersion of the heavenly bodies in the immensity of the nothingness. Sacrifice of the monstrous sovereignty in order that the universal dispersion be a cosmos. In order that the movements of time depart.

As servility is constituted in receiving more than one can give in return, monstrous sovereignty consists in giving more than one's existence, giving in order not to receive. One has, to be sure, received one's existence from the universe. In giving more than one is to the universe, one perceives more than exchange-value in one's existence. The monstrous splendor of the absolute value no longer has the phenomenal form of value, exchange-value. The giving, with one's existence, of more than one is was the exorbitance to which the Aztecs destined themselves.

At Cholula, on the pyramid of Quetzalcoatl, the greatest structure ever built on this planet—1600 feet square, rising over 433 acres, greater than the great pyramid of Cheops in Egypt—the sacrifice was fixed in its canonical form. The sacrifice was the most beautiful male of his year, his face painted gold, on his throat a jewel in the shape of a butterfly, wearing a jade bird's mask of the wind god, golden socks and sandals, a mantle of glittering green quetzal plumes, a diadem on his head. For forty days he went through the city dancing and singing, and the crowds adored him with flowers and exquisite food. To drink, he was given crushed coca mixed with human blood and peyotl. At length the appointed day arrived. He ascended the great pyramid, lay spread-eagled on the sacrificial stone for the black-faced priests to open his breast with obsidian daggers to pull out his heart, and for the nobles to partake of his flesh and blood. Not a nourishment, human flesh with human flesh; Eucharist of Quetzalcoatl, the departing one.

Moctezuma Xocoyotzin had been completely informed of every detail of Cortés's ships, his horses, his effectives, his arms, his acts; he had sent his priests to Cortés with a turquoise mask with quetzal plumes, that of the priest of Quetzalcoatl; he had repeatedly sent emissaries with tribute more and more in excess of what Cortés told them he had come for. Now Cortés was in the city, with his four hundred men and his fourteen pieces of firearms, surrounded by two hundred thousand armed Aztecs. One day Cortés asks for an audience with Moctezuma, seizes him and puts him under house arrest in his own palace. Moctezuma takes every precaution to make sure that his generals do nothing whatever, he accedes to all Cortés's wishes, including the desecration of the most sacred temples. Each day he conceives more and more lavish gifts of gold objects, and orders them to be brought to Cortés. Moctezuma, tall, lean, supple, elegant, refined, dressed in white embroidered robes which are worn but once and destroyed, adorned with jewels and glittering plumes, the sole Aztec proved not to be a sodomite, is, Cortés perceives, mesmerized with love for him. Cortés trims his beard, practices the most ceremonious Castillian manners, fondles his sparkling gifts like a courtesan, and speaks each time of the great love he has for him. He keeps Moctezuma from his harem, he distributes to his subalterns the princesses Moctezuma offers him. Cortés must be bought with gold, with daily gifts of ever greater piles of gold jewelry, with armies, with an empire, with a whole civilization. When Moctezuma was dead, Bernal Díaz reports that not one of the troops of Cortés received a single gold piece from the plunder; Cortés had appropriated it to the last dram. His pay for the love of Moctezuma.

What is normally called prostitution is the merchandizing of one's organism, that first and fundamental object of use-value. One does not need galleons of gold; renting a prostitute's body for the night is within the means of any sailor or student with a summer job. For one does not pay her in terms of the incalculable value of the voluptuous emotion received, but in terms of what any working woman needs to keep herself in business; as, in capitalism, one pays a factory worker not the equivalent of the surplus value his labor contributes to the raw materials, but in terms of the cost of the sustenance he requires to reproduce himself as manpower. The sometimes enormous prices prostitutes can command when marketed by procurers need not mislead us: their use-value is determined by the labor hours released for productive and commercial activity in their possessor—one hour of personality A is worth to the entrepreneur in advertising effectivity eight hundred billboards erected along freeways. One calculates how much the voluptuous emotion provoked in consumers by the body of Farah Fawcett or Mark Spitz is worth in terms of shampoo or swim trunks sold. Paying cash makes preserving human dignity possible. It is the basis of the distinction between those firm tits and bulging cock, rented out, and the person as such, transcendent focus of choice—that is, proprietor of the abstract means for the appropriation of any commodities whatever.

The word "prostitute" is little more than an epithet hurled to insult and devalue someone. Yet does not one become a value through prostitution? There are distinct forms of value, and distinct forms of prostitution. There are those who rent out their bodies for wages; that is, for the sustenance costs involved in maintaining and reproducing themselves. The organization of a mass market makes it possible to rise from this proletarian status to the status of a person; while one continues to be paid by the entrepreneur in terms of one's exchange-value in the competitive labor pool of personalities, the superior price one can command enables one to appropriate, at the limit, any commodity whatever, and thus become a faculty of choice—a person. Sade's *Nouvelle Justine* stages a third possibility: that of being driven to sell oneself not out of destitution but out of extravagant wealth. One then forces oneself on the market not as a good of exchange-value, but as that against which the use-value of all organisms is measured—that is, as money.

Such a soul, where venality is pure and nowise motivated by the material needs of human nature, we can contemplate writ large in the El Dorado imagined by Sade, and analyzed by Pierre Klossowski in *La monnaie vivante*. In the monetary economy extended across the planet outside of Sade's prison cell, each good, of real use-value, is evaluated in terms of its equivalent in gold, the least useful of available substances, less useful even than dirt or rocks. Gold is the most useless metal both by reason of its properties and because of its scarcity. Were it abundant, one could plaster one's walls with it, for though it is too soft to use in implements, it is as good a nonconductor of heat, cold, and sound as lime. Sade dreams of an economy in which entrepreneurs would be paid by consumers not in cash but in women. The entrepreneurs would in turn pay the labor force in women. The stock of women destined as currency in the economy would have to be maintained by the labor of other women, who for their labor would be paid in men.

In Sade's time English merchants on the banks of the Monomotapa and the shores of the Gulf of Guinea expressed the value of all commodities in terms of human beings. Thus four ounces of gold, thirty piastres of silver, three-quarters of a pound of coral, or seven pieces of Scottish cloth were, according to Father Labat, worth one slave.[4] But a slave is an organism; that is, a living substance organized by a political economy, the first and fundamental object of use-value. In order to function, in the El Dorado imagined by Sade, as money, the women and the men for which all usage-objects are exchanged must themselves be without use-value. Simply maintaining possession of them does not liberate the possessor of a quantum of hours to be devoted to productive and commercial activity. For example, they are not to be used for reproductive copulation, which yields the possessor potentially enterprising offspring who will liberate him of a quantity of hours to be used for productive and commercial activities. The time they are in the hands of their possessor is occupied in the production of an unprofitable and sterile voluptuous emotion.

The most generalized form of exchange-value, the monetary form, requires that all objects of use-value can be exchanged for one item absolutely indeterminate in use-value. All one can do with the inert form of currency, one's gold, is fondle it. All one can do with live currency is fondle, caress, massage, blow, rim them. These objects are without use-value by reason of their scarcity as by reason of their properties. They do not have rare physiognomy or charismatic personality that could be marketed. They have the shape of retired stock brokers, the charisma of dentists' or professors' wives. For El Dorado is, we now know, in south Florida.

By what operation would this trope of irony occur in the discourse of a society by which a living organism becomes currency? It would occur through venality—when, in a society where all things of use-value are exchanged for gold, the gold in turn is appropriated by one who gives in exchange only the gratuity of voluptuous emotion. The voluptuous emotion, evanescent and sterile discharge, acquires value in a political economy by reason of its capacity to render goods of use-value useless. The measure of its value is calibrated by the number of those it can deprive of useful goods. Juliette, through years of indefatigable asceticism, has made herself available for any conceivable debauchery; her utter contempt for all norms and rights has made her immensely rich; now she is ready to sell herself. Her compensation will be the satisfaction of knowing that she has never parted with a sou for the alleviation of any case of human misery. It is a bliss not to be underestimated; according to St. Augustine and St. Thomas Aquinas, the blessed in heaven spend their eternity watching the torments of the damned, *ut beatitude illis magis complaceat*.

There arrived in Seville, on 9 December 1519, the first ship from Anahuac laden with Cortés's gold—bells, jewels, earrings, and nose ornaments of exquisite workmanship; a gold wheel seventy-nine inches in diameter; an Aztec calendar swarming with designs hammered out in *repoussé*. In August of 1520 Albrecht Dürer came to see them, and wrote in his diary:

> I have never seen anything heretofore that has so rejoiced my heart. I have seen the things which were brought from the new *golden land*. . . . a sun entirely of gold a whole fathom broad; likewise a moon entirely of silver, equally large . . . also two chambers full of all sorts of weapons, armor and other wondrous arms, all of which is fairer to see than marvels . . . these things are so precious that they are valued at 100,000 gulden, I saw among them such amazing artistic objects that I have been astonished at the subtle *ingenia* of these people in these distant lands.

In the course of time the mints of New Spain coined some two billion dollars worth of currency, and two billion more were exported in ingots. Two-thirds of the entire silver supply of the world was eventually shipped from the port of Vera Cruz. It was the complete ruin of Spain. The intricate irrigation system of the Moors, which had made of the Iberian peninsula gardens that fed an empire in Africa, simply crumbled into ruins; famine ravaged the countryside and goats sheared the soil even of weeds, so that the topsoil was burnt and eroded leaving Spain the rocky desert that it is today. Spanish manufacture and crafts were bankrupted, the guilds were disbanded, merchants were ruined. The cities became hostages to their fifth column of subproletariat; the countryside, to bandits. Finally the Spanish throne fell to Napoleonic armies, and the creoles in New Spain, in Central and South America, completely emancipated their countries from Spain within twenty years. The race of Spaniards whose organisms figured in the economy as objects of use-value were entirely exchanged for Moctezuma's gold, which is exchanged for the figure of Hernando Cortés. Man of inestimable value.

What did the knight of faith look like? "Hernando Cortés," wrote Gomara,

> was of a good stature, broad-shouldered and deep-chested; his color, pale; his beard, fair, his hair, long. . . . As a youth he was mischievous; as a man, serene; so he was

always a leader in war as well as in peace. . . . He was
much given to consorting with women, and always gave
himself to them. The same was true with his gaming, and
he played at dice marvelously well and merrily. He loved
eating, but was temperate in drink, although he did not
stint himself. He was a very stubborn man, as a result of
which he engaged in more lawsuits than was proper to his
station. . . . In his dress he was elegant rather than
sumptuous, and was exceedingly neat. He took delight in a
large household and family, in silver service and dignity.
He bore himself nobly, with such gravity and prudence
that he never gave offense or seemed unapproachable . . .
He was devout and given to praying; he knew many
prayers and Psalms by heart. (*THCS*, 000)

What does the knight of faith look like? Kierkegaard wanted
to know.

People commonly travel around the world to see rivers and
mountains, new stars, birds of rare plumage, queerly
deformed fishes, ridiculous breeds of men—they abandon
themselves to the bestial stupor which gapes at existence,
and they think they have seen something. This does not
interest me. But if I knew where there was such a knight of
faith, I would make a pilgrimage to him on foot, for this
prodigy interests me absolutely. I would not let go of him
for an instant, every moment I would watch to see how he
managed to make the movements, I would regard myself
as secured for life, and would divide by time between
looking at him and practicing the exercises myself, and
thus would spend all my time admiring him. . . . Here he
is. Acquaintance made, I am introduced to him. The
moment I set eyes on him I instantly push him from me, I
myself leap backwards, I clasp my hands and say half
aloud, "Good Lord, is this the man? Is it really he? Why,
he looks like a tax-collector!"[5]

But not tax collecting, just a tax write-off, those pale men, those
values, are shipped off to Acapulco, to Cancun, to Barbados, to
Tangier, to Sanur, in exchange for all the gold, the diamonds,
the uranium, and the bananas.

Chapter 13

EASY BECOMING UNEASY IMAGES: A PHOTOGRAMMIC SOLARIZATION OF CAVES

James R. Watson

"Socrates"—midwife to contesting questions—and "friend" Plato are brought to us by a technology that is itself implicated

in the contestation it presents.[1] The uneasy graphic image of "Socrates" and "Plato," an image within and among others, images of the instituting and contesting of the new political authority of writing, comes to us in a multiple printing. Which is what I propose here: a photogrammic improvisation of Plato's scripting of Socrates. The improvisation is necessarily set within the Socrates-Plato contest at the same time that it sets this historical event within its own framing. Thoroughly complicitous, this is not an easy set(ting) of images. But because photography is for us today what writing was for Plato, it is with such uneasy images that the instituting and contesting of authority in Plato becomes the way we must address that issue today. This is not, however, an "objective" undertaking.

The photogrammic exposure—improvisation—we offer here results in a partly reversed image of the contest. This image comes from Plato's cave, specifically from the image of sunlight that temporarily blinds the liberated cave-dweller upon reaching the entrance of the cave—a solarization.[2] What is given and received is an unsafe exposure to the development of authority, a reversal of its power through the use of its captured power (the fire within the cave). Exposing the negative (authority) to the sun and its subsequent printing by the bound-unbound ones does not result in a duplication of power, but a mutation of power. We will call this a photogramm of authority because the results are surprising—they exceed the authority reversed in its framing.[3]

Our photogramm will attempt to reverse the image of authority that is at work in the seeming transparency and objectivity of photographic reproductive technology. We will see that photographic technology has an uneasy "bifocal" nature. On the one hand, photography easily pulls us through itself to its scenes, fixing those scenes within its transparent, unnoticed frames. This is how the Plato-Socrates contest of authority, for example, can be displaced. The transparency of the medium makes it seem that that contest is not repeated in and with the medium that reenacts it. Instead the medium "objectively" displaces the contest to a safer arena—the past. This is the aspect of photography that conquers space and time. But if this were the only way that photography works, we would "ignore" that the Postcard in our photogramm is printed without signatures before it is written on, signed, and sent by its "owner." But who can doubt that this is precisely the usual state of affairs? We don't usually see the medium that brings us the message, and this is why it has power over us.

Why do we focus on written message, signature, and address rather than the printing and other processes of appropriation that bring these messages to us? Why is the uneasy image of the productive, reproductive, and transmissive technology so easily missed? Could it be that we have been captured and played by the set-up of "freedom" which such "objective" technologies fabricate? Are we being played by powers which subject us by assigning us to roles within their scenes of freedom? If so, how is that accomplished? Can we see this setting-up? How can the ob-scene be seen within the scenic display? How can we "read" Plato's writing of Socrates in a way that sees the uneasiness of its images? And not just Plato-Socrates.

Can we imagine performers as creators, as improvisors, as mutations rearranging, recomposing, the stage set-ups? Actors on culture's stage, recomposing both their lines and the staging, mutating, disrupting the authority of scripts—all of this an unnoticed play of backgrounds for audiences unfamiliar with the scripts and their directions. Except, perhaps, for declamations that break the spell of contexts, audiences remain captivated by the seven ages or acts directed by Shakespeare on the world's stage.[4] But Shakespeare was both playwright and actor and his plays are an actor's declamations to audiences captivated by something other than Shakespeare's scenes. Scenes within, with, and against the world's stage, the Shakespearean theater is a questioning critique of set-ups. But Shakespeare cared little for the literary publication of his plays. His art was verse-speaking. Can Shakespeare's art still work in the age of photographic reproduction? Or, perhaps, photographic reproduction is like the re-forming of theatrical art that Hamlet praises as he admonishes the players of the play that he hopes will catch the conscience of the King: "And let those that play your clowns speak no more than is set down for them; for there be of them that will themselves laugh, to set on some quantity of barren spectators to laugh too, though in the meantime some necessary question of the play be then to be considered. That's villainous, and shows a most pitiful ambition in the fool that uses it."[5] Here Shakespeare has Hamlet express what is contrary to Shakespeare's art—that the play should be a perfectly figured mirror of the world's stage.

Like *Hamlet* there are those who believe we need not know the art of the world's stage to stage that stage. This belief derives from another tradition, a spiritual tradition that derives its powers from beyond the world's stage. It also began with slaves, actors within prescribed scenes, but, unlike the slaves who improvised their master's tools of subjection, they appealed to a power above all worldly conditions and powers. They were, in other words, slaves that wanted to get out of set-ups altogether. These were the "players" who did not mutate. Instead they took their roles so seriously that they became "autonomous" works of art within the master set-ups. *L'art pour l'art* is one result of this tradition analyzed in *The Genealogy of Morals*, a tradition to which Nietzsche attempted to assign Plato and Socrates. It is the "Postcard" that both affirms and negates that assignment.[6]

Together with the "Postcard" image we have the *Apology* images of Socrates: a cultured individual; a normal person; a good citizen of Athens. Within the cultural framework of Athens, as set forth by Plato, "Socrates" felt comfortable with no noted difficulty regarding the laws (or walls) of this great city. But "Socrates," comfortable with his own fit, made others uncomfortable with their fit (and fitness). "Comfortable Socrates," so comfortable that he dies for Athens, was discomforting for others who felt they had as much right to a comfortable fit as Socrates. "Socrates" did not deny his opponents their right to a comfortable fit, he just made it difficult for them to fit into anything permanent— You can't fit into the same "Athens" twice. Thus did "Plato" stage-write (improvise on) the Athenian stage.

When, in the presence of youthful followers, "comfortable Socrates" began to examine what authoritative others took for granted (themselves), there were tremors and much uneasiness among those who had been comfortable. "Socrates" thought that being an Athenian had something to do with cultivation, learning—*paideia* (and *paidia*)—and this required a rather thorough examination of everything that appeared solid and well-established. He was thus comfortable with the uneasiness of being an Athenian. He was, in other words, comfortable with his Athenian unsettledness. Plato's writing of "Socrates" makes being an "Athenian" uneasy, unless one is comfortable with Socrates being so easy that he dies (is written) for the state.

"Plato" was also unsettled and unsettling, especially after the upset settlers put his easy friend and teacher Socrates to rest. "Plato" brought Socrates back by making the Socratic dialogue even more upsetting. He connected it with an explosive new technology—writing. Plato put Socrates's words in our eyes: he "pictured" Socrates. Thus Plato rescued "Socrates" from those who put him to rest; he re-presented Socrates, transformed him, with a complex set of visual word images. We have "Socrates" but not Socrates, or Socrates became an intricate composite of visual (word) images that went where Socrates never did. Socrates was easy when he died for the state, but uneasy when Plato brings him back in writing. You can't read the same "Socrates" twice.

We might say that writing the spoken word was a "mixed" media performance that many found, and still find, confusing. Socrates had been put to rest, but then "Socrates" appeared. Is this what "Socrates" was referring to when he warned those who had condemned him that "others" less moderate than he would come to haunt them? Or, is this "Socrates" "speaking" in a way that confuses us? Confusing because once improvisation sets in, there can't be any closure of the script?

"Plato" also tells us that writing is a dangerous technology, different in kind from the dangers of speaking because writing involves the use of inanimate mediations. He likens writing to the practice of medicine—the administration of poisons, which can heal or kill—and thus "represents" himself and "Socrates" as physicians of the soul. These pharmaceutical images are powerful . . . and dangerous.

We have, however, become accustomed to the use of inanimate mediations. We are comfortable with medical practices that open our bodies to technical interventions, and we are not too uncomfortable with the practice of transforming the human body with inanimate "transplants." There are dangers, to be sure, but we take these dangers as ones of degree rather than kind. We are comfortable in the world of technical mediations in a way that Plato was not.

Yet there is a strange and perhaps unsettling common interest

between us, our technological embraces, and "Plato's phar-
macy." The question of the danger of writing, for Plato, was the
question of its control. Look at his images of "Socrates." It was, in
other words, a matter of administration, dosage, and allocation.
Writing was a political program for Plato, one that concerned the
administrative, educational, and technical apparatus for assuring
that only good writing be allowed. What is unsettling is that
many still do not "see" just how powerful "Plato's" pharmaceutical images have been for controlling the "body" politic. Writing
well is the same as being a good (read: behaving) citizen. At the
same time, however, Plato's writing is set forth as a *pharmakon*—
a poison. Just say "No" to "illegal" drugs and their administra-
tions.

Why isn't this usually "seen"? What keeps us from "seeing"
what controls us? Is it because a really great performance "capti-
vates" us? Did Plato know our souls that well? Or, is it because
we "read" Plato exactly the way he thought we would if we failed
to "see" the danger of writing? The danger was the fix that brings
contentment and easy readings—the fix that brings such easy
readings as:

> Plato's philosophy is perhaps the most notable effort in the
> history of Western thought to construct a doctrine of
> absolute and objective values. According to Plato, there is a
> true right and wrong, which is a universal principle for all
> times. We do not make values or truths; we find them;
> they do not alter with races, places, or fortunes. Thus,
> there are two worlds; the world of absolute beauty, and the
> world of opinion, with its conventions and delusions.[7]

But there are no two worlds in Plato's writings, only images
within images. Speaking of which, shouldn't we note that the
writing of the dialogue called "the Republic" places that dialogue
and its narration outside the laws/walls of Athens at the Piraeus
and in the private house of Cephalus? Or, *pace* Jowett, should
we discount such images? That would be easier, and that would
be a misreading leading to the recommendation that we adopt
this "easier" "Republic" as a model for our city-state. But, then,
what about "easy Socrates" who died for Athens? Is the "easier
Republic" Plato's revenge for the political misuse of "easy Socrates," or is "uneasy Socrates" the guiding spirit of the new and

easier Republic with a heavenly foundation? Let me suggest here that our common interest and patriotic enthusiasm today lies with our not seeing Plato's images within images (not "representation") of the Socratic dialogue.

Much has been done to make Plato (and not just Plato) unsettling once again, but much has been done to make sure that doesn't work. This latter reactive and antideconstructive enterprise employs various techniques of capturing, freezing, framing, for the purposes of instituting "bodies of knowledge" transparent to those properly trained in cultural assimilation. The culture of freedom, the "easy Republic"—imperial America, its presidency, and those who covet these—attempts to make uneasy images easy, transparent, and assimilable—in a word, consumable. Photography is central to both enterprises; it is the pivotal power of reenacting authority and the poison (*pharmakon*) which weakens and sometimes kills authority.

We have been "developed" by the photographic industry for more than a century, and nothing is more "natural" for us than to see the way the products/codes of that industry teach us to see. Optical and chemical images are easy for us. So easy, in fact, that they are hardly "seen" as dangerous. We naturally see imperially—we will accept nothing less than "freedom," nor anything more. The imperial president proclaims that Saddam Hussein is worse than Hitler. Yes, we can accept that, but we can't "see" that "worse" refers to the "interrupted flow of oil." While Billy Graham spends the night at the White House in spiritual solidarity with the leader of free peoples, television brings us the Iraqi sky lighting-up in a glorious pyrotechnic display. So glorious that the "pilots of freedom" describe it as a Fourth of July celebration a hundred times over. The same pilots pronounce the connection of state-industry (culture-entertainment-deception): the glorious display is like something out of Disney World. Let freedom ring in the magic kingdom! We see and hear that and consume petro-culture's nihilistic-spiritual commitments. It is so easy that we don't "see" the connection between oil, burning children (annihilation of futures), and "freedom." Raised with the many idols of Jowett's "Plato," our otherworldly soul says that "easy Socrates's" children must die for the "free state" while our earthy body craves the petro "fix." We are murderous schizophrenics who sooner or later become Salmon

Rushie's "Chamcha" and cry out "Fix me, Jesus." For us, it's all too easy—so easy that our heavenly spirits can make the monstrous connection: the reenactment of "Holocaust." "Sadim," as Bush calls him, is worse than Hitler! Images within images that the state and its agencies disentangle and separate for our needy consumption.

But if Plato were here today, I believe that he would attempt to photogramm all the people and things put to rest (and sleep) by state powers. Photogramms are our new kind of writing, at least as dangerous as older kinds of writing. He would do this because photography is also imperial, a statist device with a political program. And that is the program that our photogrammic Plato would try to unsettle with its "own" images. Thus, we do to Plato what he did to Socrates: give (re)birth to "Plato," a postmodern photogrammic dis-easer of settled-in youth, youth made so easy that they are off to die for the state. And not just youth.

Actually, there have been and still are quite a few photogrammic "Plato's." There are of course more settling photographers than unsettling photogrammers. But the distinction between writing and photograph has been unsettled by the photogramm. Barbara Kruger, for example, combines writings and photographs in one image, one which works differently than each in separation. Such photogrammic writing brings us closer to the danger of writing that Plato alerted us to. It is always the uneasy image that shows us the danger of the easy ones.[8] This is the *mise en abîme*, the writing of the disaster, the image within images of authority, the Iraqi skies seen otherwise than a Disney production. This is also a joy, but not one apart from anguish. Nothing can be the same after the disaster writes and is written.[9] But the disaster writing us is different from our writing of the disaster.

The photographic industry makes profits by providing the techniques and equipment for producing easy images—decidable images that can be read directly, clearly and distinctly. This is the "snapshot" business, and a political program ("point and shoot") not seen by easy and unwary readers. It all seems so natural, so easy. It is a program that goes back to the refinement of certain photographic processes in the mid-nineteenth century, most notably the discovery of the chemical fixation of photographic images.

By the late nineteenth century, subsequent improvements in film speeds and lens give rise to the optimistic view that photographic science and industry have solved the central problem in the quest for accurate reproductions of nature. The biological limit of human visual experience had been broken with permanent records, and the dream of conquering space and time seemed to be no more than a matter of time. So perfect were the photographic reproductions that when people were "exposed" to daguerreotypes, they were "at first frightened to look for any length of time at the pictures produced. They were embarrassed by the clarity of these figures and believed that the little, tiny faces of the people in the pictures could see out at them."[10] Thus, Mathew Brady's photographers brought the horrors of the Civil War into the homes of soldiers' parents. Such photographs were immediately credible depictions of the horrors of war. They were also easy images, showing nothing of the connections of war and politics, industry, and the deadly contradictions of capitalist expansion. They were, in fact, so easy that they had no influence or counterinfluence on the war.

In 1871 hundreds of photographs were taken of the celebrating Communards of the Paris Commune. But celebration turned to anger when after their defeat, these photographs were used by the police to identify the Communards, who were then executed. In 1890 Jacob A. Riis's *How the Other Half Lives* was published. The sociologist-photographer Lewis W. Hine photographed the exploitation of children in American factories from 1908 to 1914, although not without a little staging and sideline coaching. These photographs were so convincing, they brought the first child labor laws.[11] The liberals praised the power of the new photography to bring about reform, without the slightest suspicion that Hine's photographs were as easy and as decontextualized as Brady's. It seemed, to the unsuspecting, that photography was indeed objective; that it simply recorded what was there, the good as well as the bad.

All of this came together in the belief that photography was the accurate reproduction of nature and society. The political program had put on a technical mask. While cutting through the limits holding us back from the conquest of space and time, the photographic industry developed ideological masks which hid behind the "liberal" uses of photography—uses which never drew the lines of flight between industrial and state powers. Photography, like all technical things, is value-free. Photographs don't kill, people do.

But while Kodak was promoting its No. 1 Kodak Camera with the "You press the button, we do the rest" slogan, others were trying to show that the photographic image was something other than a value-free technical affair. The technical mask had never been accepted by all photographers. Its rejection and the various forms thereof have a rather complex history of their own, but for our purposes here it is sufficient to focus on the period when photographs began to be explicitly used as political tools. It was during this period that the "objective" and "accurate" reproductions of nature and society were used for contradictory purposes by attaching to them different texts or captions. A picture may be worth a thousand words, but different words make the same photograph worth a different thousand words. The World Wars and the propaganda thereof bought the age of photographic innocence (objectivity) to an end. It is not that photographic images are no longer pure, but rather the recognition that they never were.

It was, of course, disillusioning to discover that photographs could be credibly "used" contrary to the photographer's intentions. Gisèle Freund confesses her astonishment when one of her photographs of share trading at the Paris Stock Exchange was used in two different newspapers with contradictory captions: "The two publications had used my photographs in opposite ways, each according to its own purpose. The objectivity of a photograph is only an illusion. The captions that provide the commentary can change the meaning entirely."[12] If, however, the photograph is not objective, neither are the words which reveal its complicity in deceptive enterprises. Images within images are not easy.

What are we to make, then, of a contemporary school of thought which regards photography as another modern obsession with objectivity? Members of this school of "medium analysis"[13] include Rudolf Arnheim, Thomas Mundro, Susanne Langer, Theodore Greene, Siegfried Kracauer, Lewis Mumford, Stanley Cavell, Susan Sontag, and André Bazin. Their theoretical position is that photography is a complex of automatic, mechanical processes that produces mimetic, optical representations: the photographic image is a function of the photographic medium, its raw materials and processes, which, like all media, have a specific potentiality. This "theoretical" position sounds like something the Kodak tech people might have put together for a promo—"learn the photographic potential at Rochester."

Medium analysis is an accommodating position that links up quite nicely with the state-industry-military attempt to reappropriate photography. A reappropriation that could not be attempted without the reign of the subject-object duality, indeed, without all the staggered and swaggering hierarchies of patriarchy. The proposition that photography is objective is complicitous and collaborative with the imperial appropriation of photography as the production of easy images.

Which is not to say that medium analysts consciously support this statist "use" of photography. Behind the "theoretical" propositions of medium analysis is a modernist agenda: to restore the purity of art and language after their foul contamination by the association with photography. Sontag, for instance, bemoans the obvious: we are besieged by an endless barrage of photographic images.[14] There is a glut of images that must be condemned on the elitist grounds of art itself. Any idiot can take a picture these days. Photography has a common pedigree, and it shows in all its images. On the highest ground the solution comes as a breeze: to preserve what remains of art and language, hand photography back to the charlatans and their industries.

It "matters" not that their own "pure writings" are handed over to the charlatans for printing, reproduction, and distribution: their purity is preserved by the sacrifice of photography. Looking backwards, they do not see the print effect. Nostalgically, they ask us to see their "printed" words as nothing but slavish, mechanical and objective reproductions, but never as things transformed and signed by the charlatans and mule workers of photographic "reproduction." No, indeed, their words work the way they worked before photography contaminated the arts, the way words conveyed meanings before photography "exposed and printed" the line separating art from the common folks. Only the highest works of art illustrate their books, except for those "pictures" that must now and then be used to show

the bad taste of common intrusions. "Know what they mean?"—
what Marx wrote concerning commodity fetishism was never
"meant" to apply to the appropriation of photography by the
culture industry and never, never, to those who hand new writing tools back to the captains of that industry for the sake of
preserving cultural literacy as its episcopal best.

However, this modernist agenda can do nothing to alter the
fact that photography has changed. Photography is postmodern
and the modernist agenda of the medium analysts can do nothing
to change that. Their elitism can be effective only in collusion
with other elitisms, but such collusions only serve to exclude
them from the writing which Derrida quite accurately says
"shows signs of liberation all over the world, as a result of decisive efforts."[15]

This liberation is not that of those who stand within the tradition that speaks in Jowett's "Plato." Photogrammic writing is an
extension of postmodern photography's irresistible tendency to
connect with everything, especially with those things marked
"Private, do not trespass," "Sacred, hands off," "Art, high bid-
ders only," "Concepts, institutionally trained thinkers only."
But contrary to modernist agendas, this is not the revenge of
philosophy's other, only the "other" pulling "philosophy" into
the dance. Postmodern photography does not subsume or con-
quer philosophy, it "simply" reconnects, recontextualizes the
fragments—which is why the postmodern body is a mutation
which carries "bad genes" along with it.

Connecting philosophy and photography is simultaneously a
deconstruction of the classical philosophical opposition governing the subordination of image to concept. But that deconstruction must always remain suspicious of its results lest the hierarchical opposition recur as a recontextualization parading as
something more than a fragment. "Bad genes" appear as easy
images.

Suspiciously, then, I would like to propose photogrammic
writing as a possible response to what Schürmann calls for in the
following passage:

> Responding and corresponding to the essence of
> technology cannot be an individual affair. How could a
> natural language be private? If, in its essence, technology is

still principial in stature but already anarchic in germ, how could words free themselves from their metaphysical order without subverting the most basic speech patterns of our civilization as it discovers itself relocated, by that germinal power, outside of onto-theo-logy? And if, in order to experience the "limits" of technology, our being-there is to open itself up to that bifrontal essence, how could *Dasein* in any way designate the individual subject? That it is still impossible for us to string words together in an order other than *pros hen*, should say something about the time it may take to free the post-modern economy of any principial overdetermination, about the time necessary to prepare an a-principial economy. Still more, it might be asked whether we are even prepared to learn the language of our own time, an *anti-principial* language, a double-talk as bifrontal as the anarchy principle. According to Heidegger, a transference, a setting-across, a translation is necessary for us even to enter the constellation of our own age. We must *über-setzen* toward the economy of the twentieth century the way one sets over to another shore. In general, "in a given epoch of the destiny of being, an essential translation corresponds each time to the way a language speaks within that destiny." Either we learn to speak as the contemporary economy of presence speaks to us, or what is propitious in advanced technology will be lost. To put it negatively: either we unlearn the *pros hen* grammar, or the technological grip will be fatal for us.[16]

"Photogrammic writing" is itself a vacillating image—easy and uneasy—because it is connected with the easy images generated by the principial economy. It is, in other words, not "free" from principial determination. When it becomes simply easy, photogrammic writing has been overdetermined by the principial economy; which is to say, it is no longer photogrammic.[17]

"So," you properly object, "all this talk about photogrammic writing is nothing more than strings of words à la the *pros hen* order."

"Yes," I respond "but to what are you then ob-jecting? The irony? This is why neither idea nor image can work without the other, and neither is victorious in the product which says something different. It's like planned parenthood that fails, producing mutations who are, strangely, still lovable."

"But," you insist, "you can't use strange terms (controversial images), like 'photogrammic writing,' without first defining them."

"Fair enough," I say, "although I could 'quote' Hegel here about prefaces by-passing the necessary labor of the concept. Instead, let me here play the fool 'Euthyphro' and give some 'examples.' "

The SS Fun House

"Yes, yes," you continue "they're interesting and all that, but we need a definition of 'photogrammic writing' before we can see that these are examples of such."

"But don't you see that asking for definitions is part of a tradition that began with the easy images of 'Plato'? Essences kill. That's why Plato never gave any—only ironic effects of the desperate attempts to do so."

"Why, then, is Euthyphro *portrayed* as a foolish pretender to religious knowledge?"

"Is he? Compared to whom? Us, the wise readers of those who could only pose the 'essential' questions?"

The Voluntary and the Involuntary Making a Thought

Writing writes us writing, leading our fear of this gripping transformative power to "secretly venerate the ideal of a language which in the last analysis would deliver us from language by delivering us to things."[18] If we could get to things, we could stop our imagining, our transformation. Fixed signs are our ideal because with them we can step out of our vulnerable fluidity and get substantial. This vampiric ideal would drain away the power of the images that have had their way with us. Actually this ideal, vampiric and incestuous, is the desire for purity.[19] The desire to get out of the implication is the one that leads to writing against writing, which is still implication but with a vengeance that hates itself hating us.

Vengeance is the only way the pure ones acknowledge that they have our "genes." We become part of that vicious circle when we *deny* our "bad genes." Yes, we must be suspicious of results; our postmodern body is a collage of fragments, including the same ones that make up Jesse Helms, Reverend Wildmon, and Charles Keating. We are them, and others just as well. The circle of vengeance is broken every time we refuse any fragment or coalition of fragments the right to rule over the others. All are of the earth—no two worlds and different lines of descent. Miscegenation—first a crime, then a dirty word—is now replaced by "mutation."

The principal economy and industry, the substantial, the pure, attempts to prescribe the bounds of sense. But in doing this, the substantial desubstantializes itself in the wars it so desperately needs. Writing against writing is the contradiction of the principial economy and its state: irony becomes a repressive strategy whenever it is picked up by the state. This is why Derrida argues—very carefully, yet forcefully, and suspiciously—that always behind (and ahead of) the force of law is the idea of justice, inseparable from yet not the same as the law.[20] What animates writing against writing is positivism. And we have seen what the state is capable of accomplishing with legal positivism.

At the recent "Obscenity Trial" of Dennis Barrie, director of Cincinnati's Contemporary Arts Center, we have a repressive strategy foiled by the same folks the "New Moral Majorities" were divinely commissioned to protect from the postmodern condition. Barrie was indicted after he decided to include sexually explicit photographs by Robert Mapplethorpe in the exhibition "The Perfect Moment" (Spring 1990). Behind the arrest of Barrie stood the respectable (and indictable) figure of Charles H. Keating, Jr., who founded the Cincinnati Citizens for Decent Literature in 1956. Keating, it seems, has a very keen eye for filth and, as we now know, our lucre as well. Barrie was charged with "pandering obscenity" and "illegal use of minors." Since Mapplethorpe's photographs included some showing male anal penetration and children with exposed genitals, the charges against Barrie were really images within images, and a Barrie-Mapplethorpe mutation that the jury would find quite impressive.

Now Cincinnati is not known for its progressive and liberal attitudes, and we could fairly characterize its inhabitants as sharing (with the rest of us) the hard surfaces of Plato's cave. We could also say that the prosecutors of Barrie were like Plato's manipulators of the people. They also insisted that the jurors view only reproductions—decontextualized shadows—of Mapplethorpe's photographs. After listening to inept "experts" trying to explain why Mapplethorpe's photographs were dirty portrayals of a non-American life-style, the jurors decided to let Barrie go, and hang-on to "Mapplethorpe." Mapplethorpe's "shadows" had somehow solarized the cave—with considerable assistance from defense witnesses such as Jacquelynn Baas who understood how photographs work. Photogrammic writing doesn't have to leave the cave to work, and that's why the state doesn't like it. As Jennifer Loesing recalls,

> Going in, I would never have said the pictures have artistic value. . . . Learning as we did about art, I and everyone else thought they did have some value. We were learning about something ugly and harsh in society that went on. . . . it seemed like Robert Mapplethorpe had talent and had a story to tell behind each one of the pictures. I would have liked to see the ones he did of flowers.[21]

NOTES

CHAPTER 1 THE TRUTH OF HERMENEUTICS

1. On the decisive sense of this term in Heidegger, and the continuation of his thought in the direction of a way out of metaphysics, cf. the final chapter of my *The End of Modernity: Nihilism and Hermeneutics*, trans. and intro. Jon R. Snyder (Baltimore: Johns Hopkins Press, 1988) and my contributions to *Filosofia* 86 and *Filosofia* 87, ed. Gianni Vattimo (Torino: 1986 and 1987).

2. Apart from the pages dedicated to Heidegger in Hans-Georg Gadamer's *Truth and Method* (New York: Crossroads, 1984), an important document in this respect is Gadamer's meeting with Adriano Fabris published in *Teoria* (fasc. 1, 1982) in which Gadamer insists on his closeness to the "second Heidegger," but also that the second Heidegger must be related back to the first, since it is ultimately a matter of retranslating into the language of *Being and Time* what the later works presented under the form of "visions."

3. See Richard Rorty, *Philosophy and the Mirror of Nature* (Ithaca: Cornell University Press, 1979).

4. See Rorty, *Philosophy and The Mirror of Nature*.

5. For example, this is Foucault's position, at least according to Paul Veyne's radical interpretation, of which one should see above all "E possibile una morale per Foucault?" in *Effeto Foucault*, ed. P. A. Rovatti (Milano: Feltrinelli, 1986), pp. 30–38.

6. For a wider illustration of this point, see my contribution to the Royaumont Colloquium in 1987, "L'impossible oubli," in ed. *Usages de l'oubli*, Yosef H. Yerushalmi et al. (Paris: Seuil, 1988).

7. Cf. Vattimo, *Filosofia* 86 and 87.

8. Speaking of "arbitrary" strategies of the thought of difference, Derrida explicitly evokes Mallarmé's *coup de dès*, and this reference has

more than a casual significance: see Jacques Derrida's "Différance," in *Margins of Philosophy*, trans. Alan Bass (Chicago: University of Chicago Press, 1982).

9. I am using the Lacanian terminology here without any pretense to fidelity to his text; all the more since alongside the imaginary and the symbolic, he proposes also the "real," which in my schema only seems to have a place on the side of the imaginary.

10. Cf. Karl Mannheim, *Ideology and Utopia* (San Diego: Harcourt Brace Jovanovich, 1985), in which historical relativism is limited by the view that ideological points of view can be integrated into a "comprehensive totality" that serves as the basis for a scientific politics.

11. A fuller discussion of this can be found in my essay "Ethics of Communication or Ethics of Interpretation?" (forthcoming)

12. This is the theme of Martin Heidegger's "On the Essence of Truth," in *Martin Heidegger: Basic Writings*, ed. David Farrell Krell, trans. John Sallis (New York: Harper and Row, 1977).

CHAPTER 2   TRUTH AS FUNDAMENTAL AND TRUTH AS FOUNDATIONAL

1. Martin Heidegger, *Zur Sache des Denkens* (Tübingen: Max Niemeyer Verlag, 1976), p. 66.

2. Jacques Derrida, *Of Grammatology*, trans. Gayatri Chakravorty Spivak (Baltimore: Johns Hopkins University Press, 1976), p. 20. Henceforth cited as *OG*.

3. John Rajchman, "Philosophy in America," in *Post-Analytic Philosophy*, ed. J. Rajchman and Cornel West (New York: Columbia University Press, 1985); cf. also Richard Rorty, "Solidity or Objectivity" in the same volume.

4. Richard Rorty, *Philosophy and the Mirror of Nature* (Ithaca: Cornell University Press, 1979), pp. 5–7, 365–72, 393–94.

5. Discussed in Martin Heidegger, *The Basic Problems of Phenomenology*, trans. Albert Hofstadter (Bloomington: Indiana University Press, 1982), pp. 218–22. Henceforth cited as *BPP*.

6. It is more usual nowadays to talk about sentences rather than propositions. This avoids the unclarity of the status, identity conditions, and abstract character of propositions as abstract entities "meant by" or "stated by" sentences. In fact the term "sentence" raises equally intractable problems, together with the tendency to look as if it meant something more concrete and unproblematic than it does. In fact, "sentence" means a sign-sequence *with* its meaning, and that meaning must be such that it is a "declarative" (truth-valued) sentence, so that the problems of how meaning is established and

whether it is determinate are just as pressing as they are for propositions. Therefore, I shall use "proposition," except where I mean an
uninterpreted sign-sequence whose formal-syntactical role is that
appropriate for being interpreted as the bearer of truth-values; but
nothing important hangs on this choice except adherence to the
standard translations of Heidegger.

7. Except in the purely technical sense of replacing it by the term
"satisfaction," i.e., the relation of an object to a predicate which
holds just in case the predicate is true of that object.

8. See David Wiggins, "Truth, Invention and the Meaning of Life,"
Proceedings of the British Academy 62 (1976); also in *Needs, Values,
Truth; Essays in the Philosophy of Value* (Oxford: Oxford University
Press, 1987), pp. 87–137.

9. Cf. Derrida's critique of Searle in *Limited Inc.* (Evanston: Northwestern University Press 1988); note especially the "Afterword." Henceforth cited as *LI*.

10. Martin Heidegger, "Letter to Frings," in *Heidegger and the Quest for
Truth*, ed. M. S. Frings (Chicago: Quadrangle Books, 1968). Henceforth cited as *HQT*.

11. Cf. Derrida's analyses of such texts in "The Purveyor of Truth," in
The Post Card: From Socrates to Freud and Beyond (Chicago: University
of Chicago Press, 1987) or in *D'un ton apocalyptique adopté naguère en
philosophie* (Paris: Galilée, 1982).

12. Jacques Derrida, "The Principle of Reason: The University in the
Eyes of its Pupils," *Diacritics* (Fall 1983), p. 20.

13. Martin Heidegger, *Grundfrage der Philosophie*, in *Gesamtausgabe*, vol.
45 (Frankfurt: Klostermann, 1984). Henceforth cited as *GP*.

14. Martin Heidegger, *Logik: die Frage nach der Wahrheit*, in *Gesamtausgabe*, vol. 21 (Frankfurt: Klostermann, 1976).

15. For the importance of the modern phase of metaphysics within
metaphysics as a whole, cf. Dominique Janicaud, "Heideggeriana,"
in *La métaphysique à la limite* (Paris: Epiméthée, 1983), sections 13,
14. Henceforth cited as *ML*.

16. Martin Heidegger, *What is a Thing?*, trans. W. B. Barton, Jr. and
Vera Deutsch (South Bend: Gateway, 1967), passim.

17. Martin Heidegger, "Platons Lehre von der Wahrheit," in *Wegmarken*
(Frankfurt: Klostermann, 1967), p. 223.

18. Marlene Zarader, *Heidegger et les paroles de l'origine* (Paris: Vrin, 1986).
Henceforth cited as *HPO*.

CHAPTER 3   SCIENCE AS FOUNDATIONAL?

1. An exception is Ian Hacking, *Representing and Intervening* (Cambridge: Cambridge University Press, 1983).

2. Karl Popper, *The Logic of Scientific Discovery* (New York: Harper and Row, 1968), p. 111. Henceforth cited as *LSD*.
3. An anti-empiricist position that does attempt to take the role of experimentation seriously, however, is Robert Ackermann, *Data, Instruments, and Theory* (Princeton: Princeton University Press, 1985). See also Robert P. Crease, "The Problem of Experimentation," in *Phenomenology of Natural Science*, ed. Lee Hardy and Lester Embree (Washington, D.C.: Center for Advanced Research in Phenomenology and University Press of America, 1990) and *The Play of Nature: Experimentation as Performance* (Bloomington: Indiana University Press, 1993).
4. These authors include: Robert Ackermann, *Data, Instruments and Theory*; Alan Franklin, *The Neglect of Experiment* (New York: Cambridge University Pres, 1986); Peter Galison, *How Experiments End* (Chicago: University of Chicago Press, 1987); David Gooding, *Experimentation and the Making of Meaning* (Cambridge: Cambridge University Press, 1990); Gooding, Trevor Pinch, and Simon Schaffer, eds., *The Uses of Experiment* (New York: Cambridge University Press, 1989); Ian Hacking, *Representing and Intervening*; Patrick A. Heelan, *Space-Perception and the Philosophy of Science* (Berkeley: University of California Press, 1983); Don Ihde, *Technics and Praxis* (Boston: Reidel, 1979); Andrew Pickering, *Constructing Quarks* (Chicago: University of Chicago Press, 1984); Joseph Rouse, *Knowledge and Power: Toward a Political Philosophy of Science* (Ithaca: Cornell University Press, 1987); Steven Shapin and Simon Schaffer, *Leviathan and the Air-Pump: Hobbes, Boyle, and The Experimental Life* (Princeton: Princeton University Press, 1985).
5. See, for instance, Peter Galison, "History and the Central/Metaphor," *Science in Context* 2 (1988).
6. Many of those who call for a "feminist" approach to science are cited in Sandra Harding, *The Science Question in Feminism* (Ithaca: Cornell University Press, 1986).
7. This point is nicely made by Joseph Rouse, in *Knowledge and Power*, p. 64. Henceforth cited as *KP*.
8. Martin Heidegger, *Discourse on Thinking*, trans. J. M. Anderson and E. H. Freund (New York: Harper and Row, 1966), p. 50.
9. Maurice Merleau-Ponty, *Phenomenology of Perception*, trans. Colin Smith (Atlantic Highlands: Humanities Press, 1962), p. ix.
10. Hans-Georg Gadamer, *Truth and Method* (New York: Seabury, 1975), p. 409. Henceforth cited as *TM*.
11. See, for instance, Patrick A. Heelan, *Space-Perception and The Philosophy of Science* (Berkeley: University of California Press, 1983), and "Experiment and Theory: Constitution and Reality," *Journal of Philosophy* 85, no. 10, pp. 515–24. Henceforth cited as *ETCR*.
12. On the concept of theatrical production, see Zev Trachtenberg, *A Theory of Drama*, M. Phil. thesis, University College, London, 1980.

13. For a discussion of the use and abuse of theater as metaphor, see Bruce Wilshire, *Role Playing and Identity: The Limits of Theatre and Metaphor* (Bloomington: Indiana University Press, 1982).
14. Thus the difference between this use of the theatrical metaphor and that of Arthur Fine, who in *The Shaky Game: Einstein, Realism, and the Quantum Theory* (Chicago: University of Chicago Press, 1986), refers to science as "a sort of grand performance, a play or opera, whose production requires interpretation and direction"; moreover, "audience and crew play as well."

CHAPTER 4   DELETION OR DEPLOYMENT: IS THAT ANY WAY TO TREAT A SIGN?

1. Edmund Husserl, *Logical Investigations*, trans. J. N. Findlay (Atlantic Highlands: Humanities Press, 1970) v.II. Cf. Investigation 1, sections 5–15 and Investigation 5, section 19.
2. Jacques Derrida, *Speech and Phenomena and Other Essays on Husserl's Theory of Signs*, trans. and intro. David B. Allison, preface Newton Garver (Evanston: Northwestern University Press, 1973). Henceforth cited as *SP*.
3. Ernst Tugendhat, *Traditional and Analytical Philosophy: Lectures on the Philosophy of Language* (Cambridge: Cambridge University Press, 1982).
4. Probably the best introductory account is to be found in G. E. Hughes and M. J. Cresswell, *An Introduction to Modal Logic* (London: Methuen, 1968).
5. Ludwig Wittgenstein, *Philosophical Investigations*, trans. Elizabeth Anscome, (Oxford: Blackwell, 1953), section 38. Henceforth cited as *PI*.
6. Cf. Newton Garver's "Preface" to *Speech and Phenomena*, which connects Derrida's incipient deconstruction with analytic philosophy.

CHAPTER 5   AUTONOMY AS FOUNDATIONAL

1. Michel Foucault, *The Order of Things*, (London: Tavistock, 1974), p. 385. Henceforth cited as *OT*.
2. Friedrich Nietzsche, *The Gay Science*, (New York: Vintage, 1975), section 125.
3. Foucault argues that the "modern" period is characterized by an impossible attempt to "think the unthought," and to ground all of our knowledge of the world upon the being who knows. "Man" is regarded as the active subject of knowledge; but paradoxically, his

very activity is then esteemed as the final *object* of all inquiry—thus ensuring the continual removal or "retreat" of the origin as thinking attempts, impossibly, to step behind itself.

4. Jacques Derrida's essay is included in *Writing and Difference*, trans. Alan Bass (Chicago: University of Chicago Press, 1978), pp. 278ff. Henceforth cited as *WD*.

5. For a thoughtful attempt to untie some of these knotty issues, however, see Kate Soper, *Humanism and Anti-Humanism* (London: Hutchinson, 1986). On the issue of "modernism" and "postmodernism" in this context, see David Hoy, "Foucault: Modern or Postmodern?" in *After Foucault*, ed. Jonathan Arac, (New Brunswick: Rutgers University Press, 1988), pp. 12ff.

6. In what follows, I have used the terms "autonomy," "sovereignty," and "self-appropriation" more or less interchangeably. Given its specific Kantian connotations, the use of "autonomy" alone might predispose us to view this whole debate in exclusively Kantian terms—something which I am anxious to avoid.

7. Of course, this requires a very long argument, especially since Foucault, among others, has discussed the various ideals of "self-cultivation" existing in the *pre*-Christian world. I would not deny that such ideals existed, but with Christianity the task becomes a universal one. If God counts every hair on our heads, then the drama of *every* individual existence becomes supremely important. Historians of autobiography—such as Karl Weintraub in *The Value of the Individual* (Chicago: University of Chicago Press, 1978); and Georges Gusdorf in "The Conditions and Limits of Autobiography," in *Autobiography: Essays Theoretical and Critical*, ed. J. Olney (Princeton: Princeton University Press, 1980)—have also shown that in classical times, self-cultivation was usually in accordance with some *impersonal* principle of reason or nature. With Christianity, however, it is the *uniqueness* of each individual which becomes the very focus of concern and the cause for celebration. I think this point holds good, even if it is also the case that for Christianity the goal of self-appropriation is used for the end of "self-denial."

8. See Hannah Arendt, *The Life of the Mind* (New York: Harcourt Brace, 1978), pp. 55–63.

9. As Weintraub remarks in *The Value of the Individual*, before 1789 the number of autobiographies is really quite limited. Since then, thousands and thousands have been written. And I think this goes along with the emphasis upon individuality as a value in itself, which characterizes the "modern" age. By the literature of "self-reliance," I mean the work of ideologues such as Samuel Smiles, Ayn Rand, Dale Carnegie, etc.

10. Such a date is more symbolic than real. But thinkers like Hegel (and

Foucault by implication) have recognized that the French revolution initiated a dramatic reorientation in thinking, in which men and women seized hold of the material forms and circumstances of their own existence, and attempted to reorder them in their own image. Thus, the rhetoric and theory of the "social contract" was used to assert the collective reason of mankind against the tyranny of arbitrary privilege and decree, while the revolutionaries also reordered the government of France, the system of weights and measures, and even the days of the week and the months of the year, so that everything might now follow the imperative of human reason. According to Kant, this age of "enlightenment" represents "man's release from his self-incurred tutelage"; for it could now be argued that prior to this time individuals had simply been the passive recipients of heteronomous values and laws.

11. Immanuel Kant, *Critique of Practical Reason*, trans. L. Beck (Indianapolis: Bobbs Merrill, 1956), p. 33. Henceforth cited as *CPR*.
12. See, for example, the famous "Hymn to Duty," where Kant speculates on the origin of the moral law: "It cannot be less than something which elevates man above himself as a part of the world of sense, something which connects him with an order of things which only the understanding can think, and which has under it the entire world of sense, including the empirically determined existence of man in time" (*CPR*, 89).
13. For example, he argues that: "Freedom itself thus becomes in this indirect way capable of an enjoyment . . . at least in origin, it is analogous to the self-sufficiency which can be ascribed only to the Supreme Being" (*CPR*, 123).
14. "Kant held that man was his own law (autonomy), i.e., bound himself under the law which he gave himself. In a deeper sense that means to say lawlessness or experimentation." *Journals* entry 1041, cited by Calvin Schrag in *Existence and Freedom*, (Evanston: Northwestern University Press, 1961).
15. In *The German Ideology*, for example, Marx argues that Marxism looks forward to bringing about an "individual" whose unalienated activity "will coincide with material life, which corresponds to the development of individuals into complete individuals." Karl Marx, *The German Ideology* (New York: International Publishers, 1947), p. 68. This is one of several passages cited by Paul Smith in his *Discerning the Subject* (Minneapolis: University of Minnesota Press, 1988). Both Smith and Soper offer thoughtful discussions of Althusser's "antihumanist" reading of Marx.
16. Freud's remark appears in "Dissection of the Psychical Personality," in *The Complete Works of Sigmund Freud*, vol. 22, ed. James Strachey (London: Hogarth Press, 1973), p. 80. In "Towards a Relational

Individualism: The Mediation of Self through Psychoanalysis," contained in the excellent collection, *Reconstructing Individualism*, ed. Thomas Heller, et al. (Stanford: Stanford University Press, 1986), Nancy Chodorow offers an interesting discussion of Freud's inherent individualism and the alternatives to it.

17. This is pointed out by D. Kellner in his essay, "Authenticity and Heidegger's Challenge to Ethical Theory," in *Thinking About Being* ed. Robert Shahan and Jitendra Mohanty (Norman: University of Oklahoma Press, 1984), pp. 159ff.

18. Martin Heidegger, "Letter on Humanism," in *Basic Writings*, ed. David Farrell Krell (New York: Harper and Row, 1977), pp. 209–10.

19. Martin Heidegger, "Overcoming Metaphysics," in *the End of Philosophy*, trans. Joan Stambaugh (New York: Harper and Row, 1973), p. 93.

20. Martin Heidegger, *Discourse on Thinking*, trans. J. Anderson and E. Freund (New York: Harper and Row, 1966), p. 85.

21. Heidegger's discussion of Nietzsche may be found in his *Nietzsche*, 4 vols., trans. David Krell, et al. (San Francisco: Harper and Row, 1982); and in "The World of Nietzsche," in *the Question Concerning Technology*, trans. W. Lovitt (New York: Harper and Row, 1977), pp. 53–112. In the latter work, for example, he writes of a univocal Will to Power in essentially negative terms: "in deliberately willing the Will to Power as the being of whatever is; and . . . in rebelliously withstanding and subjugating to itself every necessary phase of the objectifying of the world [willing as Will to Power] makes the stably constant reserve of what is for a willing of the greatest possible uniformity and equality" (102). Here, Heidegger is simply oblivious of any affirmative account of the Will to Power as a principle of individual sovereignty and difference.

22. Jacques Derrida, "Limited Inc.," in *Glyph* 2 (1977), pp. 162ff. My discussion of Derrida has benefitted from Paul Smith, *Discerning the Subject* and Peter Dews, *Logics of Disintegration* (London: Verso, 1987).

23. Jacques Derrida's "Otobiographies" appears in *The Ear of the Other*, ed. Christie McDonald (New York: Schocken Books, 1985). "Interpreting Signatures" is in *Philosophy and Literature* 10, no. 2 (1986).

24. Consider the following passage from Derrida's essay, "Shibboleth," in *Midrash and Literature*, ed. Geoffrey Hartman and Sanford Budick (New Haven: Yale, 1986), p. 314, which is also cited by Dews: "This you, which may be an I, like the *'er als ein Ich'* of a moment ago, always figures an irreplaceable singularity—one which is thus replaceable only by another irreplaceable singularity which takes its place without substituting for it." Surely there is quite a distance between such "irreplaceable singularity" and the complete dispersion of the subject and her proper name.

25. The discussion appears in *Reflexive Water*, ed. F. Elders (London: Souvenir Press, 1974), pp. 135ff.
26. See the interview with Foucault in *Technologies of the Self*, ed. Luther Martin, et al. (Amherst: University of Massachusetts Press, 1988), p. 15.
27. Michel Foucault, *Discipline and Punish*, trans. Alan Sheridan (New York: Vintage, 1979).
28. See Charles Taylor's discussion of this point in *Foucault: A Critical Reader*, ed. Jonathan Arac (Oxford: Basil Blackwell, 1986), pp. 69ff.
29. For example, see Dominique Lecourt, *Marxism and Epistemology* (London: New Left Books, 1970).
30. See for example, Foucault's comments in *Power/Knowledge*, ed. Colin Gordon (New York: Pantheon, 1980), p. 98. "The individual is not to be conceived as a sort of elementary nucleus, a primitive atom, a multiple and inert material on which power comes to fasten or against which it happens to strike, and in so doing subdues or crushes individuals. In fact it is already one of the prime effects of power that certain bodies, certain gestures, certain discourses, certain desires come to be identified and constituted as individuals."
31. See the interview with Foucault, "On the Genealogy of Ethics," included in Herbert Dreyfus and Paul Rabinow, *Michel Foucault: Beyond Structuralism and Hermeneutics*, 2d ed. (Chicago: University of Chicago Press, 1982), p. 237.
32. This idea of the subject as a fold within power is Gilles Deleuze's formulation in his book, *Foucault*, trans. Sîan Hand (Minneapolis: University of Minnesota Press, 1988), pp. 94ff.
33. This is not the place for a survey of recent feminist thinking. However, it does seem that there is at least a possibility of a creative interchange between the two "wings" of contemporary feminism. On the one hand, the (primarily Anglo-American) approach, which tends to emphasize *women's* experience, *women's* history, etc.; on the other hand, the (continental) approach, which is informed by deconstruction and psychoanalysis and remains deeply suspicious of all "essentialist" accounts of "woman." Perhaps the conjunction of these two moments could provide us with a critically renewed conception of the self. See Smith, *Discerning the Subject*; and Linda Alcoff, "Cultural Feminism Versus Post-Structuralism: The Identity Crisis in Feminist Theory," *Signs* 13, no. 3, pp. 405–36.
34. Friedrich Nietzsche, *Beyond Good and Evil*, trans. Walter Kaufmann (New York: Vintage, 1966), section 12, p. 20.
35. Friedrich Nietzsche, *On the Genealogy of Morals*, trans. Walter Kaufmann (New York: Vintage, 1969), second essay, section 2, p. 59.
36. I would like to thank Deborah Chaffin, Dennis Rohatyn and Brian Seitz for their helpful comments on an earlier version of this essay.

CHAPTER 6   INTENTIONALITY, ONTOLOGY, AND
EMPIRICAL THOUGHT

1. Maurice Merleau-Ponty, *Phenomenology of Perception*, trans. Colin Smith (Atlantic Highlands: Humanities Press and London: Routledge and Kegan Paul, 1962). Henceforth cited as *PP*.

2. Alfred J. Ayer, *Philosophy in the Twentieth Century* (New York: Random House, 1982), p. 221. Henceforth cited as *PTC*.

3. See Reiner Schürmann, *Heidegger on Being and Acting: From Principles to Anarchy* (Bloomington: Indiana University Press, 1987), who uses this term in connection with the different attitudes of Husserl and Heidegger toward the transcendental. Henceforth cited as *HBA*.

4. Maurice Merleau-Ponty, *The Visible and the Invisible*, trans. Alphonso Lingis (Evanston: Northwestern University Press, 1968), p. 115. Henceforth cited as *VI*.

5. George Lakoff and Mark Johnson, *Metaphors We Live By* (Chicago: University of Chicago Press, 1980), p. 25. Henceforth cites as *ML*.

6. See also Edmund Husserl, *Logical Investigations II*, trans. J. N. Findlay (Atlantic Highlands: Humanities Press and London: Routledge and Kegan Paul, 1970), pp. 730–34.

7. Maurice Merleau-Ponty, "The Metaphysical in Man," in *Sense and Non-Sense*, trans. Herbert and Patricia Dreyfus (Evanston: Northwestern University Press, 1964). Henceforth cited as *SNS*.

8. Donald Davidson, "Psychology as Philosophy," in *The Philosophy of Mind*, ed. J. Glover (Oxford: Oxford University Press, 1976), pp. 101–110.

9. Maurice Merleau-Ponty, *The Structure of Behaviour* (London: Methuen, 1965), pp. 148–49.

10. Michel Foucault, *The Order of Things* (London: Tavistock, 1970), p. 326.

11. Michel Foucault, *The Archaeology of Knowledge*, trans. Alan Sheridan (London: Tavistock, 1972), p. 203. Henceforth cited as *AK*.

12. Maurice Merleau-Ponty, "The Primacy of Perception and Its Philosophical Consequences," trans. James Edie, in *The Primacy of Perception and Other Essays* (Evanston: Northwestern University Press, 1964), p. 25. Henceforth cited as *PrP*.

13. Alan Chalmers, *What is This Thing Called Science?* (Milton Keynes: Open University Press, 1983), p. 25.

14. Michel Foucault, *The Use of Pleasure: The History of Sexuality*, vol. 2 (London: Penguin, 1987), pp. 7–8.

15. Michel Foucault, *Discipline and Punish*, trans. Alan Sheridan (New York: Vintage Books, 1979).

CHAPTER 7   REHABILITATING THE "I"

1. Michel Foucault, *The Order of Things*, trans. anon. (New York: Vintage Books, 1973), p. 387.

2. Karl Marx, *The German Ideology*, trans. S. Ryazanskaya, in *The Marx-Engels Reader*, ed. Robert Tucker (New York: W. W. Norton, 1978), p. 170.

3. Karl Marx, *Economic and Philosophic Manuscripts of 1844*, trans. Martin Milligan, in *The Marx-Engels Reader*, p. 98. Henceforth cited as *MER*.

4. Michel Foucault, "The Subject and Power," in Hubert Dreyfus and Paul Rabinow, *Michel Foucault: Beyond Structuralism and Hermeneutics* (Chicago: The University of Chicago Press, 1983), p. 208. Emphasis added.

5. Michel Foucault, *Discipline and Punish*, trans. Alan Sheridan (New York: Vintage Books, 1977), p. 137. Henceforth cited as *DP*.

6. Michel Foucault, "On the Genealogy of Ethics," interview with H. Dreyfus and P. Rabinow, in *Michel Foucault: Beyond Structuralism and Hermeneutics*, pp. 251–52. Henceforth cited as *GE*.

7. Stephen Toulmin, "The Inwardness of Mental Life," in *Critical Inquiry* 6 (Autumn 1979).

8. Norbert Elias, *The Court Society*, trans. Edmund Jephcott (New York, Pantheon Books, 1983), p. 253. Henceforth noted as *CS*.

9. The process by which "court rationality" and other aspects of court life made their way from elite social circles to the culture at large is a complicated one, and obviously this article is not the place to attempt to explicate it. Maurice Keane, in *Chivalry* (New Haven: Yale University Press, 1985), devotes his conclusion to a discussion of the question, and Elias offers some help in this connection as well. Mario Moussa's dissertation *The Exemplary Subjectivity of Francis Bacon* (University of Chicago, Committee on Social Thought) takes up the question in the course of analyzing the emergence of the modern interiorized self.

10. Of course it is not only Foucault and Elias who argue in this direction. Among many other sources, for example, is the especially illuminating five-volume *History of Private Life*, ed. Philip Aries and Georges Duby, the first two volumes of which have so far been translated into English by Arthur Goldhammer (Cambridge: Harvard University Press, 1987 and 1988).

11. Carolyn Merchant, *The Death of Nature* (San Francisco: Harper and Row, 1980); Brian Easlea, *Witch-Hunting, Magic and the New Philosophy* (Atlantic Highlands: Humanities Press, 1980); Evelyn Fox Keller, *Reflections on Gender and Science* (New Haven: Yale University Press, 1985); Sandra Harding, "Is Gender a Variable in Conceptions of Rationality," *Dialectica* 36, pp. 225–42; Susan Bordo, *The Flight to Objectivity* (Albany: SUNY Press, 1987).

12. Jacques Derrida, "Choreographies," an interview with Christie McDonald, in *Diacritics* 12, no. 2 (Summer 1982), p. 76.

13. Jacques Lacan, *The Four Fundamental Concepts of Psychoanalysis*, trans. Alan Sheridan, ed. Jacques-Alain Miller (New York: W. W. Norton, 1981), p. 20. Henceforth cited as *FFC*.

14. Jacques Derrida, "Structure, Sign and Play," in *Writing and Difference*, trans. Alan Bass (Chicago: University of Chicago Press, 1978), p. 280. Henceforth cited as *WD*.

15. Jacques Derrida, "Cogito and the History of Madness," in *Writing and Difference*, p. 59.

16. Some of the ideas in this section are more extensively developed in Susan Bordo, "Feminism, Postmodernism and Gender-Skepticism," in *Feminism/Postmodernism: The Politics of Method*, ed. Linda Nicholson (New York: Routledge, 1989).

17. Thomas Nagel, *The View from Nowhere* (Oxford: Oxford University Press, 1986).

18. Nancy Chodorow, *The Reproduction of Mothering* (Berkeley: University of California Press, 1978); Carol Gilligan, *In a Different Voice* (Cambridge: Harvard University Press, 1982); Dorotohy Dinnerstein, *The Mermaid and the Minotaur* (New York: Harper and Row, 1977); Hélène Cixous, "The Laugh of the Medusa," *Signs* 1 (Summer 1976), pp. 875–93, and *The Newly Born Woman* (with Catherine Clement) (Minneapolis: University of Minnesota Press, 1986); Luce Irigaray, *Speculum of the Other Woman* (Ithaca: Cornell University Press, 1985).

    A great deal of feminist scholarship in many disciplines has issued from these perspectives, and in turn a large critical literature has emerged as well. It is impossible here to review, or even to adequately cite, the development of feminist scholarship along these lines. Interested readers are referred to relevant issues of the *American Philosophical Association Newsletter on Feminism and Philosophy*, ed. Nancy Tuana (inaugural issue, and issues on "Feminism and Science," "Reason, Rationality and Gender," "Feminism and Aesthetics," "Feminism and Moral Theory," and "Feminism and the Environment") for literature reviews and bibliographies. (The articles printed in the *Newsletter on Feminism and Philosophy* have far greater interdisciplinary breadth than the title of the Newsletter suggests, covering developments in literature, social science, and physical science as well as philosophy.)

19. Such a "reconstructive" moment is found in the work of many feminists. To refer the reader to just a few sources: Nancy Hartsock, *Money, Sex and Power* (New York: Longman, 1985); Hilary Rose, "Hand, Brain and Heart: A Feminist Epistemology for the Natural Sciences," *Signs* 9, no. 1 (1983); Dorothy Smith, "A Sociology for Women," in *The Prism of Sex: Essays in the Sociology of Knowledge*, ed.

J. Sherman and E. T. Beck (Madison: University of Wisconsin Press, 1979); Sara Ruddick, "Maternal Thinking," *Feminist Studies* 6, no. 2 (1980); and the following collections: Sandra Harding and Merrill Hintikka, eds., *Discovering Reality: Feminist Perspectives on Epistemology, Metaphysics, Methodology, and Philosophy of Science* (Dordrecht: Reidel, 1983); Eva Kittay and Diana Meyers, eds., *Women and Moral Theory* (Totowa: Rowman and Littlefield, 1987); Alison Jaggar and Susan Bordo, eds., *Gender/Body/Knowledge: Feminist Reconstructions of Being and Knowing* (New Brunswick: Rutgers University Press, 1989).

20. Again, the relevant literature here is extensive. See, for example, Angela Davis, *Women, Race and Class* (New York: Random House, 1983); bell hooks, *Ain't I A Woman: Black Women and Feminism* (Boston: South End Press, 1981), and *Feminist Theory: From Margin to Center* (Boston: South End Press, 1984); Barbara Smith, ed., *Home Girls: A Black Feminist Anthology* (New York: Kitchen Table Press, 1984); Cheri Moraga and Gloria Ansaldua, eds., *This Bridge Called My Back: Writing by Radical Women* (New York: Kitchen Table Press, 1983).

21. Works which discuss issues related to the development of "postmodern" and "poststructuralist" feminism include: Linda Alcoff, "Cultural Feminism versus Post-Structuralism: The Identity Crisis in Feminist Theory," *Signs* 13, no. 3 (Spring 1988); *Feminist Studies* 14, no. 1 (issue devoted to "Feminism and Deconstruction"); Seyla Benhabib and Drucilla Cornell, eds., *Feminism as Critique* (Minneapolis: University of Minnesota Press, 1987); Irene Diamond and Lee Quinby, eds. (*Feminism and Foucault: Reflections on Resistance* (Boston: Northeastern University Press, 1988); and Linda Nicholson, ed. *Feminism/Postmodernism: The Politics of Method,* (New York: Routledge, 1989).

22. Susan Suleiman, "(Re)Writing the Body: The Politics and Poetics of Female Eroticism," in *The Female Body in Western Culture,* ed. Susan Suleiman (Cambridge: Harvard University Press, 1986), pp. 7–29.

23. Nancy Fraser and Linda J. Nicholson, "Social Criticism Without Philosophy: An Encounter Between Feminism and Postmodernism," in *Feminism/Postmodernism: The Politics of Method.*

24. One of the authors of this piece was made freshly aware of this recently, when she presented a talk discussing some consequences of the fact that the classical philosophical canon has been dominated by white, privileged males. After the talk, a member of the audience, feminist philosopher Bat-Ami Bar-On, pointed out that they have also been overwhelmingly Christian—a fact utterly overlooked by the (Jewish) speaker, and of no little significance for the ideas she

had been developing. Certainly, this "exclusion" was not the result of ethnocentric identification with the Christian world. And yet it was not entirely innocent or arbitrary either. The determinants of these "selections" are complex and ever-shifting; no theoretical formula (e.g., "attending to x, y, and z axes") can clean up our act here—only unceasing self-reflection and readiness to listen and learn.

25. Barbara Christian, "The Race for Theory," *Feminist Studies* 14, no. 1 (Spring 1988), pp. 67–79. Henceforth cited as *RT*.

26. Stephen Toulmin, "The Recovery of Practical Philosophy" in *The American Scholar* (Summer 1988), pp. 337–52.

27. Cf. Alison Lurie, "A Dictionary for Deconstructors" in *The New York Review of Books* 37 (23 November 1989), pp. 49–50.

28. Paul Smith, *Discerning the Subject* (Minneapolis: University of Minnesota Press, 1988), p. 134. Henceforth cited as *DS*.

29. See, for example, Wlad Godzich's forward to Michel de Certeau's *Discourse on the Other*, trans. Brian Massumi (Minneapolis: University of Minnesota Press, 1986), especially p. xii.

30. Friedrich Nietzsche, *The Gay Science*, trans. Walter Kaufmann (New York, Vintage Books, 1974), p. 345.

31. The bulk of this paragraph and the next are taken from Mario Moussa's "Foucault and the Problem of Agency: Or, Toward a Practical Philosophy," delivered at the annual Society for Phenomenology and Existential Philosophy Conference, 12–14 October 1989, Duquesne University, Pittsburgh.

32. Michel Foucault, "Clarifications on the Question of Power," an interview with Pasquale Pasquino, in *Foucault Live* (New York: Semiotext(e), 1989), p. 191. Henceforth cited as *FL*.

33. Michel Foucault, "Revolutionary Action: 'Until Now,' " in *Language, Counter-Memory, Practice* (Ithaca: Cornell University Press, 1977), p. 231.

34. Michel Foucault, "How Much Does It Cost for Reason to Tell the Truth?," an interview in *Foucault Live*, p. 252.

35. Michel Foucault, "L'hermeneutique du sujet" in *Résumés des cours 1970–1982* (Paris: Juillard, 1989), p. 148.

36. Michel Foucault, "The Concern for Truth," an interview with Francois Ewald, in *Foucault Live*, pp. 293–308.

37. Pierre Bourdieu, *Outline of a Theory of Practice*, trans. Richard Nice (Cambridge: Cambridge University Press, 1987), pp. 106–107.

38. Jean-François Lyotard, *The Postmodern Condition: A Report on Knowledge*, trans. Geoff Bennington and Brian Massumi (Minneapolis: University of Minnesota Press, 1985), p. 15.

39. Minnie Bruce Pratt, "Identity: Skin, Blood, Heart," in *Yours in Strug-*

gle, eds. Elly Bulkin, Minnie Bruce Pratt, and Barbara Smith (New York: Long Hall Press, 1984), p. 18. Henceforth cited as *ISBH*.

40. Friedrich Nietzsche, *Beyond Good and Evil*, trans. Walter Kaufmann (New York: Vintage Books, 1966), p. 53. Henceforth cited as *BGE*.

41. Alexander Nehamas makes this point in *Nietzsche: Life as Literature* (Cambridge: Harvard University Press, 1985). See pp. 58–59. The general drift of this entire paragraph owes much to Nehamas's reading of Nietzsche.

42. Quoted in Jean Starobinski, *Montaigne in Motion*, trans. Arthur Goldhammer (Chicago: University of Chicago Press, 1985). Starobinski's entire discussion in chapter 2, from where this passage is taken, is relevant here.

CHAPTER 8   CRITICAL EXCHANGES: THE SYMBOLIC AND QUESTIONS OF GENDER

1. Portions of this essay, which was written in 1988, were published in *Gender Trouble: Feminism and the Subversion of Identity* (New York: Routledge, 1990). Some of the views proposed here have been reformulated in subsequent publications. For my reevaluation of Lacan, see "Lacan's 'Imitation,' " in *Genders*, 8 (Winter 1990) and "The Lesbian Phallus," *Differences*, 4:1 (1992), pp. 133–171.

2. See Claude Lévi-Strauss, "The Principles of Kinship," in *The Elementary Structures of Kinship* (Boston: Beacon Press, 1969), p. 496.

3. See Jacques Derrida, "Structure, Sign, and Play," in *The Structuralist Controversy*, ed. Richard Macksey and Eugenio Donato (Baltimore: Johns Hopkins University Press, 1964); "Linguistics and Grammatology," in *Of Grammatology*, trans. Gayatri Chakravorty Spivak (Baltimore: Johns Hopkins University Press, 1974).

4. See Lévi-Strauss, *The Elementary Structures of Kinship*, p. 480: "Exchange—and consequently the rule of exogamy which expresses it—has in itself a social value. It provides the means of binding men together."

5. One might consider the literary analysis of Eve Sedgwick's *Between Men* (New York: Columbia University Press, 1985) in light of Lévi-Strauss's description of the structures of reciprocity within kinship. Sedgwick effectively argues that the flattering attentions paid to women in romantic poetry are both a deflection and elaboration of male homosocial desire. Women are "objects of exchange" in the sense that they mediate the relationship of unacknowledged desire between men through becoming an ostensible object of discourse.

6. See José Guilherme Merquior, *From Prague to Paris: A Critique of*

Structuralist and Poststructuralist Thought (London: Verso, 1986), pp. 12–13.

7. For a feminist account of how historical work can uncover the modes of meaning-constitution within a given historical-discursive field, see Joan W. Scott, *Gender and the Politics of History* (New York: Columbia University Press, 1988), especially chapters I–II.

8. See Julia Kristeva, *Desire in Language*, ed. Leon Roudiez (New York: Columbia University Press, 1980). For impressive commentaries on Kristeva's efforts to displace the symbolic, see Andrea Nye, "Woman Clothed with the Sun: Julia Kristeva and the Escape from/ to Language," *Signs* 12, no. 4 (1987), pp. 664–86; and Iris Marion Young, "Impartiality and the Civic Public: Some Implications of Feminist Critiques of Moral and Political Theory," in *Feminism and Critique*, ed. Seyla Benhabib and Drucilla Cornell (Minneapolis: University of Minnesota Press and Oxford: Basil Blackwell, 1987), pp. 56–76.

9. Of course, Lévi-Strauss himself suggested the parallel between structural anthropology and psychoanalysis at the close of *The Elementary Structures of Kinship*.

10. A similar reading of the unconscious as a destabilizing force of resistance is to be found in Leo Bersani, *The Freudian Body* (New York: Columbia University Press, 1986).

11. Kristeva, *Desire in Language*, p. 136. Henceforth cited as *DL*.

12. For a fuller discussion of the limits of the semiotic's subversive potential in Kristeva's work, see my "The Body Politics of Julia Kristeva," special issue on French Feminism, *Hypatia* (December 1988).

13. For a lucid analysis of the political and philosophical consequences of Kristeva's distinction between the symbolic and the semiotic, see Iris Young, "Impartiality and the Civic Public."

14. Frederick Engels, *The Origins of the Family, Private Property and the State*, ed. Evelyn Reed (New York: Pathfinder Press, 1972), pp. 71–72.

15. Gayle Rubin, "The Traffic in Women: Notes Toward a "Political Economy of Sex," in *Toward an Anthropology of Women*, ed. Rayne R. Reiter (New York: Monthly Review Press, 1975), pp. 157–210. Henceforth cited as *TAW*.

16. Luce Irigaray, "When the Goods Get Together," in *New French Feminisms*, ed. Elaine Marks and Isabel de Courtivron (New York: Schocken, 1978), pp. 107–110 (originally published as "Des marchandises entre elles," in *Ce sexe qui n'en est pas un* (Paris: Minuit, 1977). Henceforth cited as *NFF*.

17. Michel Foucault, *The History of Sexuality*, Volume 1, trans. Robert Hurley (New York: Vintage, 1980), p. 101.

18. It is difficult to resist the allusion to Kafka's parable, "Before the Law" and Derrida's skillful deconstruction of the spatial and temporal meanings of the "before." If the law is performative, as Derrida suggests, then it creates the "before" retroactively, as it were. Although Derrida's engagement with Kafka does not address the psychoanalytic postulation of an infantile pleasure "before the law," his reading nevertheless suggests a skeptical stance toward the status of such a state. See Derrida's essay, "Kafka's Before the Law," in *Kafka and the Contemporary Critical Performance*, ed. Alan Udoff (Bloomington: Indiana University Press, 1987).

19. See Gayle Rubin, "Thinking Sex: Notes for a Radical Theory of the Politics of Sexuality," in *Pleasure and Danger: Exploring Female Sexuality*, ed. Carole Vance (Boston: Routledge and Kegan Paul, 1984), pp. 267–319.

CHAPTER 9   FOUNDATIONS AND CULTURAL STUDIES

1. A shorter version of this essay is included in *Literary Theory Today*, ed. Peter Collier and Helga Geyer-Ryan (Cambridge: Polity Press, 1990), pp. 219–44.

2. I have discussed this at greater length in "Derrida/Foucault," forthcoming in a collection edited by Thomas Wartenberg (Albany: SUNY Press).

3. In "Representing the Colonized: Anthropology's Interlocutors," Edward Said is quite correct in reminding us that "We should first take scrupulous note of how . . . the United States has replaced the great earlier empires as *the* dominant outside force." *Critical Inquiry* 15 (Winter 1989), p. 215. It seems to me that the displacements entailed by this shift in conjuncture must also be kept in mind. The "West," in other words, is also not a founded monolith, however desperately it might want to establish this claim.

4. See Carl Pletsch, "The Three Worlds, or the Division of Social Scientific Labor, circa 1950–1975," *Comparative Studies in Society and History* 23, no. 4 (October 1981) pp. 565–90.

5. Folker Froebel, et al., *The New International Division of Labor: Structural Unemployment in Industrialized Countries and Industrialization in Developing Countries*, trans. Peter Burgess (Cambridge: Cambridge University Press, 1980); Nigel Harris, *The End of the Third World: Newly Industrializing Countries and the Decline of an Ideology* (London: Penguin, 1986).

6. Michel Foucault, *Language, Counter-Memory, Practice: Selected Essays and Interviews*, trans. Donald F. Bouchard and Sherry Simon (Ithaca: Cornell University Press, 1977), p. 145. Henceforth cited as *LCP*.

7. It is incorrect to say that "Aryanism" was simply a "European High

Tory search for original homelands." "Aryanism" is a strong tendency in the Hindu sector of the violent and divisive religious communalism which is part of the Indian sociocultural formation today. Radical historians of ancient India such as Romila Thapar are most scrupulous in the avoidance of this element in their estimation of the historian's role in forging "national identity." I will cite here a text immediately involved in these political realities, where we can appreciate how a group of historians by no means nonfoundationalist in their disciplinary approach are obliged by situational exigency to become practical nonfoundationalists: Sarvapalli Gopal, et al., *The Political Abuse of History: Babri Masjid-Rama Janmabhumi Dispute* (New Delhi: Centre for Historical Studies, JNU, 1989). I have pointed at a similar gesture on the part of Maxine Rodinson in *Islam and Capitalism,* in my "Constitutions and Culture Studies," *Yale Journal of Law and the Humanities* (forthcoming). See also Jean-François Lyotard, "Notes on Legitimation," in *The Public Realm: Essays on Discursive Types in Political Philosophy,* ed. Reiner Schürmann (Albany: SUNY Press, 1989). In fact, every identification of Indian ethnicity with the Brahminical tradition, pervasively practiced in mainstream Indology and its cultural offshoots, is contaminated by Aryanism.

8. Edward Said, *Orientalism* (New York: Pantheon Books, 1978).
9. For a more detailed consideration of the attendant pedagogical situation, see Spivak, "The Making of Americans, the Teaching of English, and the Future of Culture Studies," *New Literary History* (forthcoming). For a brief checklist of required reading, see Chinua Achebe, "Colonialist Criticism," in *Morning Yet on Creation Day: Essays* (Garden City: Anchor Press, 1975); Ngugi Wa Th'iongo, *Writers in Politics* (London: Heinemann, 1981); Ashis Nandy, *The Intimate Enemy: Loss and Recovery of Self Under Colonialism* (New York: Oxford University Press, 1983); Ranajit Guha and Gayatri Spivak, eds., *Selected Subaltern Studies* (New York: Oxford University Press, 1988); Stuart Hall and James Donald, *Politics and Ideology* (London: Open University Press, 1985); Hazel Carby, *Reconstructing Womanhood: The Emergence of Afro-American Women Novelists* (New York: Oxford University Press, 1987); Sneja Gunew (with Uyen Loewald), "The Mother Tongue and Migration," *Australian Feminist Studies* 1 (Summer, 1985); Trinh-Ti-Minh-Ha and Jean-Paul Bourdier, *African Spaces: Designs for Living in Upper Volta* (London: Holmes and Meier, 1985); Paulin J. Hountondji, *African Philosophy: Myth and Reality,* trans. Henri Evans (Bloomington: Indiana University Press, 1983); Henry Louis Gates, Jr., *Figures in Black: Words, Signs and the "Racial" Self* (New York: Oxford University Press, 1986); Lata Mani, "Contentious Traditions: The Debate on Sati in Colonial India," *Cultural*

Critique (Fall, 1987); Mick Taussig, *Shamanism, Colonialism and the Wild Man: A Study in Terror and Healing* (Chicago: University of Chicago Press, 1987); Mary Louise Pratt, "Scratches on the Face of the Country; or What Mr. Barrow Saw in the Land of the Bushmen," *Critical Inquiry* 12 (Autumn 1985). Of the numerous journals appearing in the field, one might name *Cultural Critique, New Formations, Criticism/Heresy/Interpretation,* and *Third Text.*

10. For a superb analysis of this phantasm in the context of the United States, see Barbara Herrnstein Smith, "Cult-Lit: Hirsch, Literacy, and 'The National Culture,' " *South Atlantic Quarterly* (Winter 1990).

11. Foucault, *The History of Sexuality,* vol. 1, trans. Robert Hurley (New York: Vintage Books, 1980), pp. 99–100. Henceforth cited as *HS.*

12. The Freudian term *Beziehung,* translated "cathexis" in the Standard Edition, is translated as *investissement* (literally "investment") in French. The Freudian term means, roughly, "to occupy with desire." Since Foucault did not use Freudian terms in their strict sense, "cathecting" or "occupying with desire" might be inadvisable here. On the other hand "invest" has too restricted a sense in English and the psychoanalytic usage is never far below the surface in poststructuralist French writers. I decided on the somewhat odd "switch it on."

13. For interesting speculations on "moral luck," see Bernard Williams, *Moral Luck: Philosophical Papers, 1973–1980* (Cambridge: Cambridge University Press, 1981), pp. 20–39. But moral luck is an after-the-fact assignment. "The justification, if there is to be one, will be essentially retrospective" (ibid., 24). The impossible and intimate "no" might thus involve our considering the historical production of our cultural exchangeability. Why does it involve the long haul toward a future? I attempt to answer this in the text. (I am also aware that the delicacy of Williams's concern with the individual moral agent is travestied when transferred to something like "the culture of imperialism." It would be interesting to "apply" Williams's brilliantly inconclusive speculations to individual imperialist reformists.)

14. This argument is laid out in greater detail in Spivak, "Theory in the Margins: Coetzee's *Foe* Reading Defoe's *Crusoe/Roxana,*" in a collection edited by Jonathan Arac (forthcoming).

15. For a discussion of the metaphors of electricity in Foucault's descriptions of the force-field subtending power/knowledge, see Spivak, "Derrida/Foucault."

16. Pierre Bourdieu, "The Philosophical Institution," in *Philosophy in France Today,* ed. Alan Montefiore (Cambridge: Cambridge University Press, 1983), p. 1.

17. The *OED* defines "catachresis" as "abuse or perversion of a trope

or metaphor." We appropriate this term to indicate the originary "abuse" constitutive of language-production, where both concept and metaphor are "wrested from their proper meaning" (*OED*: "catachrestical"). Thus, in the narrow sense, a word for which there is no *adequate* referent to be found. See also Derrida, *Glas*, trans. John P. Leavey, Jr., and Richard Rand (Lincoln: University of Nebraska Press, 1986), p. 2b(i).

18. Whenever someone attempts to put together a "theory of practice" where the intending subject as absolute ground is put into question, catachrestical master-words become necessary, because language can never fully bypass the presupposition of such a ground. The particular word is, in such a case, the best that will serve, but also, and necessarily, a misfit. (There can, of course, be no doubt that the Marxian theory of ideology put into question the intending subject as absolute ground.) The choice of these master-words brings along the history of their meanings (paleonymy). Thus "value" (as "writing" in Derrida or "power" in Foucault) must necessarily also mean its "ordinary language" meanings: material worth as well as idealist values. The name "value" thus creates the productive confusion that can, alone, give rise to practice. It must be said, however, that these master-words are misfits only if the ordinary use of language is presupposed to have fully fitting cases. Thus "to fit" is itself a catachresis and points to a general theory of language as catachrestical that must be actively marginalized in all its uses. For a development of the idea of "active marginalization," see Spivak, "Versions of the Margin."

19. Karl Marx, *Capital: A Critique of Political Economy*, vol. 1, trans. Ben Fowkes (New York: Vintage Books, 1977), p. 90. Henceforth cited as *Cap*.

20. Karl Marx, *Selected Correspondence* (Moscow: Progress Publishers, 1975), p. 228.

21. Williams uses "currency" in this sense in *Moral Luck*, p. 35. Yet because he can only see value-coding as singular and rational, rather than heterogeneous and coherent, he dismisses it as impossible in the moral sphere, and indeed is skeptical about the possibility of a moral philosophy on related grounds. I am in basic sympathy with his position, though I cannot accept his presuppositions and conclusions about "currency." Here perhaps attending to the metaphoricity of a concept would help. See Jacques Derrida, "White Mythology: Metaphor in the Text of Philosophy," in *Margins of Philosophy*, trans. Alan Bass (Chicago: University of Chicago Press, 1982), pp. 207–71.

22. I have discussed this in "Scattered Speculations on the Question of

Value," in Spivak, *In Other Worlds: Essays in Cultural Politics* (New York: Methuen, 1987).

23. Gayle Rubin, "The Traffic in Women: Notes on the 'Political Economy' of Sex," in *Toward an Anthropology of Women*, ed. Rayna R. Reiter (New York: Monthly Review Press, 1975), pp. 157–210.

24. See, for example, Kalpana Bardhan, "Women: Work, Welfare and Status. Forces of Tradition and Change in India," *South Asia Bulletin* 6, no. 1 (Spring 1986). Because of the heavy weight of positivist empiricism in her discipline (development economics), she has to be read somewhat against the grain.

25. Tim Mitchell, "The World as Exhibition," *Comparative Studies in Society and History* 31, no. 2 (April 1989).

26. Jean-François Lyotard, *The Postmodern Condition: A Report on Knowledge*, trans. Geoff Bennington and Brian Massumi (Minneapolis: University of Minnesota Press, 1984).

27. Jacques Derrida, "Signature Event Context," in *Glyph–1*, trans. Samuel Weber and Jeffrey Mehlman (Baltimore: Johns Hopkins University Press, 1977), p. 194.

28. For an extraordinary staging of this pervasiveness and ubiquity, and indeed a reinscription of "India" from that perspective, see Mahasweta Devi, "Douloti the Bountiful," in *Imaginary Maps*, trans. Gayatri Spivak (New York: Routledge; Calcutta: Thema, both forthcoming).

29. *The Bhagavadgita in the Mahabharata*, trans. Johannes Adrianus Bernardus van Buitenen (Chicago: University of Chicago Press, 1981), p. 87.

30. Karl Marx, "Economic and Philosophical Manuscripts," in *Early Writings*, trans. Rodney Livingstone and Gregor Benton (Harmondsworth: Penguin, 1975), p. 20.

31. Antonio Gramsci, "The Study of Philosophy," in *Selections from the Prison Notebooks*, trans. Quintin Hoare and Geoffrey Nowell Smith (New York: International Publishers, 1971), p. 324.

32. I take this distinction from Foucault, *The Archeology of Knowledge*, trans. A. M. Sheridan Smith (New York: Pantheon Books, 1972), pp. 88–105.

33. The *OED* defines *parabasis* as "going aside," "address to the audience in the poet's name, unconnected with the action of the drama." We appropriate this as a transaction between postcolonial subject-positions, persistently going aside from typical allegorical continuity.

34. For a treatment of the Armenian case from the point of view of catachrestical claims to nationhood, see Anahid Kassabian and David Kazanjian, "Theorizing Armenian Genocide," *New Formations*

(forthcoming); Boris Kagarlitsky, *The Thinking Reed: Intellectuals and the Soviet State: 1917 to the Present*, trans. Brian Pearce (London: Verso, 1988), fast becoming *the* text on the new USSR, does not yet take into account the breaking open of the available value-coding of ethnicity and nationalism. I have written elsewhere, at greater length, of the problems of cultural representation of central and eastern Europe and central and western Asia. See Spivak "Cultural and Political Power of Cinematic Language," paper delivered at conference on "Problems of Cultural Representation in Global Cinema" (Boston Film/Video Institute, 26–30 April 1990); also see "Constitutions and Culture Studies," *Yale Journal of Law and the Humanities* (forthcoming).

35. This seems particularly apposite when, in the wake of the reterritorializations and recodings of central and eastern Europe, "Europe" itself can once again legitimize itself as a project: "Europe is an idea in the making, the product of an uncompleted history. It must be built. The efforts of political, economic and social leaders must be complemented by the creative thinking of intellectuals. Europe has been predicted by history, but history does not dictate a pre-established destiny for it. History should help to realize it, clarifying the decisions needed to accomplish the work." Jacques Le Goff, speaking as editor of a new series, Making Europe, cited in "Liber 2, p. 6," *Times Literary Supplement*, 15–21 December 1989.

36. Umberto Melotti unwittingly exposes this in *Marx and the Third World*, trans. Pat Ransford (London: Macmillan, 1977), pp. 28–29.

37. For "truth" as one case of a general iterability, see Derrida, *Limited Inc. a b c . . .* trans Samuel Weber (Baltimore: Johns Hopkins Press, 1977).

38. Jacques Derrida, *Of Grammatology*, trans. Gayatri Spivak (Baltimore: Johns Hopkins University Press, 1976), p. 46. Henceforth cited as *OG*.

39. I am naturalizing Derrida's general description. Derrida's next sentence makes clear that this concern is more subindividual than the level of language-acquisition.

40. Marcel Proust, *Cities of the Plains*, trans. C. K. Scott Moncrieff, (New York: Vintage Books, 1970), p. 99. Professor Jessie Hornsby's extraordinary knowledge of Proust helped me locate a merely remembered passage.

41. Star: "This *Ursprache* as German scholars termed it . . . which we might term Proto-Indo-European . . . could be reconstructed. . . . The asterisk being used by convention to indicate reconstructed parent words which were not directed attested by any language known. . . ." Colin Renfrew, *Archeology and Language: the Puzzle of Indo-European Origins* (New York, Cambridge University Press,

1988), p. 14. Caught between two translations: "Indeed it was not until 1947 that a good bilingual inscription was found at the site of Karatepe, written in Phoenician (a well-known Semitic language) as well as in hieroglyphic Hittite, so that real progress could be made with it" (ibid., 51). Japhetic: "the story in the book of Genesis of the three sons of Noah, Ham, Shem and Japheth were taken as perfectly acceptable explanation of the divergence of early languages. The languages of Africa were thus termed Hamitic, those of the Levant Semitic, and those to the land of the north Japhetic" (ibid., 13). Since "Semitic" is still in use, I am using "Japhetic" within the allegorical frame of the authority still given to the Biblical myth in certain situations of global politics. See Volosinov's underscoring of a differentiated origin for "Japhetic languages" in his discussion of N. Ja Marr in *Marxism and the Philosophy of Language,* trans. Ladislav Matejka and I. R. Titunik (New York: Seminar Press, 1973), pp. 72, 76, 101.

42. Frederick Engels, *The Origin of the Family, Private Property, and the State,* ed. Evelyn Reed (New York: Pathfinder Press, 1972). Henceforth cited as *OF.* Gayle Rubin's sympathetic critique of Engels in "Traffic" (cited above) is exemplary.

43. This is in striking contrast to the story's "source," Samaresh Basu's "Uratiya," a poignant semi-phantastic staging of patriarchal conflict. Another case of the narrativization of an alternative history that will not allow the verification of a possible world by the actual world is brilliantly telescoped in the tribal half-caste woman's utterance in Mahasweta Devi's "The Hunt": "If my mother had killed her white daughter at birth . . . I would not have been." "The Hunt," forthcoming in *Women in Performance.*

44. For my statement of the argument, see Spivak, *In Other Worlds,* pp. 241–47; for a dismissal where concept and rhetoric are resolutely identified with the disciplines of "Philosophy" and "Literary Criticism (Aesthetics)," see Jürgen Habermas, *The Philosophical Discourse of Modernity,* trans. Fredrick Lawrence (Cambridge: MIT Press, 1987), pp. 161–210.

45. For a taxonomy of possible diversity here, see for example the articles in *Cultural Critique* 6 and 7 (Spring and Fall 1987).

46. For a detailed study of Marx and Foucault, see Barry Smart, *Foucault, Marxism and Critique* (London: Routledge, 1983).

CHAPTER 10 *GRUND* AND *ABGRUND*: QUESTIONING POETIC FOUNDATIONS IN HEIDEGGER AND CELAN

1. Martin Heidegger, "The Origin of the Work of Art," in *Poetry, Language, Thought,* trans. Albert Hofstadter (New York: Harper and Row, 1971), p. 89. Henceforth cited as *OWA.*

2. The word for "destiny" which Heidegger uses in the German text is *Geschick*. Destiny as a preordained or teleological development is not implied in the term. Rather, *Geschick* hovers between contingency and necessity—it is "sent," but its sending is not "from without." Rather, the sending arises out of the very grounding of the historical epoch within its own occurrence. Such a destiny sketches out the possibilities of a given epoch and so precedes the individual's taking up with those possibilities as his or her own. See Martin Heidegger, *Being and Time*, trans. John Macquarrie and Edward Robinson (New York: Harper and Row, 1962), p. 436.

3. Otto Pöggeler, *Martin Heidegger's Path of Thinking*, trans. Daniel Magurshak and Sigmund Barber (Atlantic Highlands: Humanities Press, 1987), p. 171. Henceforth cited as *HPT*.

4. See Martin Heidegger, *Wegmarken* (Frankfurt: Klostermann, 1978). Henceforth cited as *WG*.

5. Even though Zionism has reclaimed a homeland for the Jews, the temple precinct remains in the hands of devout Moslems, who have built the Temple of the Rock over that area where the original temple is said to have stood. Celan addresses the displacement of the Jewish temple in his poem "Die Pole" in *Zeitgehöft*.

6. Alan Mintz, *Hubran: Responses to Catastrophe in Hebrew Literature* (New York: Columbia University Press, 1984), p. 50.

7. See Alan Udoff, "On Poetic Dwelling: Situating Celan and the Holocaust," in *Argumentum e Silentio*, ed. Amy Colin (Berlin: Walter de Gruyter, 1987), pp. 345–46.

8. See the text to Claude Lanzmann's film, *Shoah: An Oral History of the Holocaust* (New York: Pantheon Books, 1985), p. 13:

> When we first opened the graves we couldn't help it, we all burst out sobbing. But the Germans almost beat us to death. We had to work at a killing pace for two days, beaten all the time and with no tools. The Germans even forbade us to use the words "corpse" or "victim." The dead were blocks of wood, shit, with absolutely no importance. Anyone who said "corpse" or "victim" was beaten. The Germans made us refer to the bodies as *Figuren*, that is as puppets, as dolls, or as *Schmattes*, which means "rags." . . . The head of the Vilna Gestapo told us: "There are ninety thousand people lying there, and absolutely no trace must be left of them" (the witness of Motke Zaïdl and Itzhak Dugin).

9. "Radix, Matrix" by Paul Celan from *Poems of Paul Celan* translated by Michael Hamburger, copyright © 1972, 1980, 1988 by Michael

Hamburger, reprinted by permission of Persea Books, Inc. 1988 edition, pp. 186–189.

10. *"Aber-du"* is difficult to translate. In French translations it has been rendered *"non-toi,"* "not you," but Hamburger chose to translate the expression as "multi-you," a choice which reflects the German expression *"abertausend,"* "thousands and thousands." *"Aber"* can also indicate an intensification of whatever it modifies.

11. See Paul Celan, *Poems of Paul Celan* (1988), pp. 174–75.

12. See Hofstadter's footnote, OWA, p. 85.

13. See Martin Heidegger, *Introduction to Metaphysics* (New York: Doubleday, 1959), p. 6.

14. See Martin Heidegger, "A Dialogue on Language," in *On the Way to Language*, trans. Peter Hertz (San Francisco: Harper and Row, 1971), pp. 35–136:

> I: To experience in this sense always means to refer back—to refer life and lived experience back to the "I." Experience is the name for the referral of the objective back to the subject. The much-discussed I/Thou experience, too belongs within the metaphysical sphere of subjectivity.

> J: And this sphere of subjectivity and of the expression that belongs to it is what you left behind when you entered into the hermeneutic relation to the two-fold.

This passage argues the poverty of I/You discourse by pointing out it is still rooted in an egology, in which what is experienced is necessarily referred "back to the 'I,' " The use of "experience" to characterize the relationship of I and Thou is already a blaring misinterpretation of Buber's own analysis in which You *as* You can never be "experienced" by the I. The Buberian vocative necessarily does not "refer back" to an ego, an 'I,' as if this 'I' could somehow comprehend or enfold the 'You.' Likewise, in Celanian address, nothing of the other returns to the I. The I is caught in a hesitation, within which the I's *loss* of the other, the You to be addressed, is all that can be given. The You does not return as an "object" of experience to the I, but as an other whose power to address cannot be experienced and must be addressed in turn. The You, as the other, ruptures the contained self and ruptures as well all attempts of that self to let the other appear within the world.

For another view of the Celanian vocative as a metaphysical category see Emmanuel Levinas, "De l'être à l'autre," in *Noms Propres* (Paris: Fata Morgana, 1976), p. 61 (translation mine):

The poem goes toward the other. It hopes to rejoin the liberated and vacant other. . . . The poem "becomes dialogue, it is often a lost dialogue . . . meetings, path of a voice toward a vigilant you"—the categories of Buber! Might these be preferable to so much brilliant exegesis descending upon Hölderlin, Trakl and Rilke from the mysterious *Schwarzwald* in order to show poetry opening up the world, and the place between earth and sky? . . . Buber is preferable, without any doubt. The personal will be the poetry of the poem: "the poem speaks! Of the date which is its own . . . of the unique circumstance which properly concerns it."

15. "Only God Can Save Us: *Der Spiegel's* Interview with Martin Heidegger," trans. Maria Alter and John Caputo, in *Philosophy Today* (Winter, 1976), p. 277: "Only a God can save us. The sole possibility that is left for us is to prepare a sort of readiness, through thinking and poetizing, for the appearance of the god or for the absence of the god in the time of foundering [*Untergang*]; for in the face of the god who is absent we founder."

Heidegger's emphasis upon the preparatory nature of thinking, leads him to emphasize with increasing vigor the need for *Gelassenheit*, for an active waiting upon the healing nature of Being, of yet another dispensation of its excess into history. But in the words of Otto Pöggeler (in regard to Celan's poem *Todtnauberg*, which records Celan's visit with Heidegger in 1967):

> Celan had not forgotten that Heidegger balked at all hasty attempts for a solution, that he would withdraw with his only preparatory thinking before he to whom one day the saving word falls. But Celan urges and admonishes: we must bring our affairs into order within the limited time of our lives; so runs a variant reading of that word that comes delayed. (Otto Pöggeler, *Spur des Wortes* [Freiburg: Karl Alber, 1986], 265)

16. In the later Heidegger, where *Grund* is now thought of as *Ereignis*, one speaks of a "difference" across which one gives one's "response, as receptive listening." Such response "is attuned to this restraint that reserves itself." Martin Heidegger, "Language," in *Poetry, Language, Thought.* Henceforth cited as *L*. In such a thought, Heidegger is, in a certain manner, not so distant from Celan's silence in the wake of the murder of the other and the experience of a loss beyond restitution that such a death brings with it. Heidegger speaks of a "pain" within the *dif–ference* between that which speaks and that

which listens. Could not such a pain be thought as Celanian loss? But precisely the "rift" of the *dif–ference*, as that in which the pain is articulated, "makes the limpid brightness shine" (*L*, 205). For Heidegger, the listening across a *dif–ference* is the listening to the "command" of the *dif–ference*, a command which "expropriates world and things into the simple onefold of their intimacy" (*L*, 210).

Again, a certain saving excess has entered through the *dif–ference* in Heidegger's thinking, one which again is anonymously articulated, this time in the sentence "Language speaks." Would Celan find it true that "man speaks only as he responds to language"? For Celan, poetic speaking must "move itself toward something," namely, "toward a You able to be addressed" (Paul Celan, *Gesammelte Werke*, vol. 3, p. 186). Only such a *particular* You, whose particularity always brings with it an "otherness" (*Anderssein*) and a vulnerability to violence, can serve as the destination for Celanian address. The particularity of the Other, rather than the Being of beings, serves as the opening of difference across which address would occur.

17. "*Emeth*," a word from ancient Hebrew, is often translated as truth and appears in Celan's poems as "*das Offene*." But this rendering of "truth" ought not be confused with Heidegger's Greek notion of aletheic truth which emphasizes the "showing-forth," the appearing of beings. *Emeth* is best characterized by loyalty, *Treue*, in which the commitment of one person to another establishes a covenant as its "truth." *Emeth* is ethical rather than ontological in its root meaning; it calls persons into conversation rather than beings into their "showing-forth." Interestingly, when the "*E*" is dropped from the word, the remaining syllable, *Meth* signifies death. Thus, buried within truth is the death which gives truth its force, as well as its fragility. These observations come from a discussion with Otto Pöggeler, held on 26 February 1988.

18. Paul Celan, *Der Meridian*, in David Brierly, "*Der Meridian*": *Ein Versuch zur Poetik und Dichtung Paul Celans* (Frankfurt: Peter Lang, 1984), p. 31.

CHAPTER 11   GENEROSITY AND FORGETTING IN THE HISTORY OF BEING

1. Maurice Merleau-Ponty, *In Praise of Philosophy*, trans. John Wild and James M. Edie (Evanston: Northwestern University Press, 1963), pp. 26–27. Henceforth cited as IPP. Translation of *Eloge de la philosophie* (Paris: Gallimard, 1953), p. 33. Henceforth cited as *EP*. References to passages from Merleau-Ponty's writings will be given in the text

with the reference to the English translation first, then the original French.

2. Paul Claudel, *Art Poétique*, in *Oeuvre Poétique* (Paris: Gallimard, 1957), p. 145. The passage is invoked by Maurice Merleau-Ponty in *The Visible and the Invisible*, trans. Alphonso Lingis (Evanston: Northwestern University Press, 1968), p. 179. Henceforth cited as VI. Translation of *Le Visible et l'invisible* (Paris: Gallimard, 1964), p. 233. Henceforth cited as *VI*.

3. Maurice Merleau-Ponty, *Signs*, trans. Richard C. McCleary (Evanston: Northwestern University Press, 1964), p. 21. Henceforth cited as S. Translation of *Signes* (Paris: Gallimard, 1960), p. 30. Henceforth cited as *S*.

4. Maurice Merleau-Ponty, *The Primacy of Perception and Other Essays*, trans. James Edie (Evanston: Northwestern University Press, 1964), p. 187. Henceforth cited as PriP. "Eye and Mind," translated from *L'Oeil et l'esprit* (Paris: Gallimard, 1964), p. 84. Henceforth cited as *OE*.

5. Maurice Merleau-Ponty, *Phenomenology of Perception*, trans. Colin Smith (London: Routledge and Kegan Paul, 1962), p. 398. Henceforth cited as PhP. Translation of *Phénoménologie de la perception* (Paris: Gallimard, 1945), p. 456. Henceforth cited as *PP*.

6. Cf. Henri Birault, *Heidegger et l'expérience de la pensée* (Paris: Gallimard, 1978), p. 533.

7. Jean-Paul Sartre, *Being and Nothingness*, trans. Hazel E. Barnes (New York: Simon and Schuster, 1956), p. 246. Henceforth cited as BN.

8. Merleau-Ponty discusses the meaning of *ecstasis* in relation to Heidegger's account of historical time. In *Phenomenology of Perception*, he writes:

If time is an *ek-stase*, if present and past are two results of this *ek-stase*, how could we ever cease completely to see time from the point of view of the present. . . . It is always in the present that we are centred. . . . There can therefore be no question of deriving time from spontaneity. We are not temporal beings *because* we are spontaneous and because, as consciousness, we tear ourselves away from ourselves. On the contrary, time is the foundation and measure of our spontaneity. (*PhP*, 427–28; *PP*, 489)

9. Cf. David Wood, "Nietzsche's Transvaluation of Time," in *Exceedingly Nietzsche: Aspects of Contemporary Nietzsche Interpretation*. eds. David Farrell Krell and David Wood (New York: Routledge, 1988), p. 42.

10. For extended elaboration of temporal sedimentation within bodily action and inhabited places, cf. my *Earth and Sky, History and Philoso-*

phy: Island Images Inspired by Husserl and Merleau-Ponty (New York: Peter Lang Publishing, 1989), chapter 2.

11. Cézanne's search for the "world's instant" is also cited by Merleau-Ponty in "Cézanne's Doubt," in *Sense and Non-Sense*, trans. Hubert L. Dreyfus (Evanston: Northwestern University Press, 1964), p. 17. Translation of *Sens et non-sens* (Paris: Editions Nagel, 1948; 4th ed. 1963), p. 29.

12. Maurice Merleau-Ponty, "Christianity and Ressentiment," trans. Gerald Wening, in *Texts and Dialogues*, eds. Hugh J. Silverman and James Barry, Jr. (Atlantic Highlands: Humanities Press, 1992), pp. 85–100. Merleau-Ponty's original essay was published as "Christianisme et ressentiment," in *La Vie Intellectuale*, 7 année, nouvelle serie, 1935, Tome 36, pp. 278–308. Cf. p. 278.

13. Friedrich Nietzsche, *Thus Spoke Zarathustra*, trans. Walter Kaufmann, in *The Portable Nietzsche* (New York: Viking Press, 1968), part 1, section 9, p. 214.

14. Nietzsche, *Zarathrustra*, part 2, section 7, pp. 211, 214. Also cf. Friedrich Nietzsche, *The Geneology of Morals*, trans. Francis Golffing (New York: Doubleday, 1956), p. 172.

15. Friedrich Nietzsche, *The Use and Abuse of History*, trans. Adrian Collins (Indianapolis: Bobbs-Merrill Company, 1949), p. 6.

16. Gilles Deleuze, *Nietzsche and Philosophy*, trans. Hugh Tomlinson (New York: Columbia University Press, 1983), p. 113.

17. Jacques Derrida, *Spurs: Nietzsche's Styles*, trans. Barbara Harlow (Chicago: University of Chicago Press, 1979), pp. 141–43.

18. Jacques Derrida, *Edmund Husserl's "Origin of Geometry": An Introduction*, trans. John P. Leavey, Jr. (Stony Brook: Nicolas Hays, and Lincoln: University of Nebraska Press, 1978), p. 93. (The French text may be found in Derrida, *Edmund Husserl, L'origine de la géometrie": Traduction et introduction* [Paris: Presses Universitaires de France, Epiméthée, 1974], p. 91.) The "Origin of Geometry" was edited and published by Eugen Fink in *Revue internationale de philosophie* 1, no. 2 (1939) under the title "Der Ursprung der Geometrie als intentionalhistorisches Problem." It appears as Appendix 6 in Edmund Husserl, *The Crisis of European Sciences and Transcendental Phenomenology: An Introduction to Phenomenological Philosophy*, trans. David Carr (Evanston: Northwestern University Press, 1970).

19. As Jacques Derrida has pointed out, "forgetfulness" is a word that Husserl rarely employs in the *Crisis*, and never used at all in the first text of "The Origin of Geometry," no doubt due to the possible suggestion that sense (*Sinn*) can be annihilated. Cf. Jacques Derrida, *Edmund Husserl's "Origin of Geometry:" An Introduction*, p. 93, note 99 (French: p. 92, note 3). Without some idea of forgetfulness,

however, there is no explanation of the possibility of a crisis in the history of reason. Cf. Suzanne Bachelard *A Study of Husserl's "Formal and Transcendental Logic,"* trans. Lester E. Embree (Evanston: Northwestern University Press, 1968), p. 144.

20. Martin Heidegger, *Being and Time,* trans. John Macquarrie and Edward Robinson (New York: Harper and Row, 1962), p. 478.

21. Friedrich Nietzsche, *The Gay Science,* 2d ed., trans. Walter Kaufmann (New York: Random House, 1974), Preface, p. 38. In "Philosophy and Non-Philosophy," Merleau-Ponty quotes, with extensive elisions, from sections 2, 3, and 4 of Nietzsche's "Preface." Cf. Merleau-Ponty, "Philosophy and Non-Philosophy Since Hegel," trans. Hugh J. Silverman, *Telos* 29 (1976), pp. 44–47. A substantially reworked translation, also by Hugh J. Silverman, can be found in *Continental Philosophy, I: Philosophy and Non-Philosophy Since Merleau-Ponty* (London and New York: Routledge, 1988). The original French course notes, edited by Claude Lefort, are found in *Textures,* nos. 8–9 (1974) and nos. 10–11 (1975).

22. Nietzsche, *The Gay Science,* p. 241.

23. Nietzsche, *The Use and Abuse of History,* p. 39.

24. Friedrich Nietzsche, *Thus Spoke Zarathustra,* trans. Walter Kaufmann, in *The Portable Nietzsche,* part 3, section 2, pp. 269–70.

25. VI, 179; VI, 233. Cf. Friedrich Nietzsche, *Beyond Good and Evil,* trans. Walter Kaufmann (New York: Random House, 1966), section 56, p. 68.

26. Cf. John Sallis, *Phenomenology and the Return to Beginnings* (Pittsburgh: Duquesne University Press, 1973), pp. 21–23, 112–16.

27. Cf. David Wood's discussion in "Nietzsche's Transvaluation of Time," in *Exceedingly Nietzsche,* pp. 51–54.

28. Merleau-Ponty cites this passage from Paul Claudel's *Art Poétique,* (p. 145) in VI, 179; VI, 233. *Sigè* means silence.

29. Cf. Franz Cumont, "La Grande Inscription Bachique du Metropolitan Museum," *American Journal of Archeology,* 2nd series, 37 (1936), pp. 262–63.

30. Cf. Walter F. Otto, *Dionysus: Myth and Cult* (Bloomington: Indiana University Press, 1965), pp. 93–94.

CHAPTER 12   TENOCHTITLAN

1. Bernal Díaz del Castillo, *True History of the Conquest of Spain,* ed. and pub. Genaro Garcia, trans. Alfred Percival Mandslay (London: Printed for the Hakluyt Society, 1908–16), vol. 5, p. 213. Henceforth cited as *THCS.*

2. Kenelm Burridge, *Some One No One; An Essay on Individuality.* (Princeton: Princeton University Press, 1979) p. 96.
3. Bartolemé de las Casas, *Apologetica Historia Summaria,* ed. Edmundo O'Gorman (Mexico: Universidad National Autonoma de Mexico, Instituto de Investigaciones Historicas, serie de historiadores y cronistas de Indias, 1, 3d ed., 1967), p. 183.
4. Fernand Braudel, *Capitalism and Material Life, 1400–1800,* trans. Miriam Kochan (New York: Harper and Row, 1973), pp. 330–31.
5. Søren Kierkegaard, *The Sickness Unto Death,* ed. Robert L. Perkins (Macon: Mercer University Press, 1987), p. 49.

CHAPTER 13   EASY BECOMING UNEASY IMAGES: A PHOTOGRAMMIC SOLARIZATION OF CAVES

1. I would like to thank Hugh J. Silverman for his patience, encouragement, and insightful suggestions on earlier versions of this essay. I would also like to thank Jesse W. Nash for suggestions that helped me clarify the central points.

2. The following description of photographic solarization suggests some of things that happen in our "photogramm":

> The effect commonly referred to as solarization is produced when a negative is exposed to too strong or unsafe darkroom illumination during development. The already developed image acts as a negative through which the rest of the silver bromide is exposed. Some reversal of the image occurs and the result is part negative and part positive. If the exposure is heavy enough the resulting positive will, at any rate in the shadows, develop up to a greater density than the original negative image. . . . While a solarized negative is often the result of an error, it can be produced intentionally for effect. Negatives with large areas of dark tone and simple outlines are most suitable for the process. (*The Focal Encyclopedia of Photography* [London: Focal Press, 1958], 1079)

3. We choose the term "photogramm" because it is an example of a photographic designation whose use reflects the change of photography and thus its "bifocal" nature. The term "photogramm" was first used as a description of photographs that were consciously artistic as opposed to mechanical records. This was the usage at the same time that photogrammetry developed as "the science of taking measurements from photographs." Later, however, "photogramm" was used to describe photographs made without the use of a cam-

era—the "making of a photogramm is an uncertain business: it is not easy to tell beforehand how it will turn out, but therein lies the fascination. After a series of dull and disappointing results, the surprisingly beautiful effects that come quite unexpectedly can more than make up for the failures" (*Focal Encyclopedia of Photography*, 834, 836). With all mixed modesty, this does indeed describe the writing-printing of my photogramm. "Photogramm" obviously owes a debt to Derrida, one which may well make him uneasy. It is part of the "new mutation in the history of writing, in history as writing." *Of Grammatology*, trans. Gayatri C. Spivak (Baltimore: The John Hopkins Press, 1977), p. 8. Which is not to mention that like the "sponge," photographic emulsions are writings that while "unable to choose between the proper and the improper," they do have an economy (see note 15) "better able to resist the oppressor." *Signéponge/Signsponge*, trans. Richard Rand (New York: Columbia University Press, 1984), p. 66.

4. *As You Like it*, act 3, scene 7.

5. *Hamlet*, act 3, scene 2.

6. *L'art pour l'art* has its political homologues. Rousseau's *The Social Contract* is one. See Derrida's reading of this under the heading "The Theorem and the Theater," in *Of Grammatology*, pp. 302–313.

7. Benjamin Jowett's introduction to his translations of Plato, *The Dialogues of Plato*, vol. 1 (New York: Random House, 1937), p. ix.

8. This is how I understand the activity of "deconstruction." Lest the image of "deconstruction" be imperialized as a negative, nihilistic activity, it should be pointed out that deconstruction is part of the truth that "is not the conclusion of a system," but rather the truth that "is joying" (*la verité jouit*) (*Signéponge/Signsponge*, 94–95). But such joying, like that of the bedroom, is not of the spiritual, unmixed variety.

9. Maurice Blanchot, *The Writing of the Disaster*, trans. Ann Smock (Lincoln: University of Nebraska Press, 1989).

10. William Crawford, *The Keepers of Light* (New York: Morgan and Morgan, 1979), p. 9.

11. See Gisèle Freund, *Photography and Society* (London: Gordon Fraser, 1980), pp. 103–114.

12. Freund, *Photography and Society*, p. 163.

13. See Norman Peterson, *Photographic Art: Media and Disclosure* (Ann Arbor: UMI Research Press, 1984). This is a good, although somewhat repetitious discussion of medium analysis and its theoretical defense against the disclosive potential of photographic art. Peterson's constructive arguments are based on Heidegger's treatment of the art work in "Der Ursprung des Kunstwerkes," in *Holzwege*

(Frankfurt: Klostermann, 1963), pp. 7–68. English translation by Albert Hofstadter in Martin Heidegger, *Poetry Language Thought* (New York: Harper and Row, 1971), pp. 17–87.

14. Susan Sontag, *On Photography* (New York: Farrar, Strauss and Giroux, 1978).

15. Derrida, *Of Grammatology*, p. 4.

16. Reiner Schürmann, *Heidegger on Being and Acting: From Principles to Anarchy*, trans. Christine-Marie Gros (Bloomington: Indiana University Press, 1987), p. 241.

17. I would like to append Derrida's caution to Schürmann's desire for a post-principial economy: "We know what always have been the *practical* (particularly *political*) effects of *immediately* jumping *beyond* oppositions, and of protests in the simple form of *neither* this *nor* that. . . . the hierarchy of dual oppositions always reestablishes itself. Unlike those authors whose death does not await their demise, the time for overturning is never a dead letter." *Positions*, trans. Alan Bass (Chicago: The University of Chicago Press, 1981), pp. 41–42. This caution concerns not the time necessary for the transition, which Schürmann acknowledges, but the desire itself.

18. Maurice Merleau-Ponty, *The Prose of the World*, ed. Claude Lefort, trans. John O'Neill (Evanston: Northwestern University Press, 1973), p. 4.

19. A scientific concept of writing, a science of language, would be a "snapshot" of language—a "fix" whose chemistry comes from the I. G. Farben division of the culture industry. Such fixes institute foundations, cultural and otherwise. Which is why Derrida insists that "his" archē-writing cannot be *recognized* as the object of a science. See *Of Grammatology*, p. 57. This also applies to what we are calling photogramms. Photogramms can't be used for photogrammetric purposes since the position of their creators and instruments used relative to the "objects" of the negative can't be determined except by means of other photogramms. Images within images endlessly defer anything but strategic, and thus always imperiled, points of reference.

20. Jacques Derrida, "Force of Law: The 'Mystical Foundation of Authority,' " trans. Mary Quaintance, *Cardozo Law Review* 11, no. 919 (1990).

21. Robin Cembalest, "The Obscenity Trial," *ARTnews* 89, no. 10 (December 1990), p. 141; also see Jayne Merkel, "Art on Trial," *Art in America* 78, no. 12 (December 1990).

BIBLIOGRAPHY

QUESTIONING FOUNDATIONS

Hélène Volat

Achebe, Chinua. "Colonialist Criticism." In *Morning Yet on Creation Day: Essays*. Garden City: Anchor Press, 1975, pp. 3–19.

Ackerman, Robert. *Data, Instruments, and Theory*. Princeton: Princeton University Press, 1985.

Alcoff, Linda. "Cultural Feminism versus Post-Structuralism: The Identity Crisis in Feminist Theory." *Signs* 13, no. 3 (Spring 1988), pp. 405–36.

Arac, Jonathan, ed. *After Foucault*. New Brunswick: Rutgers University Press, 1988.

Arendt, Hannah. *The Life of the Mind*. New York: Harcourt Brace, 1978.

Barthes, Roland. *Critical Essays*. Trans. Richard Howard. Evanston: Northwestern University Press, 1972.

———. *Criticism and Truth*. Trans. Katrina Pilcher Kenneman. Minneapolis: University of Minnesota Press, 1987.

———. *New Critical Essays*. Trans. Richard Howard. New York: Hill and Wang, 1980.

———. *Writing Degree Zero*. Trans. Annette Lavers and Colin Smith. New York: Hill and Wang, 1968.

Benhabib, Seyla and Drucilla Cornell, eds. *Feminism as Critique*. Minneapolis: University of Minnesota Press, 1987.

Bernasconi, Robert. *The Question of Language in Heidegger's History of Being*. Atlantic Highlands: Humanities press, 1985.

Bersani, Leo. *The Freudian Body*. New York: Columbia University Press, 1986.

Blanchot, Maurice. *The Writing of the Disaster*. Trans. Ann Smock. Lincoln: University of Nebraska Press, 1986.

Braudel, Fernand. *Capitalism and Material Life, 1400–1800*. Trans. Miriam Kochan. New York: Harper and Row, 1973.

Bordo, Susan. *The Flight to Objectivity*. Albany: SUNY Press, 1987.

Bourdier, Jean Paul and Trinh-Ti-Minh-Ha. *African Spaces: Designs for Living in Upper Volta*. New York: Holmes and Meier, 1985.

Bourdieu, Pierre. "The Philosophical Institution." In *Philosophy in France Today*. Ed. Alan Montefiore. Cambridge: Cambridge University Press, 1983, pp. 1–9.

———. *Outline of a Theory of Practice*. Trans. Richard Nice. Cambridge: Cambridge University Press, 1987.

Burridge, Kenelm. *Some One No One: An Essay on Individuality*. Princeton: Princeton University Press, 1979.

Butler, Judith. "The Body Politics of Julia Kristeva." *Hypatia* 3, no. 3 (Winter 1989), pp. 104–18.

———. *Gender Trouble: Feminism and the Subversion of Identity*. New York: Routledge, 1989.

———. *Subject of Desire: Hegelian Reflections in Twentieth Century France*. New York: Columbia University Press, 1987.

Carby, Hazel. *Reconstructing Womanhood: The Emergence of Afro-American Women Novelists*. New York: Oxford University Press, 1987.

Casey, Edward S. *Remembering: A Phenomenological Study*. Bloomington: Indiana University Press, 1987.

Chodorow, Nancy. *The Reproduction of Mothering*. Berkeley: University of California Press, 1978.

Christian, Barbara. "The Race for Theory." *Feminist Studies* 14, no. 1 (Spring 1988), pp. 67–79.

Cixous, Hélène. "The Laugh of the Medusa: Viewpoint." *Signs* 1, no. 5 (Summer 1976), pp. 875–93.

——— and Catherine Clément. *The Newly Born Woman*. Minneapolis: University of Minnesota Press, 1986.

Cooper-Wiele, Jonathan. *The Totalizing Act: Key to Husserl's Early Philosophy*. Boston: Kluwer, 1989.

Copp, David and David Zimmerman, eds. *Morality, Reason and Truth: New Essays on the Foundations of Ethics*. Totowa, N.J.: Rowman and Allanheld, 1984.

Corrington, Robert. "Metaphysics Without Foundations: Jasper's Confrontations with Nietzsche." *Dialogue* 23 (July 1988), pp. 73–95.

Couvalis, Georges. *Feyerabend's Critique of Foundationalism*. Brookfield: Avebury, 1989.

Crease, Robert P. "The Problem of Experimentation." In *Phenomenology of Natural Science*. Ed. Lee Hardy and Lester Embree. Washington, D.C.: University Press of America, 1990, pp. 215–35.

Davis, Angela. *Women, Race and Class*. New York: Random House, 1983.

Deleuze, Gilles. *Anti-Oedipus: Capitalism and Schizophrenia*. Trans. Robert Hurley, Mark Seem, and Helen Lane. Minneapolis: University of Minnesota Press, 1983.

———. *Foucault*. Trans. Sandra Hand. Minneapolis: University of Minnesota Press, 1988.

———. *Kant's Critical Philosophy: The Doctrine of the Faculties.* Trans. Hugh Tomlinson and Barbara Habberjam. Minneapolis: University of Minnesota Press, 1984.

———. *Nietzsche and Philosophy.* Trans. Hugh Tomlinson. New York: Columbia University Press, 1983.

Derrida, Jacques. "Choreographies." An interview with Christie McDonald. *Diacritics* 12, no. 2 (Summer 1982), pp. 66–76.

———. *Dissemination.* Trans. Barbara Johnson. Chicago: Chicago University Press, 1981.

———. *Edmund Husserl's Origin of Geometry: An Introduction.* Trans. John Leavey. Lincoln: University of Nebraska Press, 1978.

———. *Of Grammatology.* Trans. Gayatri Chakravorty Spivak. Baltimore: Johns Hopkins University Press, 1976.

———. *Margins of Philosophy.* Trans. Alan Bass. Chicago: University of Chicago Press, 1982.

———. "Kafka's Before the Law." Trans. Avital Ronell. In *Kafka and the Contemporary Critical Performance.* Ed. Alan Udoff. Bloomington: Indiana University Press, 1987, pp. 128–50.

———. "No Apocalypse, Not Now (full speed ahead, seven missiles, seven missives)." *Diacritics* 14, no. 2 (Summer 1984), pp. 19–31.

———. *Of Spirit: Heidegger and the Question.* Trans. Geoffrey Bennington and Rachel Bowlby. Chicago: University of Chicago Press, 1989.

———. *The Post Card.* Trans. Alan Bass. Chicago: University of Chicago Press, 1987.

———. "Shibboleth." In *Midrash and Literature.* Ed. Geoffrey Hartman and Sanford Budick. New Haven: Yale University Press, 1986, pp. 307–49.

———. *Speech and Phenomena, and Other Essays on Husserl's Theory of Signs.* Trans. David Allison. Evanston: Northwestern University Press, 1973.

———. *Spurs: Nietzsche's Styles.* Trans. Barbara Harlow. Chicago: Chicago University Press, 1979.

———. *Writing and Difference.* Trans. Alan Bass. Chicago: Chicago University Press, 1978.

Descombes, Vincent. *Modern French Philosophy.* Trans. L. Scott-Fox and J. M. Harding. New York: Cambridge University Press, 1981.

Diamond, Irene and Lee Quinby, eds. *Feminism and Foucault: Reflections on Resistance.* Boston: Northwestern University Press, 1988.

Dinnerstein, Dorothy. *The Mermaid and the Minotaur.* New York: Harper and Row, 1977.

Dreyfus, Herbert and Paul Rabinow. *Michel Foucault: Beyond Structuralism and Hermeneutics.* Chicago: University of Chicago Press, 1982.

Easlea, Brian. *Witch-Hunting, Magic and the New Philosophy.* Atlantic Highlands: Humanities Press, 1980.

Engels, Frederick. *The Origin of the Family, Private Property and the State.* Ed. Evelyn Reed. New York: Pathfinder Press, 1972.

Fotí, Véronique. "The (Dis)place of the Other in the Poetics of Paul Celan." In *Ethics/Aesthetics: Postmodern Positions.* Maisonneuve Press, 1987, pp. 95–119.

Foucault, Michel. *The Archaeology of Knowledge.* Trans. A. M. Sheridan Smith. New York: Harper and Row, 1972.

———. "Clarifications on the Question of Power," an interview with Pasquale Pasquine. In *Foucault Live.* New York: Semiotext(e), 1989.

———. *Discipline and Punish.* Trans. Alan Sheridan. New York: Vintage Books, 1979.

———. *The History of Sexuality.* Vol. 1, *An Introduction.* Trans. Robert Hurley. New York: Vintage, 1980.

———. *The History of Sexuality.* Vol. 2, *The Use of Pleasure,* Trans. Robert Hurley. New York: Vintage Books, 1980.

———. *Language, Counter-Memory, Practice: Selected Essays and Interviews.* Trans. Donald Bouchard and Sherry Simon. Ithaca: Cornell University Press, 1977.

———. *The Order of Things: An Archaeology of the Human Sciences.* Trans. anon. New York: Pantheon, 1970.

Frank, Manfred. *What is Neo-Structuralism?* Trans. Sabine Wilke and Richard Garry. Minneapolis: University of Minnesota Press, 1989.

Franklin, Alan. *The Neglect of Experiment.* New York: Cambridge University Press, 1986.

Freud, Sigmund. "Dissection of the Psychical Personality." In *The Complete Works of Sigmund Freud.* Vol. 22. Ed. James Strachey. London: Hogarth Press, 1973.

Frings, Manfred, ed. *Heidegger and the Quest for Truth.* Chicago: Quadrangle Books, 1968.

Furth, Hans. *Piaget and Knowledge: Theoretical Foundations.* Englewood Cliffs: Prentice-Hall, 1969.

Gadamer, Hans Georg. *Truth and Method.* New York: Crossroads, 1989. Trans. Joel Weinsteimer and Donald G. Marshall.

Galison, Peter. *How Experiments End.* Chicago: University of Chicago Press, 1986.

Gates, Henry. *Figures in Black: Words, Signs and the "Racial" Self.* New York: Oxford University Press, 1986.

Gooding, David. *Experimentation and the Making of Meaning.* Cambridge: Cambridge University Press, 1990.

Gordon, Colin, ed. *Power/Knowledge.* New York: Pantheon, 1980.

Gramsci, Antonio. "The Study of Philosophy." In *Selections from the Prison Notebooks.* Trans. Quintin Hoare and Geoffrey Nowell. New York: International Publishers, 1971, pp. 321–43.

Gunew, Sneja. "The Mother Tongue and Migration." *Australian Feminist Studies* 1 (Summer 1985).

Hacking, Ian. *Representing and Intervening*. Cambridge: Cambridge University Press, 1983.

Hall, Stuart and James Donald. *Politics and Ideology*. London: Open University Press, 1985.

Hanson, N. R. *Patterns of Discovery*. New York: Cambridge University Press, 1958.

Harding, Sandra and Merrill Hintikka, eds. *Discovering Reality: Feminist Perspectives on Epistemology, Metaphysics, Methodology, and Philosophy of Science*. Dordrecht: Reidel, 1983.

Harding, Sandra. "Is Gender a Variable in Conceptions of Rationality?" In *Beyond Domination*. Ed. Carol Gould. Totowa: Roman and Allenheld, 1984, pp. 112–38.

———. *The Science Question in Feminism*. Ithaca: Cornell University Press, 1986.

Harris, Nigel. *The End of the Third World: New Industrializing Countries and the Decline of an Ideology*. London: Penguin, 1986.

Heelan, Patrick. "Experiment and Theory: Constitution and Reality." *Journal of Philosophy* 85, no. 10 (1988), pp. 515–24.

———. *Space-Perception and the Philosophy of Science*. Berkeley: University of California Press, 1983.

Heidegger, Martin. *The Basic Problems of Phenomenology*. Trans. Albert Hofstader. Bloomington: Indiana University Press, 1982.

———. *Being and Time*. Trans. J. Macquarrie and E. Robinson. New York: Harper and Row, 1962.

———. *The End of Philosophy*. Trans. J. Stambaugh. New York: Harper and Row, 1973.

———. *Essence of Reasons*. Trans. T. Malick. Evanston: Northwestern University Press, 1969.

———. *Existence and Being*. Chicago: Gateway and London: Vision Press, 1949.

———. *History of the Concept of Time: Prolegomena*. Trans. Theodore Kisiel. Bloomington: Indiana University Press, 1985.

———. *An Introduction to Metaphysics*. Trans. Ralph Manheim. New Haven: Yale University Press, 1959.

———. *The Metaphysical Foundations of Logic*. Trans. Michael Heim. Bloomington: Indiana University Press, 1984.

———. *On Time and Being*. Trans. Joan Stambaugh. New York: Harper and Row, 1972.

———. *The Question of Being*. Trans. W. Kluback and J. T. Wilde. London: Vision, 1959.

———. *What Is Philosophy?* Trans. W. Kluback and J. T. Wilde. New Haven: New College and University Press, 1958.

Heller, Thomas, ed. *Reconstructing Individualism*. Stanford: Stanford University Press, 1986.

Hooks, Bell. *Feminist Theory: From Margin to Center*. Boston: South End Press, 1984.

Hountondji, Paulin. *African Philosophy: Myth and Reality*. Trans. Henri Evans. Bloomington: Indiana University Press, 1983.

Husserl, Edmund. *The Crisis of European Sciences and Transcendental Phenomenology: An Introduction to Phenomenological Philosophy*. Trans. David Carr. Evanston: Northwestern University Press, 1970.

———. *Ideas Pertaining to a Pure Phenomenology and to a Phenomenological Philosophy: First Book*. Trans. Fred Kersten. Boston: Martinus Nijhoff, 1983.

———. *Logical Investigations*. Vols. 1 and 2. London: Routledge and Kegan Paul, 1970.

Irigaray, Luce. *Speculum of the Other Woman*. Ithaca: Cornell University Press, 1985.

Jaggar, Alison and Susan Bordo, eds. *Gender/Body/Knowledge: Feminist Reconstructions of Being and Knowing*. New Brunswick: Rutgers University Press, 1989.

Johnson, Conrad D. "The Idea of Autonomy and the Foundations of Contractual Liability," *Law and Philosophy* 2, no. 2 (December 1983), pp. 271–304.

Johnson, Galen. *Earth and Sky, History and Philosophy: Island Images Inspired by Husserl and Merleau-Ponty*. New York: Peter Lang, 1989.

Keller, Evelyn Fox. *Reflections on Gender and Science*. New Haven: Yale University Press, 1985.

Kittay, Eva and Diana Meyers, eds. *Women and Moral Theory*. Totowa: Rowman and Littlefield, 1987.

Kofman, Sarah. *The Enigma of Woman: Women in Freud's Writings*. Trans. Catherine Porter. Ithaca: Cornell, 1985.

Kolakowski, Leszek. *Metaphysical Horror*. Oxford: Basil Blackwell, 1988.

Krell, David F. and David Wood, eds. *Exceedingly Nietzsche: Aspects of Contemporary Nietzsche Interpretation*. New York: Routledge, 1988.

Kristeva, Julia. *Desire in Language*. Trans. Leon Roudiez. New York: Columbia University Press, 1980.

———. *Revolution in Poetic Language*. Trans. Margaret Waller. New York: Columbia University Press, 1984.

———. *Semiotikē: Recherches pour une sémanalyse*. Paris: Seuil, 1969.

Kuhn, Thomas S. *The Structure of Scientific Revolutions*. Chicago: University of Chicago Press, 1970.

Lacan, Jacques. *The Four Fundamental Concepts of Psychoanalysis*. Trans. Alan Sheridan. New York: W. W. Norton, 1981.

Lakoff, George and Mark Johnson. *Metaphors We Live By*. Chicago: University of Chicago Press, 1980.

Lecourt, Dominique. *Marxism and Epistemology*. London: New Left Books, 1970.

Lévi-Strauss, Claude. *The Elementary Structures of Kinship*. Boston: Beacon Press, 1969.

Levinas, Emmanuel. *Collected Philosophical Papers*. Trans. Alphonso Lingis. The Hague: Martinus Nijhoff, 1987.

———. *Otherwise than Being*. Trans. Alphonso Lingis. The Hague: Martinus Nijhoff, 1981.

———. *Totality and Infinity*. Trans. Alphonso Lingis. Pittsburgh: Duquesne University Press, 1969.

Lyotard, Jean-François. *The Differend: Phrases in Dispute*. Trans. G. Van Den Abbeele. Minneapolis: University of Minnesota Press, 1989.

———. "Notes on Legitimation." In *The Public Realm: Essays on Discursive Types in Political Philosophy*. Ed. Reiner Schürmann. Albany: SUNY Press, 1989, pp. 36–58.

———. *The Postmodern Condition: A Report on Knowledge*. Trans. Geoff Bennington and Brian Massumi. Minneapolis: University of Minnesota Press, 1984.

Mani, Lata. "Contentious Traditions: the Debate on Sati in Colonial India." *Cultural Critique* no. 7 (Fall 1987), pp. 119–57.

Marks, Elaine and Isabel de Courtivron, eds. *New French Feminisms*. New York: Schocken, 1978.

Martin, Luther, et al. *Technologies of the Self: A Seminar with Michel Foucault*. Amherst: University of Massachusetts Press, 1988.

Marx, Karl. *Capital: A Critique of Political Economy*. Trans. Ben Fowkes. New York: Vintage Books, 1977.

———. *Economic and Philosophic Manuscripts of 1844*. Trans. Martin Milligan. New York: International Publishers, 1964.

———. *The German Ideology*. New York: International Publishers, 1947.

———. *Selected Correspondence*. Moscow: Progress Publishers, 1975.

Melotti, Umberto. *Marx and the Third World*. Trans. Pat Ransford. London: Macmillan, 1977.

Merchant, Carolyn. *The Death of Nature*. San Francisco: Harper and Row, 1980.

Merleau-Ponty, Maurice. *Consciousness and the Acquisition of Language*. Trans. Hugh J. Silverman. Evanston, Northwestern University Press, 1973.

———. "The Experience of Others." Trans. Fred Evans and Hugh J. Silverman. In *Merleau-Ponty and Psychology*. Ed. Keith Hoeller. Atlantic Highlands, N.J.: Humanities Press, 1993, pp. 33–63.

———. *In Praise of Philosophy*. Trans. John Wild and James Edie. Evanston: Northwestern University Press, 1963.

———. *Phenomenology of Perception*. Trans. Colin Smith. London: Routledge and Kegan Paul, 1962.

————. *The Primacy of Perception*. Ed. James M. Edie. Evanston: Northwestern University Press, 1964.

————. *Signs*. Trans. Richard McCleary. Evanston: Northwestern University Press, 1964.

————. *Sense and Non-Sense*. Trans. Hubert Dreyfus and Patricia Dreyfus. Evanston: Northwestern University Press, 1964.

————. *Texts and Dialogues*. Ed. and with an Introduction by Hugh J. Silverman and James Barry, Jr. Atlantic Highlands: Humanities Press, 1992.

————. *Themes from the Lectures at the Collège de France*. Trans. John O'Neill. Evanston: Northwestern University, 1970.

————. *The Visible and the Invisible*. Trans. Alphonso Lingis. Evanston: Northwestern University Press, 1968.

Merquior, José Guilherme. *Foucault*. Berkeley: University of California Press, 1987.

————. *From Prague to Paris: A Critique of Structuralist and Poststructuralist Thought*. London: Verso, 1986.

Mitchell, Timothy. "The World as Exhibition." *Comparative Studies in Society and History* 31, no. 2 (April 1989), pp. 217–36.

Mohanty, Jitendra and Robert Shahan, eds. *Thinking about Being*. Norman: University of Oklahoma Press, 1984.

Mulligan, Kevin. "Adolph Reinach and the Analytical Foundations of Social Acts." Trans. Jean-Louis Gardies and Kevin Mulligan. In *Speech Act and Sachverhalt: Reinach and the Foundations of Realist Phenomenology*. Dordrecht: Kluwer, 1987, pp. 107–119.

Nagel, Thomas. *The View from Nowhere*. Oxford: Oxford University Press, 1986.

Nandy, Ashis. *The Intimate Enemy: Loss and Recovery of Self under Colonialism*. New York: Oxford University Press, 1983.

Nicholson, Linda J. ed. *Feminism/Postmodernism: The Politics of Method*. New York: Routledge, 1989.

Nietzsche, Friedrich. *Beyond Good and Evil*. Trans. Walter Kaufmann. New York: Random House, 1966.

————. *The Gay Science*. Trans. Walter Kaufmann. New York: Random House, 1974.

————. *The Genealogy of Morals*. Trans. Francis Golffing. New York: Doubleday, 1956.

————. *The Use and Abuse of History*. Trans. Adrian Collins. Indianapolis, Bobbs-Merril Company, 1949.

————. *Thus Spoke Zarathustra*. Trans. Walter Kaufmann. New York. Viking Press, 1968.

————. *The Use and Abuse of History*. Trans. Adrian Collins. Indianapolis, Bobbs-Merrill Co., 1949.

Nye, Andrea. "Woman Clothed with the Sun: Julia Kristeva and the Escape from/to Language." *Signs* 12, no. 4 (1987), pp. 664–86.

Odegaard, Douglas. "Foundations for Claiming Knowledge." *Canadian Journal of Philosophy* 16, no. 2 (December 1986), pp. 613–33.

Pickering, Andrew. *Constructing Quarks.* Chicago: University of California Press, 1984.

Pöggeler, Otto. *Martin Heidegger's Path of Thinking.* Trans. Daniel Magurshak and Sigmund Barber. Atlantic Highlands: Humanities Press, 1987.

Popper, Karl. *The Logic of Scientific Discovery.* New York: Harper and Row, 1968.

Pratt, Marie Louise. "Identity: Skin, Blood, Heart." In *Yours in Struggle.* Ed. Elly Bulkin, Marie Louise Pratt, and Barbara Smith. New York: Long Hall Press, 1984, pp. 122–141.

———. "Scratches on the Face of the Country; or What Mr. Barrow Saw in the Land of the Bushmen." *Critical Inquiry* 12, no. 1 (Autumn 1985), pp. 119–44.

Rajchman, John and Cornel West, eds. *Post-Analytic Philosophy.* New York: Columbia University Press, 1985.

Rapaport, Herman. *Heidegger and Derrida: Reflections on Time and Language.* Lincoln: University of Nebraska Press, 1989.

Rorty, Richard. *Philosophy and the Mirror of Nature.* Ithaca: Cornell University Press, 1979.

Rose, Hilary. "Hand, Brain and Heart: A Feminist Epistemology for the Natural Sciences." *Signs* 9, no. 1 (1983), pp. 73–90.

Rosenbaum, Alan. *Coercion and Autonomy: Philosophical Foundations, Issues, and Practices.* Westport: Greenwood Press, 1986.

Rosenthal, Sandra. "Scientific Method and the Return to Foundations: Pragmatism and Heidegger." *The Journal of Speculative Philosophy* 2 (1986), pp. 192–205.

Rouse, Joseph. *Knowledge and Power: Toward a Political Philosophy of Science.* Ithaca: Cornell University Press, 1987.

Rubin, Gayle. "Thinking Sex: Notes for a Radical Theory of the Politics of Sexuality. In *Pleasure and Danger: Exploring Female Sexuality.* Ed. Carole Vance. Boston and London: Routledge and Kegan Paul, 1984.

———. "The Traffic in Women: Notes toward a 'Political Economy of Sex.' " In *Toward an Anthropology of Women.* Ed. Rayne Reiter. New York: Monthly Review Press, 1975, pp. 157–211.

Ruddick, Sara. "Maternal Thinking." *Feminist Studies* 6, no. 2 (Summer 1980), pp. 342–67.

Said, Edward. *Orientalism.* New York: Pantheon Books, 1978.

———. "Representing the Colonized: Anthropology's Interlocutors." *Critical Inquiry* 15, no. 2 (Winter 1989), pp. 205–25.

Sallis, John. *Phenomenology and the Return to Beginnings.* Pittsburgh: Duquesne University Press, 1973.

Sartre, Jean-Paul. *Being and Nothingness.* Trans. Hazel Barnes. New York: Simon and Schuster, 1956.

Schürmann, Reiner. *Heidegger on Being and Acting: From Principles to Anarchy.* Bloomington: Indiana University Press, 1987.

Schrag, Calvin. *Existence and Freedom.* Evanston: Northwestern University Press, 1961.

Shapin, Steven and Simon Schaffer. *Leviathan and the Air-Pump: Hobbes, Boyle, and The Experimental Life.* Princeton: Princeton University Press, 1985.

Sherman, Julia. and Evelyn Beck, eds. *The Prism of Sex: Essays in the Sociology of Knowledge.* Madison: University of Wisconsin Press, 1979.

Silverman, Hugh J. *Inscriptions Between Phenomenology and Structuralism.* London and New York, Routledge, 1987.

Silverman, Hugh J., ed. *Philosophy and Non-Philosophy since Merleau-Ponty.* [*Continental Philosophy - I:*] London and New York, Routledge, 1988.

———. *Derrida and Deconstruction.* [*Continental Philosophy - II:*] London and New York, Routledge, 1989.

———. *Postmodernism—Philosophy and the Arts.* [*Continental Philosophy - III:*] New York and London, Routledge, 1990.

———. *Gadamer and Hermeneutics.* [*Continental Philosophy - IV:*] New York and London, Routledge, 1991.

———. *Piaget, Philosophy and the Human Sciences.* Atlantic Highlands: Humanities Press, 1980.

———. *Writing the Politics of Difference.* Albany: SUNY Press, 1991.

——— and Gary E. Aylesworth eds. *The Textual Sublime: Deconstruction and its Differences.* Albany: SUNY Press, 1990.

Smith, Paul. *Discerning the Subject.* Minneapolis: University of Minnesota Press, 1988.

Soper, Kate. *Humanism and Anti-Humanism.* London: Hutchinson, 1986.

Spivak, Gayatri. "Constitutions and Culture Studies." *Yale Journal of Law and the Humanities* (forthcoming).

———. *In Other Worlds: Essays in Cultural Politics.* New York: Methuen, 1987.

———. "Speculations on Reading Marx: After Reading Derrida." In *Post-Structuralism and the Question of History.* Ed. Derek Attridge and Geoffrey Bennington. Cambridge: Cambridge University Press, 1987.

———, and Ranajit Guha. *Selected Subaltern Studies.* New York: Oxford University Press, 1988.

Starobinksi, Jean. *Montaigne in Motion.* Trans. Arthur Goldhammer. Chicago: University of Chicago Press, 1985.

Suleiman, Susan, ed. *The Female Body in Western Culture*. Cambridge: Harvard University Press, 1986.

Taminiaux, Jacques. *Dialectic and Difference: Finitude in Modern Thought*. Trans. and ed. James Decker and Robert P. Crease. Atlantic Highlands: Humanities Press, 1985.

Taussig, Mick. *Shamanism, Colonialism and the Wild Man: A Study in Terror and Healing*. Chicago: University of Chicago Press, 1987.

Toulmin, Stephen. "The Inwardness of Mental Life." *Critical Inquiry* 6, no. 1 (Autumn 1979), pp. 1–16.

———. "The Recovery of Practical Philosophy." *The American Scholar* 57 (Summer 1988), pp. 337–52.

Vance, Carole, ed. *Pleasure and Danger: Exploring Female Sexuality*. Boston and London: Routledge and Kegan Paul, 1984.

Vattimo, Gianni. *The End of Modernity*, trans. Jon R. Synder. Baltimore: Johns Hopkins Univ., 1988.

Velkley, Richard. *Freedom and the End of Reason: On the Moral Foundation of Kant's Critical Philosophy*. Chicago: University of Chicago Press, 1989.

Watson, Stephen S. "Aesthetics and the Foundations of Interpretation." *The Journal of Aesthetics and Art Criticism* 45, no. 2 (Summer 1986), pp. 125–38.

Weintraub, Karl. *The Value of the Individual*. Chicago: University of Chicago Press, 1978.

Wiggins, David. *Needs, Values, Truth: Essays in the Philosophy of Value*. Oxford: Oxford University Press, 1987.

Williams, Bernard. *Moral Luck: Philosophical Papers, 1973–1980*. Cambridge: Cambridge University Press, 1981.

Wilshire, Bruce. *Role Playing and Identity: The Limits of Theatre and Metaphor*. Bloomington: Indiana University Press, 1982.

Wyschogrod, Edith. *Emmanuel Levinas: The Problem of Ethical Metaphysics*. The Hague: Martinus Nijhoff, 1974.

———. *Spirit in Ashes: Hegel, Heidegger and Man-Made Mass Death*. New Haven: Yale University Press, 1985.

NOTES ON CONTRIBUTORS

SUSAN BORDO

Susan Bordo is Associate Professor of Philosophy at LeMoyne College. She is author of *The Flight to Objectivity: Essays on Cartesianism and Culture* (SUNY Press, 1987) and coedited, with Alison Jaggar, *Gender/Body/Knowledge: Feminist Reconstructions of Being and Knowing* (Rutgers University Press, 1989).

JUDITH BUTLER

Judith Butler is Professor in the Humanities Center at Johns Hopkins University, Baltimore, Maryland. She is author of *Subjects of Desire: Hegelian Reflections in Twentieth Century France* (Columbia University Press, 1987) and *Gender Trouble: Feminism and the Subversion of Identity* (Routledge, 1990).

ROBERT P. CREASE

Robert P. Crease is Assistant Professor of Philosophy at the State University of New York at Stony Brook and is affiliated with the Brookhaven National Labs. He is coauthor of *The Second Creation: Makers of the Revolution in Twentieth Century Physics* (Macmillan, 1986) and is coeditor and translator of Jacques Taminiaux's *Dialectic and Difference* (Humanities Press, 1985).

JAMES HATLEY

James Hatley is Assistant Professor of Philosophy at Salisbury State University in Maryland. He is also an Assistant Editor of *Continental Philosophy*. His book on Heidegger, the Holocaust, and "Mourning" is forthcoming from SUNY Press.

HERBERT HRACHOVEC

Herbert Hrachovec is Professor of Philosophy at the University of Vienna, Austria. He is author of several books including *Vorbei: Heidegger, Frege, Wittgenstein* (Stroemfeld/Roter Stern, 1981) and *Vermessen* (Stoemfeld/Roter Stern, 1990).

GALEN A. JOHNSON

Galen A. Johnson is Professor and Chair of the Department of Philosophy at the University of Rhode Island. He is author of *Earth and Sky, History and Philosophy* (Peter Lang, 1989) and has coedited with Michael B. Smith, *Ontology and Alterity in Merleau-Ponty* (Northwestern, 1990).

ALPHONSO LINGIS

Alphonso Lingis is Professor of Philosophy at the Pennsylvania State University. He has translated books by Merleau-Ponty and Levinas and is author of *Excesses of Eros and Culture* (SUNY Press, 1983), *Libido: The French Existential Theories* (Indiana University Press, 1985), *Phenomenological Explanations* (Kluwer, 1986), and *Deathbound Subjectivity* (Indiana University Press, 1989).

MARIO MOUSSA

Mario Moussa teaches Philosophy at Worcester Polytechnic in Worcester, Massachusetts.

TONY O'CONNOR

Tony O'Connor teaches in the Department of Philosophy at University College, Cork, Ireland. He has written widely on Merleau-Ponty, aesthetics, and Greek philosophy and contributed an essay on Foucault to the first volume of *Continental Philosophy: Philosophy and Non-Philosophy since Merleau-Ponty*.

BASIL O'NEILL

Basil O'Neill is Senior Lecturer in the Department of Philosophy at the University of Dundee, Scotland. He writes in the areas of logic and continental philosophy. He is founder of the Scottish Phenomenological Society.

GAYATRI CHAKRAVORTY SPIVAK

Gayatri Chakravorty Spivak is Professor of English and Comparative Literature at Columbia University. She has held endowed chairs at Emory University and the University of Pittsburgh. She is translator of Derrida's *Of Grammatology* (Johns Hopkins, 1976) and author of *In Other Worlds: Essays in Cultural Politics* (Routledge, 1987), and *The Post Colonial Critic: Interviews, Strategies, Dialogues* (Routledge, 1990). She also coedited, with Ranajit Guha, *Selected Subaltern Studies* (Oxford University Press, 1988).

GIANNI VATTIMO

Gianni Vattimo is Professor of Theoretical Philosophy at the University of Turin, Italy. He is author of many books including *Introduzione a Heidegger* (Laterza, 1971/1982), *Il soggetto e la maschera: Nietzsche e il problema della liberazione* (Bompiani, 1974, 1979), *Le Avventure della differenza* (Garzanti, 1980, 1988), *Il pensiero debole* (Feltrinelli, 1983), *The End of Modernity: Nihilism and Hermeneutics in Postmodern Culture* (1985), (Johns Hopkins Univ. Press, 1988), and *La Società transparente* (Garzanti, 1989). His *Consequences of Hermeneutics* is forthcoming in the Humanities Press Series in *"Philosophy and Literary Theory."*

JAMES R. WATSON

James R. Watson is Professor of Philosophy at Loyola University in New Orleans. He is author of *Thinking with Pictures: Photographs and Essays* (Art Review Press, 1990), and previously *Louisiana Labor: From Slavery to "Right-to-Work"* (University Press of America, 1985).

RICHARD WHITE

Richard White is Assistant Professor of Philosophy at Creighton University in Omaha, Nebraska. He has published articles on Nietzsche, Heidegger, Kant, Hume, ethics, and the philosophy-literature interface in journals such as *Philosophy and Literature, The British Journal of Aesthetics, Philosophy Today,* and *International Studies in Philosophy.*

About the Editor
HUGH J. SILVERMAN

Hugh J. Silverman is Professor of Philosophy and Comparative Literature at the State University of New York at Stony Brook. He has held visiting teaching posts at the Universities of Warwick and Leeds (England), at the Université de Nice (France), the Università di Torino (Italy) and at Stanford University, Duquesne University, and New York University in the United States. He is currently Executive Director of the International Association for Philosophy and Literature. He served for six years as Executive Co-Director of the Society for Phenomenology and Existential Philosophy (1980–86). Author of *Inscriptions: Between Phenomenology and Structuralism* (Routledge, 1987) and *Textualities: Between Hermeneutics and Deconstruction* (Routledge, 1993) as well as numerous articles in continental philosophy, aesthetics, philosophical psychology, and literary/cultural theory, he has lectured widely in North America, Britain, and Continental Europe. He is editor of *Writing the Politics of Difference* (SUNY Press, 1991) and *Piaget, Philosophy and the Human Sciences* (Humanities/Harvester, 1980), and coeditor of *Jean-Paul Sartre: Contemporary Approaches to his Philosophy* (Duquesne/Harvester, 1980), *Continental Philosophy in America* (Duquesne, 1983), *Descriptions* (SUNY Press, 1985), *Hermeneutics and Deconstruction* (SUNY Press, 1985), *Critical and Dialectical Phenomenology* (SUNY Press, 1987), *The Horizons of Continental Philosophy: Essays on Husserl, Heidegger, and Merleau-Ponty* (Nijhoff/Kluwer, 1988), *Postmodernism and Continental Philosophy* (SUNY Press, 1988), *The Textual Sublime: Deconstruction and its Differences* (SUNY Press, 1990), and *Merleau-Ponty: Texts and Dialogues* (Humanities Press, 1992), as well as the first four volumes in the *Continental Philosophy* series: *Philosophy and Non-Philosophy since Merleau-Ponty* (Routledge, 1988), *Derrida and Deconstruction* (Routledge, 1989), *Postmodernism—Philosophy and the Arts* (Routledge, 1990), and *Gadamer and Hermeneutics* (Routledge, 1991).